MANCHESTER
CITY
FOLKLORE
What You Didn't Know

Gary James

CONKER

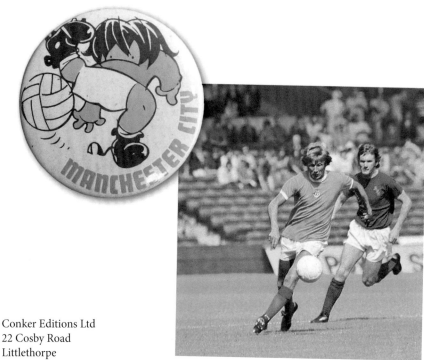

Conker Editions Ltd
22 Cosby Road
Littlethorpe
Leicester
LE19 2HF
Email: books@conkereditions.co.uk
Website: www.conkereditions.co.uk
First published by Conker Editions Ltd 2018

A CIP catalogue record for this book is available from the British Library.
13-digit ISBN: 9781999900823
Design and typesetting by Gary Silke.
Printed in the UK by Mixam.

"The fact that an Englishman has an Argentinian as an idol is very rare.
I keep watching my [title-winning] goal against QPR and every time I
get more emotional. My plan is to stay here because I'm convinced
Manchester City will be at the same level as Real Madrid and Barcelona."

Sergio Agüero

Over the years, I have researched and written several heavyweight histories of Manchester City, its players, stadia, statistics and rivals – and hopefully these books have added to our overall knowledge of the club. However, they have not always exactly been accessible to all. That's why I chose a different approach here, writing a series of features that cover some of our greatest achievements, inspirational records and statistics alongside more light-hearted or seemingly trivial information. The aim was to produce a book with a broader appeal, providing the kind of information that every City fan needs to know.

I wanted to include enough of City's DNA for it to be recognised by all. The aim wasn't to list every fact, success and record but to write an entertaining collection of pieces to bring to life City's story, shot through with colourful images, inviting readers to dip in and out.

they're about recent successes or stories of the club's initial formation in 1880. But there's also a serious reason for wanting to capture the pure essence of City, to help inform while trying to entertain every generation of fans.

Over recent years, elements of the media have been critical of City's position as a dominant club in English and European football. They have suggested that because City had not competed at the highest level of European football during the modern era, or because major trophy success eluded us for around 30 years, this was typical of the Blues' entire history. As fans, we know different; but the negative narrative was

Inside *City Folklore* I hope everyone will find some fascinating nuggets of info – great ammo for the pub, for the workplace or half-time at the match – whether growing so strong that even some of those associated with our team were taken in by the perception. This outside criticism of City's history was something I felt I had to

propelling the Blues forward at a pace that has left behind many traditional rivals. The success is certainly deserved after the rough ride of the '80s and '90s, and the enduring loyalty of the fans has finally been repaid.

act on, and this book is a tangible result of my determination to ensure that our great club's rich and eventful past never fades from memory.

Since we became the first Manchester side to earn promotion in 1899 the Blues have always been one of the country's biggest clubs. Each generation has enjoyed major success and City have established many records, even though the struggles of the 1980s and 1990s meant that Manchester's Blues were unable to compete for trophies in our accustomed manner by the 2000s. The finances of rival clubs had grown while City had lost ground. Support remained high and the Blues battled hard, but the game was changing fast.

In 2008 major investment arrived from Abu Dhabi and, over the years since, success has returned. Unlike many other clubs, however, City's rise has been built on strong foundations with investment into facilities, player development, women's football, the stadium and Manchester itself –

This book arrives at a time when Pep Guardiola has just guided City through an incredible title season, with long-standing national records tumbling – some of them worthy of a mention here.

As a fan of this club since birth, I can think of no greater time to be a Blue. Hopefully, *City Folklore* will give younger and newer fans as well as lifelong followers a timely reminder of how Manchester City became the club we all love. I hope you enjoy the book.

The Blues of '63 (far left); and David White, scorer of City's first ever Premier League goal (left).

Silverware on the Sideboard

The success of recent years has overturned many of the club's long-standing records. It has also resulted in substantial changes to the list of the Blues' most decorated players.

For comparison purposes I have highlighted the eight most decorated players based on successes at City. These details include European, League, FA Cup and League Cup successes – though they only include players who actually appeared on the pitch in finals (i.e. they either started or came on as substitute, were not unused substitutes or squad members). This excludes players who appeared in earlier cup rounds but did not make the final, and also unused substitutes as, over the years, medal eligibility rules have changed. This method allows a comparison across the decades.

These players are listed in order of total trophies won. Where two players have the same total, their ranking is based on the following order: European trophy, League, FA Cup, League Cup. All details correct at the start of the 2018-19 season.

Vincent Kompany
7 trophies won: 3 Premier League, 1 FA Cup & 3 League Cups.

Runner-up: Premier League 2013 & 2015; FA Cup finalist 2013.

City's most successful captain. He was captain for six major trophy successes (Tevez was captain for the 2011 FAC win). Kompany has demonstrated his abilities as a great leader of the club for over a decade now. He will forever be remembered as a committed, dedicated Blue and a Mancunian by choice.

David Silva
7 trophies won: 3 Premier League, 1 FA Cup & 3 League Cups.

Runner-up: Premier League 2013 & 2015; FA Cup finalist 2013.

Regarded by many as City's greatest ever player. Silva captained the Blues with distinction prior to the return of Kompany in 2017-18, and was a member of the successful Spanish World Cup side in

2010, which won the trophy 11 days after the announcement that he was joining City.

Yaya Touré
6 trophies won: 3 Premier League, 1 FA Cup & 2 League Cups.
Runner-up: Premier League 2013 & 2015; FA Cup finalist 2013.
    The man who scored the winning goal for the first trophy success of the modern era. The only final he missed was the

2018 LC final, though he did play in earlier rounds.

Sergio Agüero
6 trophies won: 3 Premier League & 3 League Cups.
Runner-up: Premier League 2013 & 2015; FA Cup finalist 2013.
    City's record goalscorer of all time. He arrived after the FA Cup final of 2011 but has appeared in every success that followed.

Mike Doyle
5 trophies won: 1 European trophy, 1 League, 1 FA Cup & 2 League Cups.
Runner-up: Football League 1977; LC finalist 1974.
    Captain of the 1976 League Cup-winning team that won the Second Division title in 1966. A determined Mancunian

Victorious: City boss Tony Book and skipper Mike Doyle at the 1976 League Cup final.

A. Oakes *(Man. City)*

whose grandson, Tommy Doyle, became a member of City's U18 squad.

Alan Oakes

5 trophies won: 1 European trophy, 1 League, 1 FA Cup & 2 League Cups. City's record appearance holder. He also won the Second Division title with the Blues in 1966 and was captain for the club's first European Cup game in 1968. Described by Bill Shankly as the most complete player he had ever seen.

Pablo Zabaleta

5 trophies won: 2 Premier League, 1 FA Cup & 2 League Cups.
Runner-up: Premier League 2013 & 2015; FA Cup finalist 2013.

Like Vincent Kompany, Zabba was signed before the takeover in 2008 and went on to become a hugely popular figure at the club. Since leaving City he has talked of his love for the club and for Manchester, and was given a great reception at the West Ham-City game in April 2018.

Fernandinho

5 trophies won: 2 Premier League & 3 League Cups.
Runner-up: Premier League 2015.

Joined City in 2013, and played a part in every major success that followed, winning the League and LC double in both his first season and the 2017-18 season. He also scored the opener in the 2016 LC final.

These players are destined to be remembered for decades, and for who knows what successes may follow. There are others who came close to the list but who missed out on the occasional cup final appearance. One of these is Colin Bell, who appeared

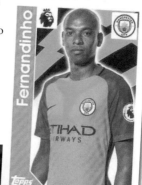

in every success between 1966 and 1979 but missed the 1976 League Cup final due to injury. King Colin's trophy haul at City is 1 European trophy, 1 League, 1 FA Cup, 1 League Cup and the Second Division title.

Zabba Dabba Don't: A frustrated Pablo sees red at the 2013 FA Cup final against Wigan Athletic.

Over Land and Sea

City's connections with UEFA go back to the beginnings of European competition. In 1956 Maine Road became the first ground in England to stage European Cup football. Back then, City offered the use of the stadium to neighbours United as the club was keen to promote European competition in England. Old Trafford was not then suitable for European games due to its lack of floodlights.

Those first games were watched by Mancunians regardless of club, and both Blues and Reds alike attended as United progressed in

GRATIS
29. APRIL 1970
EUROPACUP-FINALSPIEL
DER POKALSIEGER

MANCHESTER CITY – GORNIK-ZABRZE

HERAUSGEGEBEN
VOM ÖSTERREICHISCHEN FUSSBALL-BUND
IM AUFTRAG DER U.E.F.A.

the competition. Maine Road went on to house the largest European crowd on an English club ground – 75,598 for United v Borussia Dortmund (a capacity crowd). Apart from games at Wembley, no English home fixture has ever attracted a higher European crowd, and this was followed by the first European Cup quarter-final ever involving an English club when United beat Athletic Bilbao at Maine Road in February 1957.

United chose to make the move back to Old Trafford for the semi-final, where a much lower crowd of 65,000 witnessed their aggregate defeat. People said at the time

that the atmosphere simply could not match that experienced at the European games at Maine Road. Many questioned whether the Reds had been right to return home for the semi.

A little over a decade later, Maine Road staged its first Manchester City European Cup tie as the Blues faced Fenerbahce in a memorable game. That season, Manchester became the first British city ever to have two clubs competing in the European Cup.

The greatest of City's late '60s appearances in UEFA competitions came in 1969-70 when thrilling performances earned victories over Bilbao, Lierse, Coimbra and Schalke. This meant we were faced with the prospect of a ECWC final against Gornik Zabrze in Vienna. City won that final 2-1 and became only the 15th club to win a UEFA tournament, as well as the 4th English side (after Spurs, West Ham and United) to earn UEFA trophy success. Incidentally, for those who talk about Liverpool's great European heritage, they became the 20th club to achieve UEFA competition

success when they finally won the UEFA Cup in 1973.

City regularly competed in Europe during the 1970s

with significant victories over Milan, for example; but the hardships of the 1980s and 1990s, together with the ban on English clubs following Heysel, meant European football was not possible until 2003 when the first competitive game at our current home saw a 5-0 victory in the UEFA Cup over TNS.

Countless memorable moments have followed, including the 2009 UEFA Cup games with Hamburg and the recent Champions League seasons. Our current stadium has also entered the European record books for staging the 2008 UEFA Cup final between Rangers and Zenit.

European football has always been significant to Manchester and Mancunians. It has been in our heritage since the earliest years of organised European competition and City fans are rightly proud of everything this club has achieved in Europe's main competitions. The club has also always been keen to see UEFA-organised games take place at either Maine Road or at our current home.

It is frustrating when the media or other figures inside football suggest that City have little or no European heritage. Clearly, it has been something the club and fans have supported since the mid '50s, and City were one of the first English clubs to taste major European trophy success.

There follows just a key selection of City's proud European games, achievements and records:

European Final Appearances
1 – European Cup Winners' Cup (ECWC) v Gornik Zabrze, 1970. City won the final 2-1 in only our second season in European competition. The ECWC was a competition for the winners of each nation's major cup (FA Cup equivalents) and was deemed of higher significance than the Fairs/UEFA Cup at the time.

In 1970 City qualified for both the ECWC and the Fairs Cup (earlier UEFA Cup equivalent) but they had to compete in the ECWC due to its stature and their role as ECWC winners.

European Semi-final Appearances

3 seasons – 1969-70, 1970-71 (both ECWC) & 2015-16 (Champions League). In 1970 City defeated Schalke 5-2 on aggregate, and in 1971 Chelsea defeated City 2-0 on aggregate. In 2016 Real Madrid defeated the Blues 1-0 on aggregate.

First European Game

City 0-0 Fenerbahce, European Cup round 1 1st leg, 18 September 1968.
Attendance: 38,787.
City team: Mulhearn, Kennedy, Pardoe, Doyle, Heslop, Oakes, Lee, Bell, Summerbee, Young, Coleman.

First ECWC Tie

Atlético Bilbao 3-3 City, round 1 1st leg, 17 September 1969.
Attendance: 45,000.
City team: Corrigan, Book, Pardoe, Doyle, Booth, Oakes, Summerbee, Bell, Lee, Young, Bowyer.
Goalscorers: Young, Booth & Echebarria (og).
Since this game Bilbao have reverted to

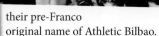

their pre-Franco original name of Athletic Bilbao.

First UEFA Cup Tie

City 2-2 Valencia, round 1 1st leg, 13 September 1972.
Attendance: 21,698.
City team: Corrigan, Jeffries, Donachie, Doyle, Booth, Oakes, Mellor, Bell, Marsh, Lee, Towers.
Goalscorers: Mellor & Marsh.

First Goal in Europe

Tony Coleman, Fenerbahce v City, European Cup round 1 2nd leg, 2 October 1968.
Attendance: 45,000.

Viennese swirl: Tony Book holds aloft the ECWC. George Heslop and Alan Oakes hold aloft Tony Book.

Mercer men plough through mud and rain

Manchester City 2 Honved 0: aggregate 3-0

MIGHTY Manchester City powered their way through pouring rain and a paddyfield of a pitch last night into the quarter-finals of Europe's Cup-winners' Cup.

European competition at the time.

Highest Maine Road Crowd

City v Atlético Bilbao, 1 October 1969. Attendance 49,665.

Highest Etihad Crowd

City v Real Madrid, 26 April 2016, Attendance 53,500.

1969-70

The 1969-70 European campaign began in September with a 6-3 aggregate

Manchester Double

The first time two sides from a British city competed in the European Cup was in 1968 when City (League Champions) and United (European Cup winners) competed.

Highest Winning Margin

Five on three occasions – 5-0 v SK Lierse, ECWC (h), 26 November 1969; 5-0 v TNS, UEFA Cup (h), 14 August 2003; 5-0 v Steaua Bucharest, Champions League, (A), 16 August 2016.

Highest Aggregate Score

8-0 v SK Lierse, ECWC round two, 1969-70. Those 8 goals were scored by: Lee (4), Bell (3) & Summerbee.

Highest Crowd

Gornik v City, 10 March 1971. Crowd is reported as between 100,000 and 110,000. This was a typical crowd for Gornik in

victory over Spanish side Atletico Bilbao. In the 2nd round SK Lierse were totally outclassed as City beat the Belgians 3-0 away and 5-0 at Maine Road in November. The third round wasn't played until March, with the first leg taking place only three days before the 1970 League Cup final. The press expected City to rest their key players, especially as their opponents were allegedly rather inexperienced students, but Mercer and Allison were keen to ensure a good result.

A grim and at times difficult match ended goalless. A whole host of travel problems followed, disrupting preparations for the League Cup final, but all of this was forgotten when the second leg ended in a 1-0 victory thanks to a goal from Tony Towers.

City's semi-final opponents were German side Schalke 04, who in the '50s had tried to sign Bert Trautmann. Despite losing the away leg 1-0 on April Fool's Day, City won 5-2 on aggregate.

The final against Poland's Gornik Zabrze was played in poor conditions on 29 April at the Prater Stadium, Vienna. In the 12th minute Neil Young gave City the lead, and shortly before half-time Lee made it 2-0 via a penalty. Gornik's captain Oslizlo pulled one back in the 68th minute, but City remained in overall control. At the final whistle Blues supporters, who numbered around four to five thousand in a crowd variously reported as anything from 7,968 to 12,000, started to celebrate. City had become the first English side to win a major domestic and European trophy in the same season. As a note, it has to be remembered that Leeds United did win the Fairs Cup and League Cup in 1968, although at that time several significant English sides had refused to enter the League Cup, and the Fairs Cup was not a UEFA-organised tournament. The 1969-70 season was the first time all League clubs had entered the competition.

City's fourth civic reception since May 1968 followed, as did a ten-mile tour of the city, starting at the airport. It was a great time to be a Blue.

City had played 61 first-team matches during the 1969-70 season. Unsurprisingly, there wasn't a single player who appeared in every match. Mike Doyle came closest, appearing in 60 games – the only one missed being a 3-1 League defeat at Chelsea in December. Tommy Booth was not far behind, having made an appearance in 59 matches.

One-way street: A police car takes a wrong turning at City's 1970 ECWC homecoming.

Love on the Terraces

Ever since reforming as Manchester City in 1894 the club has enjoyed great support, and in turn the fans have experienced a unique range of incredible highs mixed with devastating lows. No matter what, City's famous supporters have always been there, urging the club forward or sharing the frustrations.

Throughout the struggles of the '80s and '90s the loyalty and dedication of fans remained the greatest positive at the club, and the focus of so much media coverage. It was an era when City fans were rightly considered to be the most loyal supporters in the land, and the facts back this up.

But the loyalty of fans stretches right back to the beginnings of the club. As does their ability to brighten the mood or inject a bit of humour into football. As early as the 1890s City fans were known for their carnival atmosphere with Manchester's Blues wearing fancy dress for games and bringing musical instruments into the ground. The 'electric' atmosphere they created was reported on in the contemporary press, and they helped their first major star, Billy Meredith, guide the Blues on to FA Cup glory in 1904 –

Manchester's first major success.

Reports show that the 1904 homecoming was attended by "the whole population of Manchester" with every age group and every segment of Mancunian society represented. That first major triumph established the Blues as a serious force and, with a dedicated fan base, they became the second best-supported League club by 1904 (after Aston Villa), before hitting top spot for the first time in 1910-11. City's old Hyde Road ground struggled to cope with the crowds as Mancunians flocked to games, putting up with cramped conditions for years.

Eventually, after over two decades of planning a move, City finally had a stadium to be proud of as Maine Road opened in 1923. Film reports claimed

80,000 were at the opening, though the club played the figure down. Nevertheless, that first season at the new stadium saw City attract 76,166 for a cup game – this

being the largest crowd ever seen on any English club ground at the time. Ten years later the Blues beat their own record with 84,569 for another game and, even today, this remains the largest attendance on a club ground in England. City also still hold the record crowd figures for games at Hillsborough and Burnden Park, both set during this era – all the more remarkable when we remember that the Depression and financial suffering plagued Mancunians at this time.

The 1934 homecoming parade was the

first to attract one million people, and film of that day makes it abundantly clear how much Mancunians loved the Blues' achievements. In 1937 City won the League and a celebratory pitch invasion ensued, as it has for every title success that has followed.

City fans have never been afraid to demonstrate their love for a player – whether it be Pablo Zabaleta, David Silva, Colin Bell, Bert Trautmann, Matt Busby or Billy Meredith – and in the late '40s goalkeeper Frank Swift was given a special honour on the occasion of his final away appearance, at Huddersfield Town. This

was marked with a procession of vehicles travelling back across the Pennines dressed in City colours with a supporters' club coach heading the motorcade with the player himself on board.

Of course, record crowds and major successes litter City's history; but then so do periods of struggle, and it is at these times when the strength of Blue support has come to the fore. The darkest days came in the

Blues on their way to the 1974 League Cup final; behind the fences at Bradford, 1989, and in Trafalgar Square, 1969.

two decades following a shock relegation in 1983. That was the beginning of the struggles but it was also the period when fan loyalty and humour reached new heights. As football fans in general were receiving negative headlines, City fans created the inflatables craze which brought humour back on to the terraces and made every game at Maine Road something special. They also demonstrated their humour with songs such as 'We Never Win at Home,' which grew in popularity as City embarked on a miserable run of away games without a win in the mid '80s.

City was part of fans' DNA – it wasn't all about success (or failure for that matter), it was about being part of a community of like-minded people who would support their club no matter what obstacles were thrown in their way. We stood tall and proud of our City, and even in the darkest of days we were there. We knew we had a history and heritage to be proud of, and we worked tirelessly to ensure our club got the full support and backing it needed. We demonstrated against owners who abused their position – the 'Swales Out' campaign lasted for over a decade – because we knew this was our club and that Manchester City deserved better.

In the 2010s City has returned to a position of strength within football and, no matter what happens in the future, City fans will always remember their triumphs and failures. Every football club has highs and lows, and it is important to celebrate the successes while remembering the difficulties.

Above all else, throughout City's history the club's fans have been welcoming, supportive and inclusive, no matter what successes or hardships they have encountered. Long may this approach continue.

Blue Remembered Ills

The struggles may have started earlier, possibly even back in 1979 when Malcolm Allison returned; but it was 1983 when City were relegated for the first time in a generation. This was the point when the club began to be seen as a struggler instead of one of the top four or five in the country. But the 1983-2008 period never defined our club, and it is time for football to recognise it as an anomolous time, not the period since the 2008 investment that is out of character.

On relegation day 1983, only Arsenal, Everton and Liverpool had enjoyed more consecutive seasons in the top flight than City and, from their first promotion in 1899 to 1983, the Blues had only spent 10 seasons outside the top flight. As a comparison, from the Blues' establishment as Manchester City in 1894, United had spent seven fewer seasons in the top division. In fact, the only teams that had enjoyed more top-flight seasons during 1894-1983 were Everton (74), Liverpool (68), Villa (67) and Arsenal (66). City had enjoyed 63 seasons in the top flight.

In terms of trophy success, on the day City were relegated in 1983 the Blues had won nine major trophies, only three behind Manchester United.

City were a major giant of the game, and in the decade before the 1983 relegation they had regularly been the third or fourth best supported club and regarded as one of the Big Four – City, Everton, United and Liverpool. Occasionally Spurs or Arsenal would be added to make it a Big Five or Six, but City were always included prior to relegation.

City's average attendances were impressive for the period. In 1977 it was claimed the Blues had more season ticket holders than any other club, and from 1975 to 1983 we finished the season as third best supported club every year apart from 1976, 1979, 1981, 1982 and 1983, when we were fourth.

Many great moments came between 1983 and 2008, of course, but when the media and rivals talk of City today as if they achieved little prior to the investment, think back to the status of the club in 1983. No one back then would have been critical of City's traditional status within the game.

The 'Bring Back Trevor Francis' Campaign.

NO MORE SWALES RUBBISH!

Kompany is King

From our first major trophy-winning captain, Billy Meredith, through to the leadership of Vincent Kompany and David Silva in 2017-18, City has been blessed with some truly great captains. They have become legendary figures, often adopting the city and its people as their own. The majority of the men who have captained City to success have tended to live and breathe City even after their own playing careers have ended.

Vincent Kompany has now lifted more trophies than any other City captain, overtaking Tony Book during 2017-18. In order of trophy-lifting regularity the most successful captains are as follows (note: these statistics include European competition, League, FA Cup and League Cup, not Charity/Community Shield or other tournaments):

League Cups) and 2013 FAC runners-up. Also played in 2011 FA Cup final (Carlos Tevez was captain).

Total Major Trophies won: 7.

Joined City for a bargain fee of around £7.5 million in August 2008 and demonstrated game after game, year on year, his commitment to City. He joined the club before the investment, when he quickly became an adopted Mancunian and a great ambassador for the club. City fans love their captains but Kompany has become our greatest of all time and a man who recognises the significance of his role, the club and of Manchester. It is a privilege to watch him play.

Vincent Kompany
Trophies lifted: 6 (2012, 2014 & 2018 PL Championships; 2014, 2016 & 2018

Tony Book

Trophies lifted: 4 (1968 League Championship, 1969 FA Cup, 1970 League Cup & 1970 ECWC). Voted Football Writers' Player of the Year in 1969.

Still known as 'Skip' to this day. From the moment he arrived in 1966 he became established as a great leader. His achievements as a captain were unsurpassed (until Kompany came along!) but his overall career record at City may never be beaten. After his playing days ended he fulfilled a variety of roles including manager of the thrilling mid-'70s team that came close to winning the League in 1977 but also won the League Cup in 1976. He was manager of the Youth team that won the FA Youth Cup in 1986.

Played: League 242+2, FAC 28, LC 19+1, ECWC 16 & UEFA Cup 1.

Goals: League 4 & LC 1.

Mike Doyle

Trophies lifted: 1 (1976 League Cup). Also played in 1966 Second Division Championship, 1968 League Championship, 1969 FA Cup, 1970 League Cup, 1970 ECWC and 1974 League Cup runners up.

Total Major Trophies won: 6.

A determined Mancunian leader, Doyle was a key defender during the Mercer-Allison years and then went on to captain the Blues in the 1976 League Cup final success over Newcastle. He had progressed through City's junior teams and personified the spirit that most Blues want from their captain and players.

Played: League 441+7, FAC 44, LC 43, European Cup 2, ECWC 16 & UEFA Cup 5.

Goals: League 32, FAC 2, LC 4 & ECWC 2.

Carlos Tevez

Trophies lifted: 1 (2011 FAC). Also played in 2012 PL Championship and 2013 FA Cup runners-up.

Total Major Trophies won: 2

An important player during City's first successes of the modern era, lifting the first major trophy in 2011.

Played: League 97+16, FAC 10+3, LC 8, Champions League 3+3 & Europa League 6+1.

Goals: League 59, FAC 8 & LC 6.

Sam Barkas

Trophies lifted: 1 (1937 League Championship). Also captained Second Division champions (1947).

The first man to captain City to the League title, Barkas was unfortunate in that the war years prevented him and City from building on their 1937 success.

Played: League 175+7, FAC 20.

Goals: League 1.

Billy Meredith

Trophies lifted: 1 (1904 FA Cup). Also runners-up in the League (1904) and Second Division champions twice (1899 & 1903).

Football's first superstar, Meredith became idolised by City fans for his excellent wing play and superb captaincy. Another man who led by example, even playing for City at the age of 49 in an FA

www.mcfc.co.uk

Goals: League 146, FAC 5 & Test Matches 1.

Sam Cowan

Trophies lifted: 1 (1934 FA Cup). Also played in 1926 & 1933 FA Cup finals (becoming the only City player to appear in three FA Cup finals) and the 1928 Second Division championship.

Following our defeat in the 1933 FA Cup final, Cowan promised that he would lead his City side to glory the following year – and he was as good as his word! This was City's first success at the old stadium. Cowan led the Blues through an era which saw them attract phenomenal crowds and start to rival Arsenal as the decade's leading team. He also managed City to the Second Division title in 1947.

Played: League 369 & FAC 37.

Goals: League 19 & FAC 5.

Roy Paul

Trophies lifted: 1 (1956 FA Cup). Also captain for the 1955 FA Cup final.

Like Billy Meredith, Roy Paul was a Welsh international. A powerful Welsh former miner from the Rhondda Valley, he arrived at City in 1950 and became one of the club's most influential players of all time. His drive and determination pushed City forward and his never-say-die spirit encouraged others, especially in the dressing room at the 1956 final.

Played: League 270 & FAC 23.

Goals: League 9.

Roy Paul claims the Cup in 1956 – and sets a trend for cool tattoos, influencing countless modern-day stars.

Cup semi-final. After his playing career ended he watched City often and went to every FA Cup final involving the Blues from 1904 to his death in 1958 (six finals in total). Meredith helped City become a major club.

Meredith is also the longest-serving City club captain, leading the Blues for eleven consecutive seasons between 1895 and 1906. This of course only includes seasons when Meredith was the official captain, not individual games when he may have captained the side but not been the regular choice.

Played: League 366, FAC 23 & Test Matches 4.

Other great stars have lifted trophies for City or led the Blues out at Wembley, such as Johnny Crossan (1966 Second Division). In 1926 Billy Meredith's son-in-law, Charlie Pringle, became the first man to lead a Manchester side out at Wembley Stadium (opened in 1923). The last man to captain City to a major

final at 'old' Wembley was Paul Power, who led City against Spurs in the 1981 FA Cup final, which went to a replay, and the 1986 Full Members' Cup final (5-4 defeat to Chelsea). The last City captain at the 'old' Wembley was Andy Morrison, who lifted the 1999 Second Division Play-off trophy after the memorable penalty shoot-out victory over Gillingham.

Manchester giants Sam Cowan (left), Sam Barkas (above) and Mike Doyle (on his bottom).

25

Goalbangers Galore

We all know that Sergio Agüero is City's all-time record goalscorer but what about our highest League scorer? And where does Agüero stand in our list of all-time highest League goalscorers?

Of course, by the time you read this, Sergio may well have surpassed all those above him in this list but, as of 31 August 2018, here are City's record League scorers:

158 Goals	Tommy Johnson	(1919-30)
158	Eric Brook	(1927-39)
146	Sergio Agüero	(2011-)
146	Billy Meredith	
	(1894-1906 & 1921-24)	
142	Joe Hayes	(1953-1965)
126	Billy Gillespie	(1896-1905)
122	Tommy Browell	(1913-26)

120	Horace Barnes	(1914-25)
117	Colin Bell	(1966-79)
116	Frank Roberts	(1922-29)

Of these goalscorers only Joe Hayes, Sergio Agüero and Colin Bell scored for City after World War Two which means Agüero is the Blues' greatest post-war League striker. In terms of goals per game, Sergio has the best record of the lot with 0.7 goals per game, followed by Billy Gillespie's 0.58 per game over a century ago. Gillespie was a City cult hero in the 1890s and early 1900s, winning the FA Cup with the Blues in 1904. He was known for his bustling style of play which often ended with the ball and the opposition goalkeeper in the back of the nets. City fans loved his never-say-die attitude.

Here is a chart listing City's top ten League scorers based on their goals-per-game ratio:

Player	Goals per game
Sergio Agüero	0.699
Billy Gillespie	0.578
Horace Barnes	0.553
Tommy Browell	0.549
Frank Roberts	0.537
Tommy Johnson	0.481
Joe Hayes	0.429
Billy Meredith	0.399
Eric Brook	0.351
Colin Bell	0.297

In terms of the Premier League's all-time greatest goalscorers, Agüero is already 10th but his ratio eclipses all other players who have scored 100 Premier League goals or more apart from Harry Kane, though Kane has played about 40 League

COLIN BELL
MANCHESTER CITY F.C. and ENGLAND

FRANK ROBERTS
MANCHESTER CITY

E. F. BROOK

international heroes but, in terms of records, Agüero's goalscoring eclipses almost all that have gone before. Inevitably it is difficult to compare heroes from one era with another, but whenever comparisons are made between Agüero and the modern era's greatest strikers the evidence is clear. Sergio Agüero's statistics speak for themselves with few Premier League legends able to compare to the record of City's Argentinian star.

games less than the City man. Here are the scoring ratios of the top 10 Premier League scorers who have scored 100 goals or more:

Player	Goals per game
Harry Kane	0.707
Sergio Agüero	0.699
Thierry Henry	0.678
Alan Shearer	0.589
Ian Wright	0.531
Robin van Persie	0.514
Romelu Lukaku	0.462
Michael Owen	0.460
Andy Cole	0.452
Jimmy Floyd Hasselbaink	0.441
Robbie Fowler	0.430

Manchester City have had many great goalscoring figures over the years, including World Cup stars and

Kearsley's finest: Local goal ace Joe Hayes was an ex-miner and mill worker (left).
Billy Meredith with trainer Jimmy Broad and son-in-law Charlie Pringle (far left);

The Mercer & Allison Years

It was a decade that started with City's great '50s team gradually moving on, and ended with the glory years under Joe Mercer and Malcolm Allison. It paved the way for the glamour of the '70s and ensured City were perceived as a giant of the game. Here's a taster of what made the '60s one of the key decades in the club's history, when the Blues became established as a major power.

Focusing exclusively on the decade 1960-69, City:

• Won the Second Division title, the First Division Championship, the FA Cup and, as the decade ended, the club was chasing glory in the League Cup and ECWC.

• Attracted some incredible individual attendances, such as 65,981 for a game with Burnley and 63,034 for a cup tie with Everton while City were a Second Division club. In fact, that crowd against Everton was larger than any domestic attendance at Old Trafford that season.

• Brought in several players who would become legends at the club, such as Colin Bell, Mike Summerbee, Francis Lee and Tony Book.

• Relied on youth for much of the decade. Talented products of City's youth system such as Alan Oakes, Glyn Pardoe, Neil Young, Mike Doyle, Joe Corrigan, Tommy Booth and many others were given their chance to shine alongside the star purchases.

• Considered then rejected appointing first Peter Doherty

Mine, all mine: Tony Book gets his hands on the last of our 3 trophies won within a year (May 1968 to April 1969).

then Bill Shankly as manager, choosing instead former Aston Villa boss Joe Mercer. Mercer had suffered a stroke at Villa and was still recuperating when he took on the City job. Within days of accepting, he tracked down the man he wanted as his assistant – Malcolm Allison. Together, they transformed activities on the pitch.

• Under chairman Albert Alexander the Blues developed and were a highly profitable club.

• City became a stylish club and Malcolm Allison even introduced the red and black shirts which became one of the club's most memorable,

popular and iconic kits.

• Stars of the decade included top scorers Denis Law (1960-61), Peter Dobing, Alex Harley, Derek Kevan, Neil Young, Colin Bell and Francis Lee, plus Ken Barnes, Harry Dowd, Mike Summerbee, Bert Trautmann, Alan Oakes, Tony Book and, let's face it, almost every member of the great late '60s squad.

The 1960s was a classic City decade, from the final years of Les McDowall's reign – with Bert Trautmann, Ken Barnes, and Joe Hayes from the great '50s side – to the crowning glories of Mercer and Allison.

The Untouchables: City supreme

NEIL YOUNG came from his sick bed to hammer in two fine goals in the first-half battering of Leicester City at Maine Road this afternoon.

Alan Oakes and Mike Doyle added two more to rip-roaring Manchester City. In a mopping-up barrage, completely flattened a Leicester side who did not quite know what had hit them.

Six hours before the kick-off ...

By
PETER GARDNER

THE TEAMS
MANCHESTER CITY: Mul-
Ireson, Book, Pardoe, Doyle,
Booth, Oakes, ...

Champion of Champions

City have won the Premier League or the original Football League on five occasions, so far. These successes have come in three significant periods for the club, although it should be stressed that we also had a few highly significant 'near-misses,' too! Here is a comparison of the five League titles (note: the 2001-02 Division One title is often recorded

MANCHESTER CITY TEAM, winners of the League Championship, 1936-37.

Back row (left to right): McCullough, Dale, T. Chorlton (trainer), Swift, Marshall, Bray.
Middle row (left to right): Toseland, Herd, Tilson, Mr. W. Wild (secretary-manager), Barkas (captain), myself, Brook.
Front row (left to right): Heale, Rodger, Clark, Percival.

A. Wilkes & Son, West Bromwich

as a League title success, however this has been excluded from this analysis as it equates to a second-tier title, similar to the one first won by the Blues in 1899).

The journey starts back in the days immediately before World War II:

1936-37
Record: P42 W22 D13 L7 F107 A61 Pts 57 (2 for a win; equivalent to 79 today).
Best unbeaten sequence: 22 games (including a 2-2 draw on last day of season).
Nearest rival: Charlton, 3 points behind (both games ended 1-1).
Highest crowd: 74,918 v Arsenal.
Highest away crowd: 68,796 v Man Utd.
Average attendance: 35,872.
Largest winning margin: 5-0 v Derby & v Liverpool.
Largest win: 6-2 v WBA & v Brentford.
Key period: April – when six games ended in victory including games against title-challenging rivals Brentford (6-2 & 2-1) and Arsenal (2-0).
Leading scorers: Peter Doherty (30), Eric Brook (20), Alec Herd & Fred Tilson (15).
Manager: Wilf Wild.
Other 'era' successes: City were the 1934 FA Cup winners & 1933 FA Cup finalists.

City were second only to Arsenal in terms of status within the decade and

the rivalry between the two clubs was intense. It tended to work in Arsenal's favour initially – in 1932 they won a FA Cup semi against City in the dying minutes to add to the agony – but it swung in the Blues' favour as the decade progressed. A record League crowd of 79,491 attended Maine Road in 1935 for the clash of the northern and southern giants, and then the Blues did the double over the Gunners in 1936-37. Arsenal finished third (Charlton were second) and the Blues won the title by 3 points.

1967-68

Record: P42 W26 D6 10 F86 A43 Pts 58 (2 for a win; equivalent to 84 today).
Best unbeaten sequence: 11 games.
Nearest rival: Manchester United, 2 points behind (games ended 1-2 home defeat & 3-1 away win).
Highest crowd: 62,942 v Manchester United.
Highest away crowd: 63,004 v Manchester United.
Average attendance: 37,223.
Largest win: 6-0 v Leicester City.
Key period: January to end of March, when Christmas disappointments were followed with a return to form and victory over title rivals Manchester United.
Leading scorers: Neil Young (19), Francis Lee (16), Colin Bell & Mike Summerbee (14 each).
Manager: Joe Mercer.

Other 'era' successes: 1969 FAC, 1970 League Cup & 1970 European Cup Winners' Cup.

After uncharacteristic struggles in the early '60s the Blues were promoted under Joe Mercer and coach Malcolm Allison in 1966. Eighteen months later they were described as the most exciting team on the planet as they demonstrated their attacking flair with brilliant football game after game. City won the League title on the last day of the season at Newcastle. This was a real team effort, with legendary footballing figures such as Bill Shankly and 'Dixie' Dean telling all who cared to listen how great this team was.

United bow to City

By IAN ARCHER: Man. Utd....1 Man. City..3
MANCHESTER
CITY made it a

the choice of champions!
jerseys, shorts and hose

as worn by Manchester City League Champions 1968

Best unbeaten sequence: 9 games (included a 6-1 victory at Old Trafford & 5-1 at Tottenham).

2011-12
Record: P38 W28 D5 L5 F93 A29 Pts 89 (equivalent to 61 under old system).
Best unbeaten sequence: 9 games (included a 6-1 victory at Old Trafford & 5-1 at Tottenham).
Nearest rival: Manchester United, same points with inferior goal difference.
Highest crowd: 47,435 v QPR.
Highest away crowd: 75,487 v Manchester United.
Average attendance: 47,044.
Largest win & winning margin: 6-1 v Manchester United & v Norwich.
Key period: Those final weeks!
Leading scorers: Sergio Agüero (23), Edin Dzeko (14) & Mario Balotelli (13)
Other 'era' successes: 2011 FAC and 2013 finalists.

A dramatic final day has become the story of this season to many, but there were so many brilliant periods during the year. Kompany's headed goal against United switched the balance City's way and set them up nicely for the final two games. Worth remembering that United had been 8 points clear of the Blues with only six games left by 11 April.

2013-14
Record: P38 W27 D5 L6 F102 A37 Pts 86 (equivalent to 59 under old system).
Best unbeaten sequence: 12 games.
Nearest rival: Liverpool, 2 points behind (won 2-1 at home but lost 3-2 at Anfield).
Highest crowd: 47,364 v Chelsea.
Highest away crowd: 75,203 v Manchester United.
Average attendance: 47,080.
Largest win & winning margin: 7-0 v Norwich.
Key period: November to January brought City from 8th to 1st but the period when City demonstrated their fighting spirit, following a 3-2 defeat at Liverpool, brought the title. City were third after Liverpool's win but 16 points out of a possible 18 in the final weeks swung the advantage back to Manchester.
Leading scorers: Yaya Touré (20), Sergio Agüero (17) & Edin Dzeko (16).
Manager: Manuel Pellegrini.
Other 'era' successes: 2014 & 2016 League Cup winners.

City swept several prominent rivals aside throughout the season with, for example, exciting victories over United (4-1 & 3-0), Arsenal (6-3 plus a 1-1) and Tottenham (6-0 & 5-1). The Blues also won the League Cup (the club's first double since 1970).

2017-18
Record: P38 W32 D4 L2 F106 A27 Pts100 (equivalent to 68 under old system).
Best unbeaten sequence: 22 games.

Nearest rival: Manchester United, trailing by a PL record 19 points (won 2-1 at Old Trafford, lost 3-2 at the Etihad).

Highest crowd: 54,452 v Newcastle United, 20 January 2018.

Highest away crowd: 80,811 v Tottenham at Wembley, 14 April 2018.

Average attendance: 54,070.

Largest win: 7-2 v Stoke City.

Winning margin: 6-0 v Watford.

Key period: The opening months of the season and City's incredible unbeaten run set the Blues up for the title. It also set the team up for an amazing array of records, many of which had stood for decades.

Leading scorers: Sergio Agüero (21), Raheem Sterling (18), Gabriel Jesus (13) and Leroy Sané (10).

Manager: Pep Guardiola.

Other 'era' successes: 2018 League Cup winners.

The Greatest?

It is impossible to compare successes across different footballing eras. And yet, it is hard to imagine a title win more stylish than that of the 2017-18 champions. There was just one blip – the second half of the Manchester derby which came in the same week as the disappointing Anfield Champions League first leg. But the 'goals for' and 'goals conceded' columns were both better than in any other City title win.

Kit launch, 1968-69 style: Malcolm Allison with Eve Atkinson and Ann Earls.

Blue Is Not the Colour...

Traditionally, football clubs would only wear a second kit when there was a colour clash, with the home side being the team expected to change. During the earliest years of City there were few clashes as our particular shade of 'Cambridge' blue only presented an issue when we played other teams

sporting a similar hue. This did not occur often and, even when there was a clash, it was only occasionally recorded which change colours were worn. Here is a selection of colours worn by City over the years:

• Cream/White – As early as 1897 there were mentions of City wearing cream jerseys, and for a period around 1903 in the Edwardian era the colour again appeared to be our regular second strip.

• Stripes – By 1901, vertical stripes were

important to the Blues and were worn at Hyde Road at times, though the exact colours are lost in the mists of time.

• Red or 'Lucky Scarlet' – It may seem unlikely now, but red was frequently worn by City back in the early days. In fact, there's evidence of red being worn in 1905 and 1913, and then regularly during FA Cup runs in the 1920s when the kit was described as 'lucky scarlet'. We wore scarlet in the 1933 FA Cup final – though many mistakenly believe we played in maroon.

• Maroon – The following year, for the successful 1934 Cup final, City actually

did turn out in maroon. This was the first time the club had won a major trophy in colours other than blue and white. Maroon has figured as a regular alternative away colour for City since then (and at times before 1934), and the colour has also often formed part of home kits – usually being used for the team numbers or as a trim on the socks and shorts. After blue and white, maroon is the colour most

Stripes at Hyde Road in 1901-02; Andy Morrison and Nicky Weaver, Wembley 1999, and Paul Hince sporting all maroon at Coventry, 1967.

A variety of white: Peter Barnes (1977), Javi Garcia (2013) and Colin Hendry (at Burnley in 1991).

often worn by City.

• Allison's Red and Black Stripes – in 1968 Malcolm Allison suggested adopting AC Milan's colours. It was not popular with fans at first but, due to a colour clash with Leicester, the colour was worn in the 1969 FA Cup final and City chose to wear it for all the successful major finals that followed including the club's first European trophy in 1970. At one point, Allison suggested making red and black the first choice kit.

• Diagonals – City were known as a stylish club by the early '70s when we started to add other modern-looking alternative kits to the kit locker. In 1972-73 City supplemented the blue and red/black kits with two containing diagonal sashes – one in white with red and blue diagonals and one in navy blue with white and red diagonals. These trendy kits even featured numbers on their arms.

• Yellow – during the late '50s and early '60s City adopted a yellow shirt for a while. At the time it was popular. Then in 1989 yellow reappeared for a humiliating 4-0 defeat at Arsenal.

• DayGlo – It has now become a kit synonymous with one of City's most crucial games, the 1999 Play-off, but the striped DayGlo kit was despised by fans when initially launched.

Traditionally, maroon has been the change colour most associated with City, but Allison's red and black stripes are also perceived by many fans as a 'true' City kit.

The Best Call in the Land

Nowadays known as 'The Best Team in the Land and All The World,' it's strange to discover this familiar chant started out as a powerful Viking call in the Kirk Douglas film *The Vikings*.

The film was shown on ITV in London a couple of days before a game at Ipswich in October 1976. Fans remember making the 'call' without any words that day. The

an easy, but highly motivational chant, and renditions at away games in the mid '80s, especially with the Viking horn leading, generated great atmosphere.

It is now one of the club's longest-running chants. Some supporters talk of the day in the late '70s when a BBC film crew arrived at Maine Road hoping to film the crowd chanting the Viking Call. The film crew tried to coax City fans to do it and, of course, they refused. Although it proved fans could never be told what to sing, it is a real shame film of the Kippax chanting the Call in all its glory were not captured for posterity that day.

following Wednesday the film was shown on Granada and, away at Norwich three days later, fans did the call again.

It soon became a great rallying cry, sometimes lasting for considerable periods of the match. At Boundary Park in 1984, shortly after another TV showing, one fan took along a Viking-style horn and repeatedly started the call whenever there was a lull. By that time the call included the word 'City,' and eventually the other words were added and the emphasis switched from the call to the second part.

In its original Viking call form, it was always a great way to get fans involved in

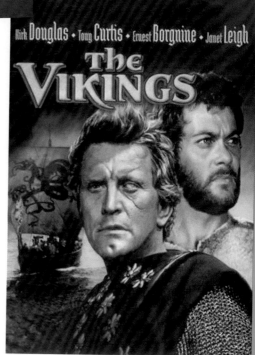

Kirk **Douglas** • Tony **Curtis** • Ernest **Borgnine** • Janet **Leigh**

The **VIKINGS**

5.45	**News. 6.0 Today. 6.30 Crossroads.**
6.55	**Film : The Vikings** (1958). Rollicking spectacular set in the days of the Vikings. It may not be historically accurate, but it's certainly cinematically effective. Kirk Douglas, Tony Curtis and Ernest Borgnine co-star.
9.0	**This Week.** Children 'on the glue'.
9.30	**N.U.T.S.** Busking on the Matterhorn to a queue of would-be climbers is one of the bizarre incidents in this comedy show, with Roy Kinnear and Barry Took.
10.0	**News at Ten.**
10.30	**The Cress** : Voices from the Past. Miss Hart has an unwelcome visitor, who shatters her contentment and revives memories of less happy days.
11.30	**Phyllis** : Leaving Home. When Jonathan Dexter's 87-year-old mother pays a family visit, Phyllis is forced to turn over her room

The Generation Game

City fans often debate the identity of City's greatest player of all time. Each generation has their own view on the matter; but the true test of a great is whether his name is remembered generation after generation.

There have been many 'greatest' players over the years, including Don Revie in the '50s and Max Woosnam in the early '20s, but post-City activities have sometimes impacted on how supporters have felt. Woosnam, for example, alienated himself with City supporters for his stance during the General Strike and this led to an angry mob of Blues confronting him at his home. Inevitably, this damaged the brilliant amateur sporting all-rounder's long-term fan status.

To be a candidate for City's greatest ever player a footballer needs to have been be an iconic Blue for many years and to have had a range of skills and match-turning abilities to enthuse the crowd. They're special players whose skills will have been recognised nationally and internationally, who opposition fans also love to see (though they may not readily admit it!).

It is impossible to directly compare a great from one era with the next due to changes to facilities, pitches and equipment, so maybe we should focus on the greatest player in each era and not search for *the* all-time greatest?

The following highlights a few of the players who have been proclaimed as the greatest at one point or another. This journey starts with Manchester's first major hero…

Billy Meredith

Appearances: 393.
Goals: 152.
Internationals (all clubs): 39 (10 goals).

Major Achievements: Captain & FA Cup winner (1904); Played until he was 49.

Reason: Meredith was the first major footballing star who helped establish City as a major force. He was idolised in three separate spells at City – 1894 to 1906; during World War I when he returned to help the club; and in the early '20s when he helped City reach the FA Cup semi-final in his final season.

He thrilled fans with his surging runs down the wing and his never-say-die, inspirational captaincy. He remains an iconic figure.

Tommy Johnson
Appearances: 354.
Goals: 176.
Internationals: 5 (5 goals).
Major Achievements: Record breaking goalscorer.
Reason: Johnson was idolised so much that when he was sold fans boycotted the club and attendances dropped by around 4,000. He became City's record seasonal scorer in 1928-29 when he netted 38 in 39 League appearances and is currently joint holder of our League scoring record.

Peter Doherty
Appearances: 131.
Goals: 80.
Internationals: 16 (3 goals).
Major Achievements: League Championship winner.
Reason: A range of skills that amazed a City crowd already used to brilliant internationals. Manchester's Blues were renowned for the brilliance of their football in the '30s and were invited to play in prestigious matches across Europe and in front of huge crowds. Doherty was a remarkable, hugely talented hero. Even though his City career was cut short by the World War II he was acclaimed as the 'greatest ever' City player into the late '70s.

Bert Trautmann
Appearances: 545.
Major Achievements: 1956 FA Cup winner, FWA Player of the year 1956.
Reason: Everyone must know the Trautmann story (if not please read about the man) but it wasn't his iconic status that made some fans view him as the greatest Blue, it was his remarkable game-turning qualities in nets. Trautmann would save the Blues often and then launch an attack with a huge throw down to a City attacker. A true legend of the game.

Colin Bell
Appearances: 501.
Goals: 153.
Internationals: 48 (9 goals).
Major Achievements: ECWC winner, League title, FA Cup & League Cup.
Reason: The first outfield player to

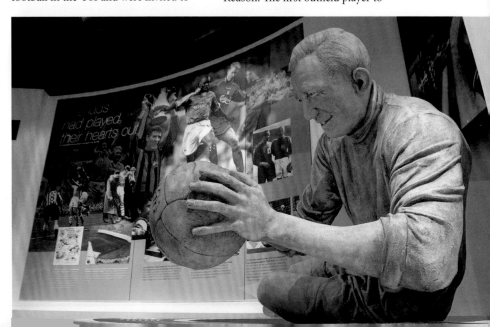

Left to right: Irish legend Peter Doherty; the much-missed Tommy Johnson, and Bert Trautmann sculpture at the City museum, 2003.

COLIN BELL
(MAN CITY)

challenge Doherty's status as the greatest with a record both for his country and for City that easily eclipsed Doherty's. Bell was often regarded as the greatest player ever by his peers. Sam Barkas, City's 1937 title-winning captain, was perhaps the first to highlight his status when he claimed that, in 1968, the 22-year-old had already matched Doherty. In the years that followed, Bell's status and accomplishments grew, before a tragic injury in the Manchester derby in 1975 seriously damaged his career for both City and England. An emotional return on Boxing Day 1977 will live with those of us there that night forever. It was the greatest ovation any Blue ever received.

Georgi Kinkladze
Appearances: 122.
Goals: 22.
Internationals: 54 (8 goals).
   Major Achievements: Remembered for his brilliance in a dismal period.
   Reason: An outstandingly talented player during the club's darkest days. Gio had everything, except the opportunity to truly

shine in a side challenging for honours. Many fans claimed he was the best they had ever seen.

Several current players are already being talked of as potential all-time 'greatest'. We already know that Agüero is our greatest-ever goalscorer but Kevin De Bruyne's contributions have brought suggestions that, in a few years' time, he may be regarded as the greatest player. Vincent Kompany is of course our greatest captain, having surpassed even Tony Book, and who knows what heights the rest of our

squad is capable of reaching?

This is truly a golden era to be Blue, blessed with an incredibly talented squad; but we should never forget the quality and talent of earlier periods. The 1900s, '30s, '50s, '60s and '70s were particularly impressive decades with a history of great players and fantastic achievements, but if you ask me to identify the all-time 'greatest ever' it has to be David Silva (and, yes, I know we still have more to come!).

winner & FA Cup winner.
Reason: Just watch him!

Another player who has already been claimed by some as the greatest they have seen is Kevin De Bruyne. We will only be able to assess his status when he has been with the club for a similar length to Silva; but he has clearly already achieved a great deal in order to earn consideration.

Kevin De Bruyne
Appearances 141.
Goals 35.
Internationals 62 (14 goals) at 11 June 2018.
 Major Achievements: 1 PL title & 1 LC winner.
 Reason: His contribution to the City cause has been impressive, and it should be noted that he has already achieved and delivered more than Kinkladze did during his time at the club.

David Silva
Appearances 346.
Goals 61.
Internationals 123 (35 goals) at 20 June 2018.
 Major Achievements: 3 PL titles, 3 LC

Going Back to Our Roots

City's Official Supporters' Club can claim a formation date as early as 1949, and is rightly proud of its 70-year history. It should be recognised for its incredible support throughout that time, especially as few other clubs followed suit until decades later. In 1968 it was reported that United's supporters' organisation was only five years old.

The roots of the current OSC go back much further than 1949, however, with evidence of an Official Supporters' Club in the '20s, continuing well into the '40s. Research is ongoing into the original set-up but the following points provide a snapshot of how City's supporter organisation has developed throughout the past century:

• The original OSC was established in 1928 and consisted of a number of branches by the '40s.

• A man called Bob Roden is believed to have been one of the founders.

• In March 1948 the City match programme listed branch meetings for Longsight (Crown Hotel), Denton (Nottingham Castle), Miles Platting (King's Arms), Gorton & Reddish (The Plough), Eccles (Duke of York), Ladybarn (Talbot), Northenden (Tatton Arms) and Chorlton (Southern Hotel).

• In May 1949 the club made special presentations to retiring goalkeeper Frank Swift, who travelled back with them in a specially decorated coach from Huddersfield Town.

• The Brooks Bar branch was established in October 1949 – the year the present OSC claims as its formation.

• Branches such as Denton were active branches in the OSC before 1949 and after its re-launch.

• By 1968 the organisation consisted of 14 branches with an annual subscription of 3 shillings (equivalent to 15p). Club ties were available at 13s 6d (65.5p).

Through the Barricades: The Supporters' Club office at Maine Road in 2002.

• Following the launch of the Junior Blues – a supporters' club for young fans – in the early 1970s, Supporters' Club branches often also established their own Junior Blues club. At the 1976 Junior Blues rally, members from Norway, Russia, France, Singapore and the UK made their presence known.

• In 1974, fans in Norway established a City supporters' club. Over the years this has evolved and is now Scandinavian Blues with many long-standing members, such as Tor Sonsteby. By 2004 it was reported that Tor had been a season-ticket holder for six years, travelling from Norway for every game. It was claimed the branch had 860 members then, and today they have over 2,100 loyal members.

• In October 1977 the Cadishead branch became the 44th OSC branch in existence.

• During the '70s and '80s the OSC would have a banner parade around the Maine Road pitch once a season, demonstrating the volume of branches in attendance.

• In 1993-94 the Supporters' Club split between branches that stayed loyal to chairman Peter Swales and those that wanted him to stand down. Nowadays the two organisations are happily reunited.

• Today, the OSC has over 170 branches around the globe, including the MCWFC Supporters' Club, and remains one of the largest football supporter organisations in the world.

❋   ❋   ❋

AN extraordinary general meeting of the City Supporters' Club will be held at the R.A.O.B. Hall, Grafton-street, on September 23 at 7-30 p.m. All are requested to attend.

Bookings should be made for the trip to Preston on October 11, fare 4s. 3d. Apply at your local branch, or to Mr. K. Souter, 46, Fovant-crescent, Reddish.

rmen. You can't beat 'em.
MANCHESTER CITY
SUPPORTERS CL
DENTON
& GORTON

HYDE

DO you come from Hyde? The Secretary of the Hyde Branch of the Manchester City Supporters' Club is Mr. T. Darling, 25, Albion Street, Hyde.

Tameside Blues: Loyal in the early '80s (main) and in 1958 (cutting).

The Inflatables Craze

In the 1980s City fans demonstrated the positive side of football during a troubled decade for the sport. Despite being one of England's top four clubs and often the third best supported side in the League, the Blues suffered a shock relegation in 1983. Financial issues and an inability to invest meant the club relied on two of its greatest strengths – youth football and the loyalty of City's fans. Young players such as Paul Simpson, Paul Moulden, Ian Brightwell, David White, Paul Lake and Andy Hinchcliffe ensured the Blues had a chance of re-establishing themselves on the pitch, while off the pitch a dedicated following was the envy of other clubs.

City fans not only turned out in their numbers – they were the sixth best supported side in 1983-84 and 1988-89 (second-tier seasons), they also brought great humour to football. The most newsworthy story involving fans during this period was the inflatable banana craze.

A dedicated City fan called Frank Newton took a 5ft 6in demonstration banana to City v Plymouth on 15 August 1987. It caused some amusement.

Newton took the banana to away games, including the match against Oldham at Boundary Park. The fans were drenched; morale was low as Oldham equalised; and yet the banana continued to be waved, bringing much-needed humour to a depressing game.

Other inflatables began appearing and by the end of the season a chant for striker Imre Varadi, to the tune of the Israeli folk song 'Hava Nagila,'

WAKE UP · Fit a smoke alarm!

was adapted with the word 'banana' replacing 'Varadi.'

For the last game of the 1987-88 season the City fanzine *Blue Print*, edited by Mike Kelly, urged fans to take a blow-up banana to Crystal Palace on the last day of the season. Around 50 bananas made it on to the terraces that day and the scene was set for supporters to enlarge on this in 1988-89.

By the time the new season began the inflatable bananas had grown in number but so too had the variety of inflatables – which now included sharks, Frankensteins, crocodiles, dinosaurs, cigarettes and many others. A surreal sight.

The cult craze continued to grow throughout 1988-89, and then on Boxing Day an appeal by the fanzines led to over 12,000 City fans, in fancy dress and carrying inflatables, descending on Stoke City's Victoria Ground. With a capacity a little over 24,000, Stoke were happy to hand over two full sides of the ground to City fans. Even the players came on to the pitch with inflatables (which they also did in the match against Leicester City in January 1989).

A company that made inflatable bananas increased production to help satisfy the craze, while Fyffes began to sponsor games at City. Thousands of inflatables appeared at some games.

The craze was copied across English football but it was City fans that were heralded as the ones who had put the fun back into football.

During a decade of disaster, tragedy and much negativity within football, City fans demonstrated there could be another way and fans became internationally renowned for their humour. The craze ultimately died out, although bananas continued to appear on occasion or in limited numbers over the years. In 2010-11 City's FA Cup run brought the bananas back as a nostalgia craze and in 2017-18 there were a number of inflatable sharks spotted at the Etihad (connected with Benjamin Mendy's comments about City being "the big shark – when teams swim with us we gobble them up").

Bananas at Stoke in 1988 (above), and comedian Eddie Large on the City bench in 1989 (left).

47

Super City from Maine Road

It was the decade that started with City's first major European trophy and ended with the Blues established as a major power. Subsequent decades saw City lose their way somewhat – and this often gets the focus when people talk of the club's modern history! – but it was the '70s that established much of what we know today as true City. For those Blues who weren't yet around (or as a nice reminder for those of us who were there), here's a sample of what was so special about 'the decade that taste forgot.'

Focusing exclusively on the span of the decade from 1970-79, City:

• Were a top four best supported side from 1975 (and on until relegation in 1983), and before that were regularly a top six best supported side.

• Could boast by 1977 over 26,000 season-ticket holders – more than any other League club.

• Won the European Cup Winners' Cup, two League Cups, appeared in another League Cup final and missed the title by a point in both 1972 and 1977. They were also ECWC semi-finalists and UEFA Cup quarter-finalists.

• The Junior Blues became established and helped to generate loyalty amongst young fans

which, during the troubles of the '80s and '90s, would ensure City's support remained high.

• Memorable European nights included beating Juventus 1-0 at Maine Road in 1976; a thrilling late goal-fest v Standard Liege in 1978; a 2-2 draw at the San Siro followed by a 3-0 victory over AC Milan in Manchester, and of course both

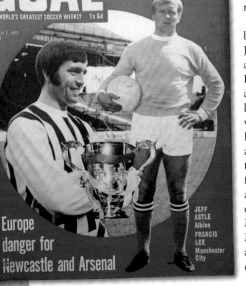

GOAL
THE WORLD'S GREATEST SOCCER WEEKLY 1s 6d

MARCH 7, 1970
No. 63

LEAGUE CUP EXTRA

Europe danger for Newcastle and Arsenal

JEFF ASTLE Albion
FRANCIS LEE Manchester City

JON'S SPORTING TYPES

'Twelve months of polishing the FA Cup and now THIS!'

48

Bobbies in helmets. Planters and nippers surrounding the tunnel. That brown Cov away kit! Willie Donachie and Brian Kidd back in the '70s.

ECWC campaigns of 1969-70 and 1970-71 when Gornik became a frequent opponent and Schalke were humbled 5-1.

• City's profile was such that the BBC did a regular series of behind-the-scenes films on the Blues, including the poignant story of Colin Bell's fight to regain fitness.

• The 'Boys in Blue' anthem was recorded in March 1972 by the players, and

became *the* City song. Written by members of Manchester chart act 10CC, it was recorded

with the band at their Strawberry Studios in Stockport.

MAN. CITY

TONY BOOK

MAN. CITY

GLYN PARDOE

MAN. CITY

RODNEY MARSH

IT'S CITY '77!

MEET the bonny bottlers of Manchester City, 1977 style. They are (back, left to right): Joe Royle, Tommy Booth, Tony Henry, Colin Bell, Willie Donachie. Centre (left to right): Gary Owen, Dave Watson, Joe Corrigan, Keith MacRae, Kenny Clements, Paul Power. Front (left to right): Brian Kidd, Gerard Keegan, Dennis Tueart (vice-captain), Mike Doyle (club captain), Asa Hartford, Peter Barnes.

• The Kippax Stand was well and truly established as the home of City's more vocal fans, every home game commencing with the 'Bring on the Champions' chant before singing the names of every player as they warmed up. Helen 'The Bell' Turner would get the atmosphere going in the North Stand.

• Stars of the decade included top scorers: Francis Lee, Rodney Marsh, Colin Bell, Dennis Tueart, Brian Kidd, and Gary Owen, plus of course Joe Corrigan, Dave Watson, Peter Barnes, Tony Book and, well, just about everybody else!

The 1970s was a classic City decade. Full of promise, hope, ambition and a few trophies along the way, too! The Kippax was vocal; Maine Road was a popular home; the Junior Blues and Official Supporters' Club were thriving; and our popular former captain Tony Book made the jump to management, proving to be the era's longest-surviving boss.

Louder Than Bombs

I t is one of City's greatest stories involving a true Blue legend, and a remarkable example of how Manchester has always been a welcoming city. Bernhard Trautmann was born in Germany in 1923 and, as a keen young athlete, he became a member of the Hitler Youth. He had high hopes of representing Germany in the decathlon at the 1940 Olympic Games and went to Berlin for several training camps. Sadly, war was to end all possibility of him becoming an Olympic hero.

Indoctrinated throughout his teenage and early adult life, Trautmann became a paratrooper during World War II. The simple facts of what followed are amazing:

- After being captured and escaping from the Russians and the Americans, Trautmann became a Prisoner of War held by the British.
- He began playing as a goalkeeper while a prisoner.
- He was signed up by St Helen's Town.
- City's goalkeeping crisis meant the Blues were desperate for a keeper – any keeper!
- Trautmann was given a chance, and joined City.
- Protests and season tickets returned in disgust but others, such as Rabbi Altmann, spoke in support.

The Goalie who Broke His Neck!

- Known as 'Bert', Trautmann soon became a hero to City fans.
- In 1955 he became the first German to play in the FAC final.
- In 1956 he helped City win the FA Cup.

In the 1956 Cup final Trautmann was outstanding, diving brilliantly at times and often showing unusual bravery in immediate danger of being hit by flashing feet. With a little over 15 minutes left to play the keeper made a daring save at the feet of Birmingham's Murphy. The collision left Bert in tremendous pain, and film of the final shows that his head and neck were left at a distinctly odd angle. The keeper bravely played on, despite obvious pain. No one knew the full extent of the dramatic injury and then a second collision occurred only a short while later.

These were the days before substitutes, and City had been forced to play with ten men the previous year. Bert knew that it had cost them the final, but the pain was excruciating.

But Bert bravely held on. City went on to win the FA Cup, and in the days that followed the full extent of his alarming injury was revealed.

TRAUTMANN: NECK BROKEN
Detained in hospital after X-ray

GREAT PAIN

BERT TRAUTMANN, Manchester City's goalkeeper, was detained in Manchester Royal Infirmary this afternoon with a broken neck.

The injury was caused when he dived at the feet of Murphy, the Birmingham forward during the last minutes of Saturday's Cup Final at Wembley.

After seeing colleagues off to-day on their foreign tour at Manchester Airport (picture—Page 5) friends persuaded him to go to the infirmary, where several X-rays were taken.

Trautmann was said to be in great pain

father-in-law said to-day: "Bert has been feeling pretty miserable and was suffering from headaches.

"As we drove to Manchester from Ringway I advised him to come with me for a check-up.

"He was unwilling at first, but was delighted he had gone when he realised how serious his condition was.

"He had ricked his neck before Saturday's game."

Saw osteopath

"The club took him to see an osteopath, and he was due to go again to-morrow.

"He didn't go with his colleagues to-day because he was not fit enough, but was expected to join them to-morrow or on Friday. He's so disappointed he can't go on this tour."

His friend said Trautmann was put to bed after having about five X-rays to find out in which places his neck was broken.

Mrs. Trautmann said: "Bert has been in terrible

47,000 fans say 'Auf Wiedersehen'

It was claimed that Trautmann had 'broken' his neck, and that the slightest further aggravation of the existing injury could have led to paralysis or killed the goalkeeper outright.

In Bert's home city of Bremen, Germany, his boyhood home is still standing, and it is possible to pay a visit to see the site where the story began. There is also a small square named after him, close by his first football club, Tura Bremen – where Bert played as a midfielder! Significantly, the square uses the English version of his name, adding to the view that Trautmann did so much for Anglo-German relations.

Bert once told me, "I was born in Germany but I grew up in Manchester." It is fitting how the city of his birth now recognises a sporting hero's significance to our city.

Singing the Blues

Chanting and singing have been a part of the matchday experience since the beginning. Here is a pitch-perfect run through the history of chanting at Maine Road and the Etihad.

Earliest Chants and Songs

During the 1890s and early 1900s City fans developed a reputation for creating an 'electric atmosphere' at home games where they would bring bugles, bells and other musical instruments. Some fans would wear fancy dress and would sing popular music-hall songs of the period. One of these, 'She's a Lassie from Lancashire,' was written in 1907 and soon found its way on to the City terraces. In fact, fans were known to be singing it as late as 1956 at the FA Cup final.

The band of St Joseph's was regularly at City games and they even went to London for the 1904 FA Cup final, parading around the pitch playing songs Mancunians were familiar with. City's opponents Bolton also brought a band,

and the two paraded around seemingly in competition pre-match. Around this time, songs dedicated to players, especially City hero Billy Meredith, appeared in sporting newspapers but whether these were actually sung at grounds is debatable. However, newspaper cartoons would often suggest that songs or even primitive chants had been heard at the ground, including one which suggested fans chanted, 'He's here, he's there...' to Bill Eadie pre-World War I!

Home Sweet Home

In 1920, after fire had destroyed the Hyde Road Main Stand, the club asked United if they could move to Old Trafford. The Reds said 'yes,' but their terms were viewed by the club and the media as being excessive.

Ultimately, City said they couldn't afford to pay United and decided to soldier on at Hyde Road. As the next City home game would be the Manchester derby much was made of both United's terms and City's need to stay at a damaged Hyde Road. The

ground was patched up and pre-match the band played 'Home Sweet Home' and 'I Wouldn't Leave My Wooden Hut for You' – fans got the message and started singing along. No doubt if that happened today City would be fined, but back then everyone recognised that these songs were a real statement by the club and its fans.

Who Said City Couldn't Play?

Throughout the period before World War II supporters used to sing along to the band of the day, usually by this point the Beswick Prize Band, either before the game or during half-time. They would also encourage the players by shouting phrases such as 'Give it to Tommy [Johnson]' or 'Play Up City!'

As Fran Parker, who first attended Maine Road around 1926, explained to me back in 2002: "It used to be a thrill to hear the crowd in those days. They'd be making lots of noise. 'Up the Blues!' and 'Come on you Blues' were two of the most popular shouts of the time."

FOOTBALL HUMOUR.
S. CHRON. NOV. 28. 1920

"I Wouldn't Leave My Little Wooden Hut for You."

There is no love lost between the two big Manchester football clubs, and the feeling has not been improved since the United first offered and then refused the City the free use of the Old Trafford ground for League matches.

Evidently a wag had been at work in the musical department prior to the match at Hyde-road yesterday, for just before the United team entered the field the band played with great pathos "I Wouldn't Leave My Little Wooden Hut For You," and followed by "Home, Sweet Home."

Songs were sung occasionally such as 'Auld Lang Syne' in the '20s while 'For he's a Jolly Good Fellow' was sung frequently to players who had married that week and enjoyed multiple airings when City won the Championship in 1937. The earliest specific City song I've been able to identify sung by fans was 'Who Said City Couldn't Play?' which appears to be based on the traditional song 'Oh My, What a Rotten Song.'

The City version was popular during the early '30s and there are recordings of it being sung at the 1934 FA Cup homecoming. It went a little bit like this:

Who said City couldn't play,
City couldn't play,
City couldn't play,
Who said City couldn't play,
City couldn't play football?

Presumably a journalist had criticised the Blues and this was the fans' response as City went on to win the FA Cup. The song remained popular until the post-war period – but maybe the time is ripe to bring it back?

The '50s and '60s

In the '50s a City version of 'Bless 'Em All' became popular:

Bless 'em all, Bless 'em all;
Bert Trautmann, Dave Ewing and Paul;
Bless Roy Little who blocks out the wing;
Bless Jack Dyson the penalty king;
And with Leivers and Spurdle so tall;
And Johnstone, the Prince of them all;
Come on the light Blues;
It's always the right blue;
So cheer up me lads;
Bless 'em all.

Another '50s favourite was 'City's the Team:'

City's the team;
They're the best team in the land;
Playing the game;
Always in Command;
We may lose a point or two;
But never do despair;
Cos you can't beat the boys in the old light blue;
When they come from Manchester.

Many of City's most recognisable chants date back to the '60s. The most important of these, from a historical context, was the terrace anthem celebrating City's triumphs under Mercer and Allison, which memorably told the story of what happened when City were relegated in 1963. The rollercoaster narrative was sung

to the tune of 'Auld Lang Syne.'

*In '63 the boys in Blue fell into Division
Two;
The Stretford End cried out aloud;
It's the end for you Sky Blues;*

*Joe Mercer came;
We played the game;
We went to Rotherham;
We won one-nil and we went back into
Division One;*

*Since then we've won the League;
We've won the Cup;
We've been to Europe too (And Won!);
And when we win the League again;
We'll sing this song to you;*

City, City, City...

From the '50s onwards, chants started to develop about specific players. According to numerous sources, Scottish centre-forward Alex Harley (who played for City from 1962 to '63) was the first player to have a chant specifically created for him although, when I interviewed them in the 1990s, supporters from the '20s and '30s claimed they were the first to specifically focus their shouted encouragement at a particular player.

'You'll Never Walk Alone'

It may seem hard to believe nowadays but the song that became linked to Liverpool was a regular at Maine Road from the '60s through to the '80s. Film of the song being sung at the 1969 and 1976 homecoming parades is held by the North West Film Archive. It is sung with real passion by City fans holding their scarves aloft. It was often trotted out to mark a triumph but, as Liverpool began winning ever more trophies, it became associated with them. It only fell out of fashion at Maine Road in the mid-'80s as Liverpool became the dominant English team.

Matchday

Once Maine Road's Kippax Stand was roofed in 1957 it became recognised as the singing heart of the club.

By the end of the '60s chanting had become a feature of every City match. At home, fans would start their singing at least 15 minutes before kick-off. With a poor quality PA system back then, those on the Kippax were able to sing freely without being drowned out. As the players gathered in the tunnel, a chant of 'Bring on the Champions!' always boomed out. Presumably, the chant had started in 1968 but it continued through to the mid '80s. The players would emerge to strains of

The Kippax, as you will remember it if you were there at Maine Road in November 1982.

Looking towards the Platt Lane from the North Stand in 1981.

opinions, of course, but the Kippax dubbed them the 'Main Stand Moaners.' As such, they were never expected to respond – but they usually did. Their chant would be an older song such as 'Singing the Blues,' for all to join in with.

'The Boys In Blue' over the PA and, once the song was over, the Kippax would chant a song for every one of the City players appearing that day – at very least, their name repeated over and over – when the player would turn and wave to the Kippax.

At away games, prior to segregation, fans would start a recognisable City chant in order to identify themselves. A massed body of fans would make their presence known by chanting about 'Colin the King' or another of his team-mates, so that other Blues could then make their way to the noisiest area in the ground.

In the 1970s to '90s the Kippax would encourage the other stands to sing. They would start with a call to the Platt Lane, City's cheapest seated stand: "Platt Lane, Platt Lane, give us a song, Platt Lane... give us a song!" The Platt Lane fans, mostly families and teenagers who hadn't yet graduated into the Kippax, would reply with a chant, typically: 'We Love You City, We Do.' This would be followed by both the Kippax and Platt Lane pointing to the slightly more expensive North Stand, chanting together: "North Stand, North Stand give us a song!" In turn, they would usually respond with 'We Are the North Stand!'

Next, all three singing stands would turn and point to the Main Stand where, for those on the Kippax, fans had a reputation for being a little negative. It was all about

During the game, a variety of chants would be heard. Often television adverts, such as British Airways' 'We'll Take More Care of You,' or popular tunes of the period such as Rod Stewart's 'Sailing' were effortlessly adapted – "We are City, we are City, super City from Maine Road." Occasionally, traditional songs such as 'Jingle Bells,' 'White Christmas,' 'You Are My Sunshine, and 'London Bridge Is Falling Down' would be converted into Blue chants.

The Kippax terracing, which stretched the entire length of the pitch, was a vibrant, boisterous space. The noisiest area was closest to the segregation fence, near the away fans. Known by a variety of names – 'Chanters' Corner' or 'the Sways'

– this area was where most (but by no means all) chants would emanate from. In 1994, after the demolition of the Platt Lane Stand and the Kippax, the North Stand became home to the more vocal fans.

The Struggles

In the '80s fans became more self-deprecating and songs such as 'We Never Win At Home' became prevalent. Supporter Peter McNally remembers singing it at West Brom in 1979 after City had failed to win in ten consecutive away games, including two 4-0 defeats at WBA. By 1987 it was sung almost every game, certainly away, as the Blues went 34 away League games without a win between January 1986 and October 1988. After every opposition goal the song would start up. It was a kind of release valve and proved popular, if that's the right word, again in 1997. Another song, 'We'll Win Away, Don't Know Where, Don't Know When' was also heard during that awful 1987-88 run, with 'Again' replacing 'Away' from time to time.

Invisible Man

Claims of when the 'We're Not Really Here' chant first started are all trumped by Prestwich & Whitefield's Don Price, who explained that it was first sung as tribute to one of their branch members who had died in 1993. A year later it was sung in Ireland along with the Cork OSC, from which point it caught on. So much so that by 1997 I mentioned it in an article as being a popular chant, peaking in 1998-99.

Blue Moon

Sung on the opening day of the 1989-90 season by a couple of Blues at Anfield post-match as fans waited to leave, 'Blue Moon' grew quickly in popularity until by the end of the season it was perceived as City's new anthem.

When the party's over:
The Kippax's Last Stand, 1994

Get Up, Stand Up

Football fans – and especially City fans – are always keen to ensure their views and feelings are heard. Whenever something happens that fans object to, the club soon finds out. Sometimes fans will chant a song or send in a few letters, tweets or radio phone-in complaints but occasionally the opinions of the fans are so strong that widespread protests, demonstrations and even boycotts occur.

The following is a brief overview of some of the big issues throughout City's history that have led to supporters expressing their views in a forceful manner. Some of these are connected with club policy, poor leadership and bad results but others provide an example of when fans felt that either society in general or a prominent body has treated the club or its fans unfairly.

The story of Blues getting riled and feeling the need to demonstrate starts way back in the 19th century:

1896 – Ticket Price Increase

Having reached the Second Division Test Matches (similar to promotional Play-offs), City's directors recognised that they were facing the most significant match

the club had ever played in. And so they decided to increase admission prices, believing the higher status of the game would be worth paying extra for. As a result, fans voiced their disapproval and many stayed away, the atmosphere was poor and City lost, making it extremely difficult to get promoted.

Normal prices returned for the next match in the Test Match series, but the damage was done. The first match against First Division West Bromwich Albion attracted approximately 6,000 only 15 days after 30,000 had watched a Second Division home game with Liverpool (then recorded as the division's record crowd).

Similar issues with ticket prices have affected other games over the years, with City's Champions League game v Paris St Germain in 2016 often being cited as one where ticket price increases led to significant fan frustration.

1904 – FA Cup Homecoming

City won the FA Cup; but this was Manchester's first big national success, and no one knew how to organise a suitable celebration! The police and City council believed too much working time had already been wasted on football, and decided there would be no homecoming parade. However, the people felt differently and the 'whole population' of Manchester got together and took to the streets to welcome the City team home.

1920 – Hyde Road Fire

The Main Stand at City's original ground was destroyed by fire. City asked United if they could move to Old Trafford on a temporary basis but United's terms were excessive and City decided to 'soldier on' at Hyde Road, patching up the ground. A week after the fire, ironically City played United at Hyde Road and the band played songs, such as 'Home Sweet Home,' aimed at 'sticking two fingers up' to United. Fans loved it.

1927-28 – Best Supported Team Despite Relegation!

City were relegated in 1926, a rather odd season when the 'Typical City' tag appears to have been established as the Blues also reached the FA Cup final. With the General Strike and other employment issues within Manchester at this time, many expected City's crowds to drop with doom and gloom filling the air.

What did City fans do? They backed the club entirely and instead of crowds dropping relative to other clubs, City's support was high. In their relegation season they were the best supported Division One club; in 1926-27 they were the third best supported club in the entire League, and they ended the 1927-28 Second Division season as the best supported team nationally with the highest average attendance of all clubs since 1921.

1929-30 – Anger at Transfers

City's star striker Tommy Johnson was sold to Everton. Supporters felt he had much more to offer and they strongly objected to the club's decision. In fact, fans were so unhappy that crowds dropped by

8,000. Johnson remained a Blue in spirit for the rest of his life and sometimes brought his Everton team-mate 'Dixie' Dean to Gorton for a night out, often in the Plough Hotel.

A similar thing happened in 1982 when Trevor Francis was sold (upset fans, that is, not Trevor enjoying the pubs of Gorton!). Francis was sold after many fans had renewed their season tickets (his face having been used in promotional material for ticket sales!) but average support still dropped by around 8,000. A 'Bring Back Trevor Francis' campaign followed a year or so later, but it was too late.

1963-64 – Merger: No Way!

Prior to the club's relegation in 1965 the shock news was leaked that a City director,

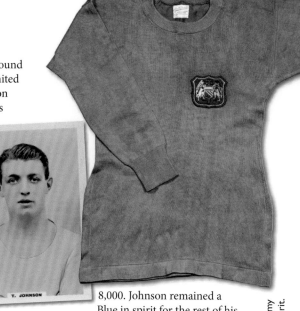

Been there, seen it, done it: Tommy Johnson's 1926 FA Cup final shirt.

CITY SOCCER ROW LOOMS OVER TEAMS "MERGER"

BY PETER GARDNER

CUP day found Manchester City fans on the receiving end of a huge shock—off the field. For a big boardroom row seems to be brewing at Maine Road over a sensational plan to link up with Manchester United.

Frank Johnson, had held meetings with directors at United to discuss the idea of a merger between the clubs. Johnson felt Manchester wasn't big enough for two clubs (how did he ever get on the City board?) and suggested that City sell Maine Road and move to Old Trafford with the long-term idea of a merger. His discussions with United started in 1963-64 but were leaked in January 1965.

The news gave a pressure group the warning they needed, and they took the opportunity to challenge the directors. Within weeks, the merger idea was dropped completely.

It seems that Johnson had acted on his own, without the support of the other board members. Johnson remained in place for the club's resurrection under Joe Mercer that followed but in 1970 his actions shook City again when he discussed selling his shareholding to a group who wanted to take over the club. A drawn-out takeover followed, led by Joe Smith, Michael Horwich, Ian Niven, Chris Muir and Simon Cussons. This caused a split between Joe Mercer and Malcolm Allison, with the new directors believing it was predominantly Allison who had been responsible for City's success. Mercer was cast aside, feeling unwanted, and City's glory days were over. Ironically, Allison also felt let down by the new directors and left nine months after Mercer.

1982-83 to 1993-94 – Swales Out!

The 1970 takeover ultimately led to Peter Swales becoming chairman. He was backed for many years by Smith, Niven, Muir, Cussons and Horwich, the takeover men. By March 1983 City fans objected to the poor management of the club, and chairman Peter Swales was the man held responsible. The truth was that the takeover had promised much but in the end had split Mercer and Allison and had seen the Maine Road stadium lose pace with its main rivals. Instead of growing the club, it was felt that City had been taken from being one of the top four English clubs to the brink of financial ruin and a life of struggle.

Peter Swales, as chairman, received most of the flak with the chant of 'Swales Out!' becoming the most popular at Maine Road for several years in the '80s. Relegation came at the end of 1982-83, but protests against Swales had begun by March that year. Thousands would gather post match outside the Main entrance, calling for him to leave. He eventually went at Christmas 1993 but the entire decade was marked by strong demonstrations and 'Swales Out!' protests. Some of Swales' supporting directors and officials remained in post in the years that followed under Francis Lee, and demonstrations returned as City failed on the pitch in the mid to late '90s.

1987-90 – Going Bananas

By the '80s, fans of most clubs were treated like animals and assumed to be violent hooligans. City fans began the banana craze to show that fans were also full of humour and decent people. The Government were planning to introduce ID cards for fans, and to curb travel. They even considered banning football, and

PETER SWALES . . City boss

Don't cry over any sacked manager —he gets a golden handshake the banana craze was perceived by some in the media as City fans' attempts at attacking the Government. Headlines such as, 'Bananas to You, Maggie' (aimed at Prime Minister Margaret Thatcher) appeared as fans demonstrated that we were not all hooligans, demanding to be treated like humans.

1990s – Standing Areas For Eastlands
In the latter part of the decade, it was City fans who kicked off the campaign for terracing to be allowed once agian at football stadia. This has now evolved into the SAFE campaign, looking at safe standing areas for all clubs.

2010s – The UEFA Anthem Booing
The booing of the Champions League anthem became a regular feature at City's Champions League games following a series of actions which fans felt were wildly inconsistent. These included City being fined more for arriving on to the pitch one minute late than other clubs were being punished for racism against our players.

As the 2017-18 season closed, the verdict on the City coach's violent welcome at Anfield angered fans further. Liverpool were fined less for the disorder which led to police injuries and a badly damaged coach than City were charged for their forgetful minute. Amazingly, it was also less than Besiktas were fined for a cat running on the pitch for one of their European games!

Here's an at-a-glance summary of the fines imposed, which sparked the UEFA anthem booing:

- £29,880 Besiktas cat incursion.
- £24,740 City one minute late for second half v Porto.
- £17,600 Liverpool attack on the Manchester City team coach.
- £17,000 Porto racist chanting at Balotelli.

While these inconsistencies continue, many City fans will continue to boo the Champions League anthem. And the intensity of the demonstration only seems to increase every time an official – whether it's a UEFA figure or a City official – asks fans to stop.

Hats Off to Josh

"**If it hadn't been for Josh, there would probably have been no Manchester City. He it was who practically alone secured their inclusion in the League in 1894. He it was, too, who after we had joined the League gave us 5 shillings bonus if we won and proceeded to take it from us again if we lost the following week. I can appreciate the humour of that better now than I did then!**" – **City legend Billy Meredith discusses Joshua Parlby in the 1920s.**

Josh Parlby's role in City's history is often overlooked, but he was the man who in 1894 got City promoted and established the club as a power in the game. In his earlier life he had been a Stoke City player and committee man, prior to arriving in Manchester to take over a public house in 1892. He soon became involved with Ardwick AFC and became one of the more vocal members of the committee. He had already started to play a part in team selection prior to taking over the role of secretary in 1893. Parlby was to become Ardwick's first paid secretary, earning 50 shillings a week.

His time in charge was a traumatic one and he was forced to 'wrangle' his way out of various financial problems that beset the club. Fare-dodging on the railways, careful manipulation of the Ardwick cheque book and many other scams managed to keep the club in existence for a while, but for much of 1893-94 Parlby wanted more and felt Ardwick offered little potential.

The final season of Ardwick saw Parlby's side finish 13th out of 15 clubs, but the club secretary had already been working behind the scenes to establish a new club, Manchester City, as he wanted to create a football team to represent Manchester – all of Manchester!

Parlby successfully guided the new club through its formative years. It was widely acknowledged that the club was only elected into the League because of an impassioned speech by Parlby at a League meeting where he boasted of City's support, ambition and drive. At that time the club did not have any players, had few backers and was without a ground but Parlby still convinced the League that Manchester City offered more than either Ardwick or its neighbours Newton Heath.

Parlby became the first secretary-manager of the new club and the opening City game ended with defeat. Nevertheless, the 1894-95 season saw the Blues finish 9th out of 16 clubs and Parlby had fulfilled his desire. He stood down in the close season due to commitments outside of football – he had now taken over a public house in Bolton – but he remained an influential committee man. In fact, the reign of his successor Sam Ormerod was noted for the constant involvement of Parlby and others. It seems Parlby continued to exert much influence over the players and other committee men during the period 1895 to 1905.

When City won the FA Cup and finished second in the League in 1903-04, many sources credited the achievement to Parlby. He was merely a director at this time, but

Star turn of the century: Second Division champions, 1899.

he was the man who had done most to establish City as a power in the game, with endless potential for further future growth.

In addition to his active involvement with Ardwick and City, he was also an influential member of the League Management committee for a period in the 1890s. He was City's first truly charismatic manager.

Managerial Record
Player Brought In: Billy Meredith – who developed into football's first superstar while at City.
First Competitive Game: Burslem Port Vale 4-2 City (goalscorers: Carson & Robinson), 2 September 1893, Division Two, attendance c.3,000.
Last Game: Grimsby 2-1 City (Milarvie), 20 April 1895, attendance 6,000.
Best Ever Result: City achieved their record score in the League during Parlby's reign. On 23 March 1895 the Blues beat Lincoln City 11-3 at Hyde Road (goalscorers: McReddie 4, Finnerhan 2, Meredith 2, Rowan 2 & Milarvie).
Points total, including League and cup fixtures:
P59 W22 D5 L32 GF 129 GA 146

Some Might Say
"There are some men whose silver tongues are said to have the power of charming song birds from the trees, and I believe 'Josh' Parlby was one of them."
– Billy Meredith on his former manager.

65

Nil Desperandum

The first goalkeeper to keep a clean sheet in the League for the Blues was Bill Douglas, who managed to repel every attack throughout the first three League games ever played by Ardwick (City) in 1892, with a 12-0 aggregate score. That season he managed to keep a total of four clean sheets. Within a couple of years, brilliant keeper Charlie Williams took the record into double figures with ten clean sheets out of 30 games. He then increased it to 13 (out of 34) in 1898-99. The progression of the club record since then is as follows:

1902-03 – 15 Clean Sheets (out of 34; percentage 0.441).

Jack Hillman, who went on to win the FA Cup with City in 1904, gave the Blues confidence with his great record, though John Edmondson had been in nets for one of the clean sheets.

1912-13 – 16 Clean Sheets (out of 38; percentage 0.421).

City used two keepers, Jim Goodchild and Walter Smith, who between them managed 12 and 4 shut-outs respectively in Division One.

1914-15 – 17 Clean Sheets (out of 38, percentage 0.447).

Goodchild and Smith pushed the record on further, although this time Smith managed 16 (a new individual record) and Goodchild one clean sheet as City challenged for the League title.

1946-47 – 20 Clean Sheets (out of 42; percentage 0.476).

The first post-war season saw Frank Swift (17), Jack Robinson (0), Alec Thurlow (3) increase the record, with Swift also establishing a new individual record.

1976-77 – 22 Clean Sheets (out of 42; percentage 0.524).

Joe Corrigan, the Blues' great goalkeeper of the late '60s to early '80s, made history by becoming the first City keeper to manage over 20 clean sheets in a League season, with ten of these coming away from home. He was an ever-present in all competitions that season, and his 22 shut-outs in the League helped the Blues to second place, missing the title by one point to Liverpool, where he would later be a well-regarded goalkeeping coach.

It is worth noting that only two other keepers have managed 20 or more League clean sheets with City in a season. In 1984-85 Alex Williams managed 21 (out of 42) in the Second Division promotion season, and in 1998-99 Nick Weaver equalled Corrigan's record with 22 (out of 45) and also had ten of these away from home; though, of course, Corrigan had achieved the record in fewer games and at a higher level.

There are several interesting aspects to keeping clean sheets. Obviously, preventing the opposition scoring means the side has a good defensive record, but there have been some notable seasons

Big Joe Corrigan with the Reds' Gary Bailey (left), 1909-10 hero Jack -yall (middle) and Nicky Weaver at Wembley, 1999(right).

with few clean sheets despite the side's success. In 1936-37, when Frank Swift helped the Blues to the League title, he only managed to keep eight clean sheets out of 42 games played. And yet, the season before, he managed 15 clean sheets in the same number of games as City eventually finished ninth.

The worst record for the club as a whole came in 1925-26. That season only two were maintained in 42 League games, which sadly contributed to the Blues getting relegated on the last day of the season. Interestingly, City managed more clean sheets in that season's FA Cup run

(three in total) before eventually losing 1-0 in the final to Bolton.

Interestingly, each record-breaking clean sheet performance is also a City record for the division played in.

Progression of Record – Most Clean Sheets by Player in a League Season				
Season	Player	CS	Games	%
1892-93	Bill Douglas	4	20	0.200
1995-96	Charlie Williams	10	30	0.333
1998-99	Charlie Williams	13	33	0.394
1902-03	Jack Hillman	13	31	0.419
1909-10	Jack Lyall	13	33	0.394
1914-15	Walter Smith	16	37	0.432
1946-47	Frank Swift	17	35	0.486
1976-77	Joe Corrigan	22	42	0.524

Corrigan's record was achieved in the top flight, while Williams was in the second tier and Weaver's in the third tier of League football. In total Weaver appeared in 55 League, Play-off and cup games during 1998-99, and kept 26 clean sheets. His record helped City achieve promotion via the Play-offs.

The shot-stopper who holds the record for most clean sheets in a season for City when all competitions are taken into consideration is Joe Hart, who managed 29 clean sheets in 2010-11 (18 in the Premier

Smith, the new idol at Ardwick.

Top 3 Clean Sheet Record holders

Season	Player	CS	Games	%
1976-77	Joe Corrigan	22	42	0.524
1998-99	Nick Weaver	22	45	0.489
1984-85	Alex Williams	21	42	0.500

League, six in the Europa League and five in the FA Cup) out of 55 appearances (percentage of clean sheets = 0.527). Hart also achieved the Blues' highest number of clean sheets from the start of the season – no less than five, in 2015-16. That run,

when combined with the final game of the previous season, constituted City's longest consecutive run of six clean sheets in the League.

In five other seasons City teams have successfully managed five consecutive clean sheets in League games – 1914-15, 1946-47, 1984-85, 2013-14 and 2015-16.

Loyal clubman Alex Williams (top left), Frank Swift (left) and Joe Hart (below).

Live Forever

City's appearance holder is Alan Oakes, and it may be some time before another player comes close to his total of 676 (plus 4 as substitute) appearances. Still, a few members of City's teams in recent years have made it on to the Top 30 appearance list.

Alan Oakes – 680
Joe Corrigan – 605
Mike Doyle – 572
Bert Trautmann – 545
Colin Bell – 501
Eric Brook – 493
Tommy Booth – 491
Mike Summerbee – 452
Paul Power – 447
Willie Donachie – 438
Neil Young – 416
Ernie Toseland – 411
Sam Cowan – 407
Billy Meredith – 394
Ian Brightwell – 382
Glyn Pardoe – 380
Frank Swift – 375
Roy Clarke - 370
Joe Hayes – 364
Bobby Marshall – 356
Tommy Johnson – 354
Richard Dunne – 352
Joe Hart – 348
David Silva – 345
David White – 340
Pablo Zabaleta – 333
Vincent Kompany – 333
Francis Lee – 330
Eli Fletcher – 326
Asa Hartford – 321

The following shows how the appearance record has evolved,

starting from the first City player to appear in 100 competitive games.

Billy Meredith (played 1894-1906; 1915-19; 1921-24)
Total Appearances: 394.

Meredith reached 100 appearances in his fourth season with the Blues, 1897-98, and by the time he was forced to leave in 1906-07 he had made 363 appearances and had captained City to FA Cup success, the Second Division title (twice) and second place in the League. He returned to City during World War I and on a permanent basis in 1921, making his final appearance at the age of 49 in the 1924 FA Cup semi-final.

Sam Cowan (1924-1935)
Total Appearances: 407.

Cowan beat Meredith's record in his final season with the Blues, 1934-35. He equalled the record on a memorable day in February, as the Blues drew 1-1 with Arsenal before the largest City League crowd of 79,491 (also then a Football League record). Cowan's 395th competitive game saw City win 2-1 at Derby County on 2 March 1935, almost a year after he had also

NEIL YOUNG
MANCHESTER CITY
INSIDE LEFT

emulated Meredith by captaining the Blues to FA Cup success.

Eric Brook (1927-39)
Total Appearances: 493

Brook appeared in Cowan's record-breaking games, and was an important member of the Blues' 1930s FA Cup fighting squad. He was also part of the 1937 League title winning team, scoring 20 League goals that season. In fact he equalled Cowan's appearance record when he played in a 5-0 victory over Liverpool at Anfield in March of that year. He also scored a hat-trick that day. He would have taken the record on further had war not intervened. It is worth noting that team-mate Ernie Toseland also eclipsed Cowan's record shortly before the war, making a total of 411 appearances by summer 1939.

Bert Trautmann (1949-64)
Total Appearances: 545

The first Blues player to appear in 500 competitive games, and the first goalkeeper to hold the record. Trautmann equalled Brook's record at home to Everton in September 1961 and made his 494th appearance three days later in a derby defeat at Old Trafford. A true legend of the game, performing heroically in the 1956 FA Cup final.

Alan Oakes (1958-76)
Total Appearances: 680

Looking back, it seems incredible that young Alan Oakes was a member of the City team at the time Trautmann broke Cowan's record,

Paul Power: a determined and dedicated City captain during the '80s.

also appearing in the team when the goalkeeper made his final appearance. By that time, Oakes had played around 100 games, but it was in the years that followed that the Winsford-born player was to become recognised as one of City's most dependable players. As Joe Mercer and Malcolm Allison re-established the club as a trophy-winning force, Oakes played a great part in every single success.

He finally overtook Trautmann's appearance record in 1972-73 with his 545th appearance coming in the goalless game at Old Trafford in April 1973.

Oakes' grand total consists of the following games: League: 561 (plus 3 as sub), FA Cup: 41; League Cup: 46 (plus 1); European Cup: 2; ECWC: 13; UEFA Cup: 2; Charity Shield: 3; Anglo-Scottish Cup: 3; Anglo-Italian Cup: 2; Texaco Cup: 3.

Notable Mentions

There are several prominent players, such as Frank Swift, Eli Fletcher, Jackie Bray and Alec Herd whose careers were interrupted by war. They did make a significant number of appearances and would still appear in the Blues' top 20 appearances list if their wartime games were included. Frank Swift would actually have held the record for a period with a total of 511 competitive and wartime appearances as City's goalkeeper.

Of all the players since Oakes moved to Chester in 1976, Joe Corrigan, Mike Doyle, Colin Bell, Tommy Booth, Paul Power and Willie Donachie established themselves as fixtures in the all-time top ten, while Ian Brightwell is the only player since Paul Power to have the consistency to break into the top 15. David White isn't too far behind however with a total of 341 appearances.

Of the 2017-18 squad David Silva is the highest placed but Joe Hart, Pablo Zabaleta and Vincent Kompany have all made it on to the record appearances table in the last decade.

Note: Competitive games are: League, FA Cup, League Cup, European Cup/ Champions League, ECWC, UEFA Cup/ Europa League, Charity/Community Shield, League Play-offs/Test Matches, Full Members Cup, Anglo-Scottish Cup, Anglo-Italian Cup and Texaco Cup. All of these counted as first-team fixtures at the time they were staged.

Transforming the Blues

Every so often a manager or coach comes along with ideas that can transform a club or a situation and at City we've been blessed with some excellent visionaries over the years. We may not always realise it at the time but some of our coaches and managers have transformed the club or even the way football is perceived.

I've decided to highlight the six men who I believe have been the greatest City coaching/managerial visionaries and the reasons why. I accept these may not be the most successful managers, but they have each achieved something way beyond expectations.

Our six visionaries are listed in chronological order. Starting with the man who established Manchester City...

Joshua Parlby

Why a visionary: Saw the opportunity to establish a 'Football Club for Manchester'.

Before Manchester City was established in 1894 there was Ardwick FC, but the club struggled in the League. Parlby arrived from Stoke City in 1892, became secretary-manager in 1893 and within a year had helped kill off the old club and launched a new one. He believed Manchester deserved a club to represent everyone, not just local district teams, and in 1894 he persuaded the Football League that Manchester City – a team which at the time had no staff, no premises or stadium, and little or no financial backing – was the club to represent the world's first industrial city. He painted a picture of a willing public desperate for an ambitious side and convinced the League – and many others – to back the new venture. Within a decade that club was finding national success, and Parlby was heralded as the visionary who established the club. His personality, drive and endeavours ensured that Manchester City became a success story.

Tom Maley

Why a visionary: Transformed MCFC into Manchester's first major trophy-winning club. A founder of Celtic Football Club, Maley brought fresh ideas from his time in Scotland. He knew what a football club could and should be, and took City from the Second Division to FA Cup glory and second place in the League. He made City Manchester's first successful club and, even 50 years after the 1903-04 season, Maley's high-achieving players were recorded as "the greatest team of the 20th century" by a 1954 football annual.

SHARP J.BROAD J.E.MAGNALL GOODCHILD MAX WOOSNAM ALLEN GODFREY TYLER
(Trainer) Secy. (Capt.)
COOKSON. BROAD. BROWELL JOHNSON. BARNES CARTWRIGHT.

system for decades, he studied Hungarian football to create tactical plans that stunned English football.

McDowall worked with his coaches to develop a deep-lying centre-forward tactic by 1954. It became known as 'the Revie Plan' (after Don Revie, City's number 9) and helped City reach successive Wembley finals. But, more importantly, it changed the way English managers thought about

Ernest Mangnall

Why a visionary: Worked tirelessly to create a stadium worthy of the club.

Mangnall was Manchester United's first successful manager, winning two League titles and the FA Cup; however in 1912 he stunned the Reds when he announced he was leaving them for Manchester City. His reason was simple – he believed that City was the bigger club with a larger fanbase and a greater opportunity for success. There was a great deal of truth in what he felt – City were the best supported club in 1911 when Mangnall's Reds won the League (United were sixth best) and were the best supported club again in 1914-15. Mangnall knew City's dominance could reach great heights and he planned to build the best stadium in England for City – yet sadly war limited his opportunities. Eventually, he was responsible for the development of Maine Road in 1923 with its 85,000 capacity. That move strengthened City as the northern force during the 1930s.

Les McDowall

Why a visionary: At a time when English football had stuck to its rigid positional

the game. New tactical plans were now needed, and the English traditional style was to be challenged.

Malcolm Allison

Why a visionary: So many reasons, but predominantly for his revolutionary approach to coaching and fitness techniques.

Allison liked to tell everyone that he wasn't merely a coach, he was also a scientist – and in his first spell at City, under manager Joe Mercer, he became recognised as the greatest coach in Britain and one of the best in Europe. He brought

that were winning trophies, no longer United. When City won the League in 1968, he said City were so good they'd be the first team to play on Mars – and when Allison said something like this fans believed him. He also introduced the red and black striped away kit that was utilised for every major final during his time at the club. He felt it made City invincible – he even suggested it became the home kit and came close to persuading others.

Pep Guardiola
Why a visionary: The records speak for themselves – just watch what he does! Mainly, his belief on the goalkeeper being his first line of attack.

It would be wrong to say too much at this stage, but it is clear from the way Pep has approached the Premier League and English football that he has already helped transform the game. His approach has been refreshing, and it is an absolute pleasure to watch any City game in these heady days. Long may they continue.

in Olympic athletes to improve fitness. Allison was a skilled tactician who enjoyed challenging the establishment. In 1966 he told Sandy Busby, the son of the United manager, that his dad had a 20-year start but, "I'll pass him in three!" – and within three years it was Mercer & Allison's City

A Jaundiced View

Although maroon has long been the foundation of City's away colours, there have been several prominent changes. There were, of course, the Malcolm Allison-inspired red and black stripes introduced in 1968-69, but before that a yellow kit was introduced.

Carrying some maroon to keep with tradition, utilising the colour on the cuffs and V-neck collar, the kit was debuted during the late '50s as an away strip. Colour clashes meant that for some games City would wear white shorts and for others they would wear maroon shorts. Black was also tried at times.

During the 1959-60 season Denis Law made his debut in the yellow shirt away at Leeds United. These colour images are

actually from later in the season, from the match against Tottenham on 16 April 1960. They are taken from film of the game but sadly the clarity is not great. Nevertheless, it shows that City did wear the kit. Notice also the fan with her yellow and maroon knitted scarf!

City ended the 1959-60 season in 15th place, but much of the season had been a struggle. In fact, it was only when Colin Barlow netted against Preston in the

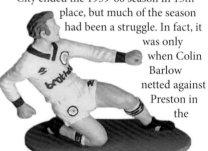

Spurs Away

PROCESSED BY Kodak

created. City lost 4-0 and the shirt was never seen again. In fact, City went as far as to vow the team would never wear yellow again, announcing that the kit would be destroyed. But still a few shirts survived to be sported by City in the Community staff. And, of course. City's stance has

dying minutes on 23 April that the Blues' safety was assured, finally avoiding relegation by three points.

Whether the yellow kit was held responsible is not known, but the outfit was dropped for first-team games in 1960-61 with maroon and white stripes, reminiscent of the 1956 final, being adopted instead.

City have used yellow on a few occasions since 1960, the most memorable being the 1999 Play-off final, although the modern version of the colour was more of a DayGlo affair. Yellow also loomed large on 14 October 1989, when Umbro designers hurriedly worked with the club to create a shirt for the meeting at Arsenal. Maroon was City's regular away kit by this time and it was felt a third strip was required to avoid a clash. In the end, a basic yellow shirt was

since softened. We have worn yellow both in the 1997-98 season and 2005-06 – the latter Reebok-designed kit said to have been inspired by the Manchester Bee.

City line up in yellow at Maine Road in 1959-60 (left); and Denis Law's debut v Leeds United (below).

Colin Barlow

PROCESSED BY Kodak

Kodachrome TRANSPARENCY

Supermac Shell-shocked

On 2 November 2013 City defeated Norwich City 7-0 to establish the club's new Premier League record score. This eclipsed the previous best achieved on 21 September 2008 when the Blues defeated Portsmouth 6-0. At the time that victory brought a significant amount of attention to the goalscoring record of the Blues, and even prompted *Match of the Day* to comment on a 10-0 win against Darwen way back in 1899.

The Darwen win is City's record winning margin in the League, however it is not the club's record score, nor is it the only time City have scored ten goals in League football.

Nevertheless, the 6-0 Portsmouth win was a significant record breaker at the time, as it simultaneously:

• Equalled City's highest score in the Premier League.

• Became City's record winning margin in the Premier League.

• Saw Shaun Wright-Phillips score City's 500th Premier League goal.

• Was the first time six separate players had scored for the Blues in a top flight game. They were Jo, Dunne, Robinho, Wright-Phillips, Evans and Fernandes.

We have had six separate goalscorers in only one earlier League game, but that was in Division Two on 9 March 1895 when the Blues beat Notts County 7-1. Six separate City players also scored in the game when we achieved our all-time record score of 11-3 (against Lincoln in 1895). However, on that day only five scored for City as our sixth, Jack Walker, netted an own goal in Lincoln's favour.

Of course, all of this was eclipsed in that

7-0 November 2013 win over Norwich City in the Premier League. That day seven players scored for the Blues. They were: Silva (20), Negredo (36), Yaya Touré (60), Agüero (71), Dzeko (86) and own-goals from Johnson and Martin (25). Johnson's goal was actually the opener in the 16th minute. Note: many City reports record Nastasic as the scorer of the third goal and not an own-goal by Martin.

Six City players scored in another thrilling Premier League game when the Blues defeated Stoke 7-2 on 14 October 2017. That day the scorers were: Jesus (2), Sterling, David Silva, Fernandinho, Sané and Bernardo Silva as City scored seven

Three hat-trick stars

NINE OUT OF TEN . . . that's the goals scored by these Manchester City hat-trick men, Tony Adcock, Paul Stewart and David White

once more in the Premier League.

City's record score and record winning margin in all major competition was actually the club's first ever appearance in the FA Cup. On that day, way back in 1890, Ardwick – as City were then known – defeated a Merseyside team called Liverpool Stanley 12-0. Clearly, the style of football has changed significantly since the 1890s, making it difficult to

understand exactly how significant that victory and others from the period actually were. Inevitably they were viewed as great results, but did the differential between winners and losers seem as significant as it would be viewed today? Many games involved high scores, and sides often took

more risks than perhaps they would in the modern era.

Victories over sides from the same division should therefore be considered more significant than high-scoring cup victories against lower-league sides. For that reason, I tend to rate all League winning scores higher than cup games, apart from when City played the part of a significant underdog. I would also suggest that victories since the mid '20s are more in keeping with the modern day as the fundamentals, such as offside laws and recognisable pitch markings, had been established by that time in the game's long development.

Many readers will remember a famous double-digit score – 10-1 v Huddersfield Town in 1987 – and, as it occurred in the modern era, this outstanding result should always rate as the benchmark, although it clearly is not the ultimate record score.

This result is rated highly because before the match many pundits predicted that Huddersfield, managed by former England star Malcolm Macdonald, would at least

Chronological Progression of Home Record (Most Goals)

Score	Date	Opposition	Competition
6-0	7/11/1891	Walsall Town Swifts	Alliance

Morris (3), Milne, Milarvie & Bogie

7-0	3/09/1892	Bootle	Division Two

Davies (3), Morris (2), Angus & Weir

8-1	7/10/1893	Burslem Port Vale	Division Two

Morris (3), Middleton, Milarvie, Steele, Yates & Own Goal

11-3	23/03/1895	Lincoln City	Division Two

McReddie (4), Finnerhan (2), Meredith (2), Rowan (2) & Milarvie

Note: This takes the first instance of City scoring and does not include details of when the Blues matched their own score.

SUPERMAC IS SHELL-SHOCKED !

10–1 is City's best since 1895

by RICHARD BOTT
Man City 10, Huddersfield T 1

MALCOLM Macdonald has never been short of a glib phrase or an arrogant boast throughout a colourful career in football—until yesterday. This extraordinary score-line rendered Huddersfield's charismatic new manager almost speechless.

"What can I say?" he asked, rhetorically, when he emerged from the debris and despair of the visitors' dressing room. "I'm shell-shocked."

"We started well, had some good chances, put them under pressure for the first goal and then became so juvenile.

"When things got bad how could you stop them? We were quite happy to get a point against Leicester on Tuesday, that's where..."

It was a joy to watch for the neutrals or the City players, though their books, particularly with THREE players, then scored 12 goals in an 73-day spell. Burnes and Brian Amber xx received hat-tricks for Wrexham against Hartlepool.

But not a City's biggest League score. Yes, but Lin and they did a without...

history They boosted League defeat was 8-0 at Middles brough 37 years ago.

Now the juvenile rattled Vatah would have found a clear off the action. You could have drawn a host of despair Margate, admitted. It could...

Bits repeatedly, when they scored 12 goals in an FA Cup first round League Margate, admitted. It could have been a different tale if...

get a draw from the game.

Macdonald had only been appointed as manager the month before, but it was clear his side were already benefiting from his vast experience. Seven days before the game, Macdonald's side had defeated a notoriously tricky Millwall side, 2-1.

City had yet to get into any kind of rhythm with two defeats, two draws and two wins coming from the previous six games and, significantly, the pre-match predictions looked accurate as City struggled early on. They appeared more likely to suffer a defeat than a victory as Huddersfield looked fairly confident from the game's outset.

For the opening ten minutes or so the Yorkshiremen seemed more capable of scoring but from the moment Neil McNab netted City's first in the 12th minute the Blues' game was transformed and they hit an unexpected patch of rampant form. By half-time it was 4-0, and there were already predictions flying around that the game could reach 8-0.

At 9-1 Huddersfield were awarded a penalty and former Blue Andy May scored to cheers from Blues and Terriers fans alike.

The game ended having established a new City record of three players scoring hat-tricks.

Nine or More Goals

Score	Date	Opposition	Competition
12-0	4/10/1890	Liverpool Stanley	FA Cup

Weir (3), Hodgetts (2), McWhinnie (2), Campbell (2), Rushton, Whittle & Own Goal

11-3	23/03/1895	Lincoln City	Div Two

McReddie (4), Finnerhan (2), Meredith (2), Rowan (2) & Milarvie

11-4	20/02/1926	Crystal Palace	FA Cup

Roberts (5), Browell (3), Austin, Hicks & Johnson

10-0	18/02/1899	Darwen	Div Two

F. Williams (5), Meredith (3), Dougal & S. Smith

10-1	29/01/1930	Swindon Town	FA Cup

Marshall (5), Tait (3), Brook & Johnson

10-1	7/11/1987	Huddersfield Town	Div Two

Adcock (3), Stewart (3), White (3) & McNab

9-0	16/04/1898	Burton Swifts	Div Two

Meredith (3), Whitehead (3), S. Smith (2) & Gillespie

9-0	28/02/1903	Gainsborough T	Div Two

Bannister (3), Gillespie (2), Turnbull (2), Meredith & Threlfall

9-0	16/04/1898	Burton Swifts	Div Two

Meredith (3), Whitehead (3), S. Smith (2) & Gillespie

9-0	18/01/1933	Gateshead	FA Cup

Tilson (3), Cowan (2), Barrass, Brook, Busby & McMullan

9-3	26/12/1938	Tranmere Rovers	Div Two

Milsom (4), Toseland (2), Doherty (2) & Herd

Chronological Progression of Away Record (Most Goals)

Score	Date	Opposition	Competition
4-4	21/11/1891	Burton Swifts	Alliance

Bogie (3) & Milarvie

5-0	7/03/1903	Burton Utd	Division Two

Bannister (2), Gillespie (2) & Meredith

6-1	21/03/1904	Wolves	Division One

Gillespie (2), Livingstone (2), Meredith & Turnbull

7-1	29/01/1938	Derby County	Division One

Heale (3) Doherty (2), Brook & Toseland

9-3	26/12/1938	Tranmere Rovers	Division Two

Milsom (4), Toseland (2), Doherty (2) & Herd

New signing Trevor Francis with manager John Bond, 1981 (right).

A Kick Up the '80s

It was the decade that brought a high-profile FA Cup final and two relegations, testing the loyalty of fans as never before. The following decade would see the Blues drop yet lower in terms of League position, but in the '80s City first became recognised as a fallen giant rather than a title-challenging club. Anyone who experienced the '80s will never forget the rollercoaster highs and lows; but for those who missed out, here's the highlights.

Focusing exclusively on 1980-89, City:
• Were a top four best supported side from 1980 through to relegation in 1983.
• Despite relegation, City remained a top six supported side in 1983-84 and ended the decade as the fifth best supported club (about 8,000 less than Liverpool who had the second highest average attendance and became League champions in 1989-90).

• The 1981 FA Cup final was the 100th in the competition's history. City took a 1-0 lead thanks to Tommy Hutchison. Sadly, the player was then unfortunate to net an own-goal, taking the game to a replay. Despite a penalty from Kevin Reeves and an impressive strike from Steve Mackenzie the Blues lost the replay 3-2. City's Joe Corrigan was declared Man of the Match.

• The aftermath of the '81 final saw City sign Trevor Francis and announce plans

for a £6 million redevelopment of Maine Road. That redevelopment would have seen white barrelled roofs erected over the Main Stand and Kippax, and the Platt Lane Stand rebuilt to match the North Stand.

It was a deeply impressive plan of action, but financial problems meant the club were forced to tear up their blueprints a short while after the Main Stand roof had been replaced.

• City's poor financial state, brought about by mismanagement on the part of the directors, led to Trevor Francis being sold approximately one year after he had arrived.

• Shirt sponsorship arrived, Swedish car manufacturers Saab being the first to have their company name emblazoned on City's shirts. The sponsorship was launched in 1982 and was reported to be worth £400,000 over two years.

• The chairmanship of Peter Swales came under intense scrutiny during the decade, especially when reports were was released in October 1985 detailing City's parlous financial state. Almost unbelievably, we were £4 million in debt and paying interest of £1,000 a day to the banks,

• Despite the 1983 and 1987 relegations there were several highs, with a Wembley appearance in the inaugural Full Members Cup Final (Chelsea won 5-4) and FA Youth Cup success against United in 1986.

• After years of community activity, City in the Community was formally established in 1986. Two years later it launched the Manchester City Ladies (now Women) team after a suggestion and

considerable effort by Neil Mather. Their first game came in November 1988 at Boundary Park, Oldham.

• Sadly, the club increased segregation and security fencing on a regular basis throughout the decade. It was the trend in football to combat hooliganism but it made attending games a difficult experience for many.

• Stars of the decade included Youth team products David White, Paul Moulden, Ian Brightwell, Paul Lake, Steve Redmond, Andy Hinchcliffe, Paul Simpson and Alex Williams along with established names such as Paul Power, Neil

McNab, Trevor Morley, Mick McCarthy and Kenny Clements.

The '80s were not the success on the pitch all Blues had hoped for, but the decade did demonstrate the loyalty of fans and brought some thrilling moments such as the 10-1 v Huddersfield Town; 5-1 v United in 1989; the last-day promotion specials at Bradford and at home to Charlton; the 1981 FA Cup semi-final v Ipswich, and a wonderful two-legged Youth Cup victory in 1986.

Three popular Youth products: Ian Brightwell, Steve Redmond and Andy Hinchcliffe.

Take a Stroll into City's Past

Throughout the period since the club's earliest known game as St Mark's in 1880, City have had an impact on the geography of Manchester. The Blues have owned and developed grounds, shops, pubs/social clubs, houses, training facilities and much more. There are plenty of locations whose stories play a part in that of the Blues, as well as

others where significant City events have occurred, such as Manchester Town Hall where homecomings and other key gatherings have taken place. Enjoy a virtual stroll into Blue Manchester's past.

East Manchester Landmarks
Clearly, the Etihad Stadium and the City Football Academy are the most obvious

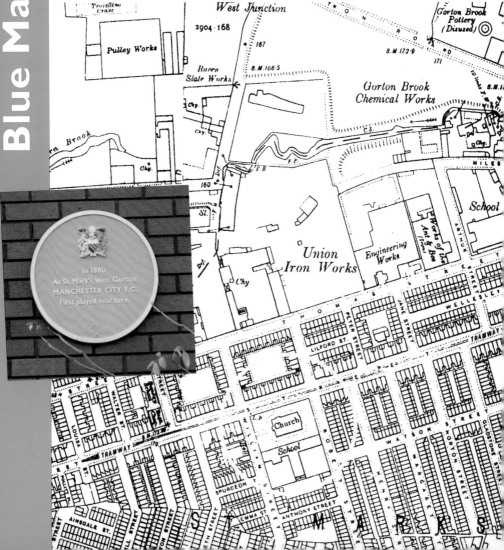

and visible symbols of the influence of the Blues, however within a mile or so of the current stadium are many other significant locations from City's past.

South of Ashbury's Station are the present-day Clowes Street and Wenlock

Way. City were initially formed as a church team and it was on Clowes Street that St Mark's Church stood. The street has been rerouted over the years and the church was located on what became Gorton Villa Walk in the 1970s – ironically, Gorton Villa were the club's biggest rivals during the 1880s! The area has been redeveloped again since then and a new road, named after William Beastow, one of the church wardens who was influential in the club's formative years, takes a similar route to the original Clowes Street.

A short distance away there used to be a blue plaque on The Aces public house (named after the Speedway team) marking City's birth, but the historical waymarker went missing around the time the pub closed down several years ago. Sadly, this was the only plaque marking City's history in Manchester and it should be more accurately placed near the tower block on Wenlock Way that used to house ICL and later Fujitsu, as this is the most likely location of the club's first pitch.

St Mark's Church played a pivotal role in the club's birth and the vast majority of early players lived in that area. Even the

great 1904 Cup final hero Billy Meredith lived on Clowes Street for several years, and he married in St Mark's Church. Incidentally, Clowes Street took its name from the Clowes family who gave land for the construction of the church.

Channel 4 used this area, including the shops located next to what was St Mark's and the houses on Gorton Villa Walk, as sets for the TV series *Shameless*.

Former Grounds
Within the Gorton area the club also played at grounds located at Pink Bank Lane; close to Redgate Lane; and at present-day Gorton Park (the only former City venue still being used for football). The club also rented a pitch from the original Bull's Head Hotel on the Reddish/ Gorton border.

In the late 1880s Ardwick (City) played a floodlit charity match at Belle Vue, and for decades up to 1923 City almost moved to the site that became the greyhound track at Belle Vue on a permanent basis.

The most significant former ground in east Manchester was behind the railway

Gorton Park, yesterday.

arches at Hyde Road, next to Bennett Street. The old Hyde Road ground staged a semi-final, inter-League games, was City's home from 1887 to 1923, and was also the first provincial football ground to be visited by a reigning monarch when King George V attended a game in 1920.

Crowds of 40,000-plus regularly attended games there, and today the site is used as a storage area for container trucks. One of the stands can still be seen, however it is currently located at The Shay, Halifax, where it was erected and remodelled after City sold it in 1923.

Public Houses

After City moved to the current stadium in 2003 several pubs, including The Kippax, Summerbee's and The Stadium, were renamed as a result of City's arrival in this area. Those three have since unfortunately closed, but the phenomenon of renaming or opening public houses after the club is not new. During the early

1900s a pub close to the Hyde Road ground was named The Manchester City Arms in a bid to take custom from its near neighbour, City's headquarters, the Hyde Road Hotel, while shops at both Maine Road and the Etihad, such as The City Chippy, clearly take their name from the Blues. There was even a 'Maine Road Joke Shop' during the '70s on the corner of Maine Road and Claremont Road.

In the '80s the Hyde Road Hotel was renamed the City Gates under landlord and ex-player George Heslop, but the venture failed. By the end of the decade

the pub was closed and falling apart. Supporters, most notably the fanzine *Blue Print* and fan Dave Scally, tried to raise awareness and save the building, and in March 2001 *The Times* newspaper featured the pub as one of their most important 'blue plaque' footballing sites. Only three Manchester locations appeared in their series – the Hyde Road Hotel; the former FA Cup final venue in Fallowfield, and the location of the first Football League meeting at Market Street. Sadly, within two months it had been demolished.

Maine Road & Platt Lane

The Platt Lane complex on the edge of Moss Side and Rusholme still exists but it now houses the Manchester FA and is used by Manchester Metropolitan University. A short distance away was Maine Road, City's home from 1923 to 2003. This has been demolished and the land redeveloped with housing and a school occupying the site of the former stadium. In the centre of the development is Gibson's Green, named after City groundsman Stan Gibson. This marker locates the old centre spot.

The Players' Estate

During 1977, eleven streets were built close to Maine Road and named after deceased City players. These walks and closes still exist in the main, and the names of past heroes can be found on the Manchester street map: look out for Horace Barnes, Eric Brook, Tommy Browell, Sam Cookson, Sam Cowan, Tommy Johnson, Jimmy McMullan, Billy Meredith, Frank Swift, Fred Tilson, and Max Woosnam. Sadly, building developments have meant the name of Frank Swift no longer appears on any street signs in that development. In Trafford another street is named after ex-Blue Matt Busby, and at various grounds around the UK other former City men – most notably Busby, Don Revie, Denis Law, Bobby Johnstone and Joe Mercer – have suites, stands or statues in their honour.

Manchester Art

City-supporting mosaic artist Mark Kennedy has done more than most to ensure a significant Blue identity within Manchester's art community. With strong support from club officials Mark has created several memorable and significant works of art featuring the Blues. These include the amazing mosaics of Joe Mercer on Joe Mercer Way at the northern end of the stadium; a redeveloped Manchester City mosaic from Maine Road; a Yaya Touré mosaic, a Stuart Pearce player mosaic and a '70s circular MCFC badge. For many months an Anelka mosaic was regularly seen on *Coronation Street*.

Another committed City artist was LS Lowry, whose paintings of matchstick men and industrial Manchester are world famous. Lowry did paint a scene at Maine Road once, although his most famous sporting painting, 'Going to the Match,' depicts Bolton's Burnden Park . This masterpiece currently resides at the Manchester-based PFA.

In the absence of any blue plaques at Maine Road, Hyde Road and other City locations, Kennedy's mosaics provide a beautiful modern Mancunian feel to the city, while Lowry's paintings show the more historical and traditional Manchester. Both Lowry's Mancunian paintings and Kennedy's City mosaics bring Manchester to life in a more significant way than traditional statues.

Joe Mercer OBE
9 August 1914 – 9 August 1990

Mood mosaics down Mercer Way.

BLUES PICTURE EXPECTED TO HIT MORE THAN A MILLION

Fans queue up to make Lowry crowd scene a record breaker

Hand in Glove

City have been blessed with some of the greatest goalkeepers football has ever known, and if there is any position that Blues fans care most passionately about it is the keeper. So many City goalies have become legendary figures at our club, such as Frank Swift, Bert Trautmann, Joe Corrigan, Joe Hart and of course Ederson.

The Stand-in Keeper

Thinking about City goalkeepers often brings to mind the heroics of Nigel Gleghorn in May 1989, when injury to keeper Andy Dibble led to Gleghorn, who had scored an eighth-minute goal, putting on the green shirt. That day Gleghorn was under immense pressure from Palace but the former north-east fireman managed to keep Steve Coppell's side at bay until the 75th minute. The game between two sides challenging for promotion ended 1-1 and meant that City retained the upper hand in the race for the second promotion spot behind Chelsea.

Gleghorn had previously fulfilled the temporary goalkeeping role at Walsall a mere six weeks earlier. That day City were losing 2-0 when Gleghorn donned the green shirt, keeping goal for about an hour during which time City fought back. They led 3-2 but a poor backpass from David

Oldfield gave Walsall the opportunity to equalise. Nevertheless, Gleghorn was the undisputed Man of the Match.

Goalscoring Goalies

The first City keeper to score from open play was Charlie Williams in April 1900 against Sunderland. The wind caught one of his goal-kicks and the opposing keeper, Scottish international Ted Doig, fumbled the ball into the net. It counted as Charlie's goal and he is recognised as the first keeper to score in League football.

Charlie's goal was scored while he was fulfilling

MANCHESTER CITY

JOE CORRIGAN

his role as goalie but in February 1964 Harry Dowd netted a City goal while playing as a makeshift centre-forward. Dowd had broken his finger and, in the days before substitutes of any kind, he was moved into attack while Matt Gray went in nets. Harry's goal came when he followed up a rebound from the bar. Incidentally, Colin Bell netted for Bury on his debut that same day.

Left to right: Bespectacled Jim Mitchell; Charlie Williams, and Bobby McDonald v Watford in 1982.

Goalie's Glasses

Maine Road's first City 'keeper Jim Mitchell always wore spectacles while playing and remains the only England goalie to have worn glasses during a game.

Scotland's Number One

Lots of outfield players have had spells in nets with Bobby McDonald, heralded as 'Scotland's Number One' after a tense yet entertaining 87 minutes in goal against Watford in 1982 (City won 1-0), being one of the best.

Niall Quinn also performed exceptionally well in April 1991 when he replaced Tony Coton (sent off) and immediately had to face a Dean Saunders penalty. Quinn saved the spot-kick and made several other great saves. City won the match against Derby 2-1 – Quinn had opened the scoring before going in nets.

Premiership Oldest

John Burridge remains the oldest player to appear for any side in the Premier League. His last appearance came at the age of 43 years and five months on 14 May 1995 when City faced QPR. Burridge will always be remembered for his extraordinary warm-up routines, which often saw him dive deliberately into muddy puddles at Maine Road before the game began.

Frank Faints

Frank Swift went on to be one of Britain's greatest goalkeepers, earning recognition across Europe, and his first season, 1933-34, ended with an appearance in the FA Cup final. The game had been difficult for him – he blamed himself for City being 1-0 down at half-time – but City went on to win the match 2-1. However, the emotion of the day was too much for Frank and as play was nearing its end the tension was taking its toll. As the whistle went, Swift turned to collect his gloves and fainted in his goal area. Later, he just about managed to collect his medal, and in the aftermath of the final King George V sent a telegram asking about his wellbeing.

Attacking Keepers

On the last day of the 2004-05 season City needed to beat Middlesbrough to qualify for the UEFA Cup. The game was heading towards a draw when manager Stuart Pearce took off Claudio Reyna, brought on goalkeeper Nicky Weaver and moved regular number one David James into attack. A specially produced outfield shirt with James's name and number was given to the keeper, proving this was a premeditated move, and James did all he could to improve City's attack, helping the Blues as they were awarded a penalty. Sadly, Robbie Fowler missed the penalty and City's hopes of European football vanished. Many left the ground muttering that James should have taken it!

This wasn't the first time City had ever been inspired to bring a second keeper into the fray. In the 1995 League Cup tie with Wycombe Wanderers an injury to Richard Edghill led to manager Alan Ball sending on goalkeeper Martyn Margetson to bolster City's attack. This unlikely masterplan paid dividends, as the game ended 4-0 to the Blues.

Do the Caballero

No exposition of City folklore could be complete without a reminder of Willy Caballero's display in the 2016 League Cup final. A great performance throughout the game was followed by his outstanding role in the penalty shoot-out. Willy was the undisputed star as the Blues won the shoot-out 3-1. As fans left Wembley, several chants highlighting Willy's role in the game could be heard booming out of the stadium and its stairwells.

FRANK SWIFT — MANCHESTER CITY

NICK WEAVER

It's a Family Affair

When City won the League in 1968 there was much talk of the club's popular chairman, Albert Alexander. He had made the bold move to bring in Joe Mercer and Malcolm Allison, and the focus on his role in City's redevelopment was appropriate. As with the dignity of current chairman Khaldoon Al Mubarak, Alexander wanted to ensure the club was both a power in the land but also a welcoming, respectful organisation. In many ways the developments since 2008 have brought back the attitude and values that Albert and his family had always encouraged.

been offered the chance to be chairman of the club – but he had refused, modestly believing he wasn't sufficiently educated to hold such an important position. Despite this he was dedicated to the Blue cause and lived and breathed City from its formation through to his death in 1953. By that time he was Life President of the club – an honour he richly deserved and one that only Lawrence Furniss had held before him.

Like his father, the younger Albert dedicated his life to the Blues. Inevitably, he spent most of his boyhood watching the club develop and, as he grew up, he

became more involved with behind-the-scenes work at the club's first home, Hyde Road. He was a member of the Ground Committee, which

Albert was the second generation of the Alexander family to play a prominent role in the development and history of Manchester City. His father, also Albert, had been involved with the club from the 1890s and had held various positions including vice-chairman, and even manager for a spell in 1925-26. He was a well-known, respected figure and had

performed crucial activities such as stewarding and ground maintenance.

Alexander also managed the club's 'A' team and provided support in whatever way necessary to ensure the Blues succeeded. He was more than happy to work through the ranks and take on any duty. His son, Eric, who was chairman in the early '70s, remembers that his father had suffered during the First World War, but that had not prevented him from pouring his energies into the Blues: "He was a very good footballer and cricketer but he was gassed in the Great War and had to give it up. It affected him throughout his life, although it's fair to say he recovered enough to fulfil a happy normal life – apart from playing, of course.

"He took up golf, but his love for football was such that he started the 'A' team at City. He started it in 1921 and ran it through until 1963. He enjoyed working with the youngsters and developing them. He gained an awful lot of satisfaction from that, particularly when players like Matt Busby developed their skills and style as part of the 'A' team."

Ultimately, after many years of loyal service, Alexander became a City director. This came after the Blues became aware that Manchester United were hoping he would join their board. It is highly likely Alexander would have turned the Reds down, and it was appropriate that he became a director at Maine Road. It was an honour he deserved for years of dedication to the City cause.

While director he felt the passion all fans feel for the Blues, as well as the pain and worries during the club's struggles in the early '60s. He wanted better and in 1965, as fans demonstrated following City's lowest-attended League game, he came out to face them and talk with them about his hopes and ambitions for the club. He apologised for City's appalling decline. It says much about his courage and the respect fans had for him that they dispersed. It is doubtful whether any other director would have been respected in this manner at such a low point.

Understandably Alexander, who was City's chairman by this point, wanted to see his side successful and later that summer appointed Joe Mercer as manager. It was a brave decision as Mercer had been out of work for a year and had suffered a stroke at Aston Villa. Other names, such as former City hero Peter Doherty and Liverpool manager Bill Shankly, had been expected to be appointed by the media, so this move could easily have been seen negatively.

Alexander guided City through the successful years of the Mercer-Allison period and was probably the first chairman to be hugely popular with fans. Everyone seemed to love 'Little Albert,' as Mercer dubbed him.

Many of City's achievements during these years were dedicated to Alexander by Mercer, while journalist Bill Fryer commented in 1970: "He is highly revered in the game and by the public, and I have no doubt good deals have been done for City out of Albert's friendships because in

ALBERT ALEXANDER
"Fit as a fiddle"

in 1958, and has been chairman since 1964.

reality the whole of football is a 'club.'"

Sadly, despite the chairman's popularity, his final years saw him suffer at the hands of the 1970 takeover battle. Alexander found out about the takeover when he received a knock on his door at breakfast one day. It was a complete shock to him.

The takeover destroyed much that was good about City at this point, including the Mercer-Allison partnership. However, it is rarely mentioned how the takeover affected Alexander, the man who had guided City with distinction through some dark days when no one else wanted to know. He had taken the club from the lowest point it had experienced since joining the League, to a position of strength with trophies galore. Those bidding for control wanted to grab some of that glory, while Alexander's motives were different – like all true fans, he wanted City to succeed no matter how it affected him.

Alexander stood down as chairman, his health unfortunately deteriorating by this point. He passed away soon after.

His son Eric, the third generation of Alexanders involved with City, was a director at the time and he worked hard to keep the club true to its values as the '70s progressed. He was a football man through and through, determined to see City develop; but those who had gained power via the takeover had their own plans. In 2015, when I interviewed Eric, he commented on his father and the changes following the 1970 takeover: "He said to me as we drove home from a board meeting, 'You know, I think I've seen the best of it all. I don't really envy you, son, but do your best and try to keep some dignity.' I've never forgotten that. As dad became ill, I became chairman, but the power at the club now lay with the men who had taken over. Dad was made Life President, as had his dad, but passed away shortly afterwards, and then in 1973 Peter Swales became chairman. I remained on the board for a few years, but Dad's words

Walter Griffiths (secretary, left), Joe Mercer (manager, right) with the directors, inc. chairman Albert (centre) and Eric Alexander (next to Mercer) in 1968.

been impressed with the discussions I have had with the current 'guardians' of the club, and am grateful that I am still welcome. When I left the board in the early 1980s Peter Swales made me an Honorary President for life, and I am proud to be still welcome at City and associated with the club. Thinking

kept coming back to me."

Eric's own achievements at City saw some significant improvements and he remains proud of what he achieved: "I've always believed that Manchester City should be a club that represents all that is good about football and Manchester. During my time I tried to improve the stadium. The North Stand at Maine Road was something I was very keen to develop and I also developed plans for a new Kippax and for a new training ground – neither idea being developed by my successor."

In the years that followed Peter Swales' appointment as chairman and the work of his supporting directors – some of whom had played their part in the 1970 takeover – the Alexander influence reduced but Eric remained very much a City attendee. He cannot get to as many games as he'd like to these days, but he is happy with the club's return to a position of power: "I'm very proud of the way the club is returning to the strengths of the past. Throughout my family's direct, 'hands-on' involvement City was always perceived as a major club with a great history and tradition. I've

of football, it's worth remembering that none of us were ever paid for our roles because, back then, football directors couldn't be paid. We bought shares, invested in the club and so on. It was all about contributing to the club. I remember my mother, who had gone to watch City herself with her father before she met my dad, saying during the successes of the Mercer-Allison era, 'At last [Albert junior] is being rewarded for the years spent travelling all over the place, far from the limelight, with the junior and budding players.'

"It had taken a lot to reach those heights by 1970 and I'm sure it has taken a great deal of effort by the club's current leaders to get City where the club is today. Personally, I'm delighted the club is back on its feet and acting with dignity, as it did in the days of my father and grandfather."

Manchester City owes a great deal to the dedication of the Alexanders. They helped guide the Blues from the 1890s through to the reign of Peter Swales, and in some ways on via the continuing involvement of Eric Alexander. Their contribution should never be forgotten.

On the Count of Three

The total number of League hat-tricks recorded by the Blues stands at 163 from 1892 to the end of the 2017-18 season, when Sergio Agüero finally overtook Fred Tilson's record. Tilson was a major star of the '30s who scored 132 goals in 275 games for City, also netting six in only four starts for England.

The Opposition

City have scored league hat-tricks against 65 different teams. Those that conceded most hat-tricks against the Blues include:

8 – Aston Villa.
7 – Everton.
6 – Derby County & Preston North End.
5 – Blackburn Rovers, Chelsea, Newcastle, Orient, Sunderland & WBA.
4 – Charlton, Huddersfield, Leicester, Liverpool, Stoke, Tottenham, West Ham & Wolves.
3 – Arsenal, Burnley, Bury, Bolton & Sheffield Wednesday.

Premier League Predators

Sergio Agüero holds the record for the most City hat-tricks in the Premier League. Up to 23 August 2018 he has scored nine. Only one player (Alan Shearer, 11) in Premier League history has scored more hat-tricks, though Agüero's career in England to date has been much shorter than Shearer's.

Nine players have scored a total of 20 hat-tricks for City in the Premier League:

9 – Sergio Agüero
4 – Carlos Tevez
1 – Nicolas Anelka, Mario Balotelli, Edin Dzeko, Robinho, Raheem Sterling, Yaya Touré & Paulo Wanchope.

Wanchope scored three against Sunderland on 23 August 2000 to become the first City man to achieve the feat in the Premier League.

Longest Gap Between Hat-tricks

The longest period without a League hat-trick (excluding wartime) is 7 years 11 months between 2 May 1992 (David White v Oldham) and 10 April 1999 (Paul Dickov v Lincoln). There were hat-tricks in cup competition during that period (Rosler, 4 v Notts County in 1995 & Ingebrigtsen, v Leicester in 1994), but none in the League.

In October 2008, when Robinho netted three goals for City against Stoke he became the first player since Nicolas Anelka in 2003 to score a League hat-trick for the Blues. The five-year gap was the second longest between League hat-tricks for City.

Ken's Penalty Hat-trick

When Ken Barnes scored a hat-trick against Everton on 7 December 1957, all his goals came from penalties and helped City achieve a 6-2 win.

Billy McAdams

ENGLAND'S CENTRE-FORWARD

S. F. Tillow.

S.F. TILSON
MANCHESTER CITY

Gillespie "on the run"

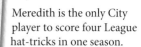

T. BROWELL

Meredith is the only City player to score four League hat-tricks in one season.

December Double
In December 1938 Jack Milsom not only scored hat-tricks in consecutive games but they were also against the same opposition and occurred on consecutive days! Tranmere Rovers were defeated 9-3 with Milsom scoring four on Boxing Day and the following day, at Maine Road, Milsom contributed three goals as Tranmere were beaten 5-2 before a crowd of 43,894.

Huddersfield
When Tony Adcock, David White and Paul Stewart each scored a hat-trick in the Second Division game with Huddersfield (10-1) in 1987, City entered the record books. It was the first time three players had netted hat-tricks in the same Division Two game and only the fifth time the feat had been achieved in all League football. Thirty-three minutes separated Adcock's first goal and his last.

Fastest
Sadly, we do not have accurate timings for the majority of hat-tricks scored, so it is impossible to pinpoint City's quickest ever hat-trick. However, we do know that Carlos Tevez's three goals against Wigan in March 2010 came in a 12-minute spell (72, 75 and 84), and that the following year he scored three in 22 minutes (v WBA, 5 February 2011). However, Sergio Agüero eclipsed these timings with a hat-trick within just 8 minutes against Newcastle in October 2015. This is the fifth fastest Premier League hat-trick of all time. He went on to score five in 20 minutes that day.

On the Receiving End
Since 1992 City have had a total of six hat-tricks scored against them in the Premier League, but did not concede any between 17 August 2008 (Agbonlahor, for Villa) and 1 May 2016 (Mané, for Southampton). Agbonlahor's hat-trick was scored in 7 minutes and 10 seconds and is the fourth fastest PL hat-trick of all time while, co-incidentally, Southampton's Mané holds the record for the fastest PL hat-trick which was scored against Aston Villa (2 minutes and 56 seconds).

Most in a Season
The 1898-99 season saw City score six hat-tricks in the League. This is a record for the Blues and the goals were scored by Billy Meredith (four hat-tricks), Billy Gillespie and Fred Williams.

Most League Hat-tricks in City Career

Player	No. of hat-tricks
Sergio Agüero	9
Fred Tilson	7
Billy Meredith	6
Tommy Browell	6
Irvine Thornley	5
Carlos Tevez	4
Billy Gillespie	4
Tom Holford	4
Horace Barnes	4
Frank Roberts	4
Tommy Johnson	4
Eric Brook	4
Bill McAdams	4
Dennis Tueart	4

HORACE BARNES
MANCHESTER CITY

Fisticuffs, Fury & Failure

Over 55 years ago one of the most controversial Manchester derby matches of all time took place. At the time both sides were struggling and heading towards relegation, so when they met head-on in City's penultimate match of the 1962-63 season there was more at stake than Manchester pride.

Prior to the game United had played 39 matches and had 31 points, while the Blues had played one more game but only had 30 points. As the game was at Maine Road, City held some advantage; but it was vital they won the match to put the pressure on to the Reds along with fellow strugglers Birmingham and Bolton.

When the game commenced, both sides were a little nervous. However the Blues seemed the more determined and, after a couple of near misses, City took the lead in the ninth minute when Alex Harley rifled a low shot passed United keeper Gaskell.

City then dominated play and after 30 minutes Harley appeared to score City's second with another splendid drive. But the referee disallowed the goal on a hair's breadth offside decision which mystified the City players and the 52,452 Maine Road crowd.

Arguments raged for some time and there were ugly scenes at half-time in the tunnel. United's Pat Crerand later admitted to punching City's David Wagstaffe as they walked through the tunnel. In 2010 Wagstaffe gave his version of what occurred: "This thing with Paddy Crerand. I must have upset him or something and we're walking up the tunnel, and he's still in a rage. He was about three yards in front of me. I had my head down and I don't know what was going through his mind but he must just have thought, 'I'll

hit him!' He turned around and did. I thought, 'What's all that about?' I didn't get it. I'd been involved with a few altercations on the pitch, as you do, but I think he just lost it. I certainly never expected it."

In the second half, the Blues remained in control but United became more desperate. Then luck was on their side as Wagstaffe attempted what was later seen as a suicidal 30-yard backpass. Denis Law, playing for the Reds, closed in and tussled with City keeper Harry Dowd for the ball. Dowd dived at Law's feet and the United man fell while the ball ran out of play. The referee pointed to the spot, and United's Albert Quixall scored the penalty in the 86th minute.

City were disgusted with the penalty decision, with Dowd telling journalists: "It was never a penalty. I scooped the ball away from Denis's feet and sent it out of play. I can't remember holding his feet but I did get a kick on the head. I'm sure the linesman was signalling for a corner."

The game ended 1-1, and following a 6-1 defeat away at West Ham in their final match, the Blues were ultimately relegated while United survived.

Another controversial derby, with Denis Law again playing a key role, followed in 1974, but on this occasion Law's solitary goal for the Blues at Old Trafford was enough to send United on their way down to Division Two.

JOY: Quixall saves United   *GLOOM: City relegation blow*

Dowd penalty tragedy

DAVID WAGSTAFFE
Manchester City F.C.   Outside Left

The Best League in the World

The Premier League was established in 1992 when the status of the top division in English league football, Division One, was changed. The clubs in the new league had greater control over the League's affairs than they had previously had in a four-division league. City's chairman Peter Swales was a keen advocate of the Premier League and was one of the men who pushed for it to be established. Since then the Blues have of course won the competition on three occasions. Here is a selection of City's Premier League firsts and records, starting with that first season in 1992-93 (all records are club records unless otherwise stated).

Famous Firsts

First Game: QPR (H), 1-1, 17 August 1992, attendance 24,471. Also first Monday night live Sky TV game.
First Scorer: David White.
First 12: Tony Coton, Andy Hill, Ian Brightwell, Fitzroy Simpson, Keith Curle, Michel Vonk, David White, Paul Lake, Niall Quinn, Ricky Holden (Mike Sheron)

& Steve McMahon.
First Win: Norwich City (H), 3-1, 26 August 1992, Attendance 23,182.
First Penalty Scored: Keith Curle at Coventry City, 3-2, 21 November 1992, Attendance 14,590.
First Manager: Peter Reid (appointed November 1990 until 26 August 1993).
First Season: Ended with City ninth; P42, W15, D12, L15, GF56, GA 51, Points 57.
First Player of the Year: Garry Flitcroft.

Full cost of a 42-game season ticket in 1992-93:

Most expensive: £230 (Main Stand Blocks B & C; concessions £170).
North Stand: £165 (concessions £140).
Kippax Stand: £125 (concessions £85).
Family Stand: £120 (children £100).

Premier League Attendance Records

The Premier League began with Maine Road at the start of a redevelopment programme. The Platt Lane Stand had been demolished and the 1992-93 season began with a reduced capacity as only three sides were available. Building issues meant that the capacity would be restricted until the final weeks of the season while the rebuilding of the Kippax from May 1994 through to the 1995 close season reduced capacity to less than 20,000 for a period. After 1995 the erection of temporary stands gradually increased the capacity to approximately 34,000 by 2003, but the permanent built capacity was marginally above 30,000. It was not until the move to the current stadium in 2003 that the capacity

increased to over 40,000.
It is in this context that the
following progression of the
record needs to be considered.

1992-93: 24,698 (8)
1993-94: 26,709 (9)
1995-96: 27,869 (10)
2000-01: 34,058 (10)
2002-03: 34,564 (11)
2003-04: 46,834 (3)
2011-12: 47,044 (4)
2013-14: 47,080 (4)
2015-16: 54,041 (3)
2017-18: 54,070 (5)

Highest Individual Home Attendance in
the Premier League: 54,693 v Leicester
City, 6 February 2016.
Highest Individual Away Attendance in
the Premier League: 80,811 v Tottenham,
14 April 2018.

Performance-related Records
City have achieved the following Premier
League Records. Many of these were in
2017-18:
Biggest Title Winning Margin: 19 points,
2017-18.
Narrowest Title-winning Margin:
0 points. City won the 2011-12
title on goal difference, finishing
with an 8-goal superior goal
difference over Manchester
United.
Most Points in a Season: 100,
2017-18.
Most Home Points in a Season:
55, 2011-12 (shared with Chelsea
2005-06 and United 2010-11).
Most Away Points in a Season:
50, 2017-18.
Most Wins in a Season: 32,
2017-18 (achieved in a 38-game
season).

Most Home Wins in a Season: 18, 2011-12
(jointly held with Chelsea 2005-06 and
United 2010-11).
Most Away Wins in a Season: 16, 2017-18.
Most Consecutive Wins: 18, (between 26
August 2017 and 27 December 2017).
Most Consecutive Home Wins: 20,
(between 5 March 2011 and 21 March
2012).
Most Consecutive Away Wins: 11
(between 21 May 2017 and 27 December
2017; held jointly with Chelsea, 6 April
2008 to 7 December 2008).
Fewest Home Defeats in a Season: 0, 2011-
12 (held jointly with several clubs).Most
Draws in a Season: 18, 1993-94 (42 game
season; held jointly with Sheffield United,
1993-94 and Southampton 1994-95).
Fewest Home Draws in a Season: 0, 2008-

Ali Benarbia and Peter Schmeichel run out for Maine Road's last City win in April 2003 (far left);
Niall Quinn at Maine Road (left; and the new Kippax during construction, 1994-95 (above).

09 (held jointly with United 2012-13 and Chelsea 2016-17).

Most Consecutive Draws: 7, 2009-10 (held jointly with Norwich 1993-94 and Southampton 1994-95).

Most Goals Scored in a Season: 106, 2017-18.

Best Goal Difference in a Season: 79, 2017-18.

Fewest Goals Scored at Home in a Season: 10, 2006-07.

Oldest Premier League Player: John Burridge, 43 years and 162 days playing for City against QPR, 14 May 1995.

Youngest Premier League Winner: Phil Foden, 17 years and 350 days.

Most Goals in a Game: 5, Sergio Agüero v Newcastle United, 3 October 2015 (held jointly).

Heaviest Defeat for the Reigning

Champions: United 1 City 6, 23 October 2011 (equalled by Spurs defeating Leicester 6-1 on 18 May 2017).
Most Individual Goalscorers in a Game: 7 v Norwich City, 2 November 2013 (held jointly with Southampton v Sunderland, 18 October 2014).
Most Consecutive Manager of the Month Awards: 4, Pep Guardiola, September to December 2017.

Youth v Experience

When Phil Foden became the youngest player ever to win the Premier League in 2018 there was a lot of talk about City's other age-related facts. So, here's a brief summary of some of the most eye-catching and surprising.

Youngest League Debutant

Glyn Pardoe was 15 years and 314 days when he made his Division One debut against Birmingham City on 11 April 1962. Incidentally, the national record stands at 15 years and 158 days (Albert Geldard, Bradford PA, in 1929 and Ken Roberts, Wrexham, in 1951).

For his debut Pardoe replaced Colin Barlow as City's centre-forward.

When I interviewed him a few years back Pardoe remembered that he wasn't too nervous: "I actually got to find out a few days before, so that helped. If I'd have found out on the morning I don't know how I'd have coped. I don't think I ever thought about my age. I'm sure others did, but to me it was just a great opportunity."

Thinking specifically about the game and his own performance, Pardoe admitted he couldn't remember too much about the game itself: "We lost 4-1 at home and I was up against a tough centre-half called Trevor Smith. I wore the number nine shirt for that game – I later played in almost every position! I don't think I did a great deal, but I do know I kept my place for the next three games.

"I remember playing on the Saturday, and then walking up to the ground on the Monday and having to knock to be allowed in. As far as everybody was concerned I was a Reserve – or even a youth player, I suppose – not a first-teamer. You never actually 'made it' until you were a first-team regular, and even then you could never be complacent. Even when we were winning all the trophies there was a very real fear that your contract would not be renewed. I remember worrying each summer, thinking that I'd be forced to move on."

Neutrals have sometimes claimed that City were struggling in the League at this time and the selection of Pardoe, and other young players, was a sign of desperation. But the truth is somewhat different. The Blues were actually doing okay. They ended the season twelfth and Pardoe's selection was simply down to his quality. In his second match – against Joe Mercer's Aston Villa – Pardoe was one of the star men. According to one press report: "I must save the last tribute for 15-year-old Glyn Pardoe who made two astonishing runs, had two headers and a shot that almost scored and even now is remarkably hard to shift off the ball. Women or no women, soccer is safe for ever in the hands of our young Pardoes."

City defeated Villa 1-0, thanks to a Neil Young goal, and the following City match programme highlighted Pardoe's contribution: "If he didn't set Maine Road alight he surely gave promise that he is going to be a menace to opposing defences in the years to come. Certainly these end-of-season games are invaluable in giving young Pardoe the experience of first-

appearance on 22 March 1924 against Preston North End at Maine Road. The gamed ended in a 2-2 draw.

Oldest Premier League Player
Goalkeeper John Burridge was 43 years and 162 days when he appeared in his final Premier League game for City against Queen's Park Rangers on 14 May 1995. This remains a Premier League record. At the time Burridge, an absolute fitness fanatic, declared: "I'm fitter now than I've ever been."

Sadly, the game ended in a 3-2 defeat and was the last managed by Brian Horton.

Oldest City Player
Billy Meredith was 49 years and 245 days when he appeared in the FA Cup semi-final against Newcastle United in March 1924. The semi final ended in a 2-0 defeat at St Andrew's, Birmingham.

team football and although there is no intention of rushing him the experience he is gaining now could well see his development stepped up and his challenge for a regular first-team place coming sooner or later."

After occasional appearances over the next season or so, Pardoe eventually became a regular choice from February 1964. He went on to be a star player during the late '60s/early '70s and scored the winning goal in the 1970 League Cup final.

During the '80s he was part of the coaching staff that helped City win the 1986 FA Youth Cup, his experience proving vital as a succession of young players made their way into City's first team. Nowadays he is more commonly known amongst younger City fans as the granddad of young player Tommy Doyle.

Oldest City League Player
Billy Meredith was aged 49 years and 238 days when he made his last League

This remains a national record for the latter stages of the FA Cup.

On 23 February 1924 Meredith scored in the 5-1 third round FA Cup victory at Brighton, which means he is also the oldest City player ever to score a first-team goal.

Youngest International Defender

After only 29 Premier League appearances, and at the age of 18 years and 144 days, Micah Richards became the youngest defender to play for England. *The Times'* Joe Lovejoy later claimed: "He has done so well that there will be few dissenters to his claim to the position on a permanent basis." Despite making eleven appearances during the reign of Steve McLaren, managerial changes were to affect Richards' claims on a regular spot. Fabio Capello only picked him once, while Roy Hodgson made it clear he preferred Phil Jones.

In total Richards made 13 England appearances and scored one goal. He also played for the 2012 Great Britain Olympic team.

Youngest Regular Captain

In 1988, at the tender age of 20, Steve Redmond succeeded Kenny Clements on a permanent basis as captain. This meant that he became the youngest regular captain for the Blues. In 2007, at the age of 19, Micah Richards became the youngest ever City captain but was not the permanent choice.

Oldest Trophy-winning Captain

City's oldest FA Cup-winning captain is Welsh international Roy Paul, who was 36 years and 17 days when the Blues beat Newcastle in the 1956 final.

Tony Book was 33 when City won the Cup in 1969 and Sam Cowan was two weeks short of his 33rd birthday when City won the Cup in 1934.

Youngest Trophy-winning Captain

City's youngest FA Cup-winning captain is Argentinian Carlos Tevez, who was 27

years and 98 days when he lifted the trophy after victory over Stoke City in 2011.

Sam Barkas was only 27 years and 123 days on the day the Blues lifted the League Championship for the first time in 1937; but Vincent Kompany was 26 years and 33 days old when he lifted the Premier League in 2012. This makes him City's youngest trophy-winning captain.

Youngest Manager

City's youngest manager is Lawrence Furniss, who is also the first man to manage the Blues in the League. When he became manager he was 31 years but the Blues were not then in the Football League. In 1892 when City staged their first League game (under the name Ardwick) Furniss was 34 years and 7 months. This means Peter Reid was actually younger when he guided the Blues

ROY PAUL
Manchester City and Wales

through his first League game. Reid was 34 years and 4 months when he took on the job in November 1990.

Oldest Manager

When Manuel Pellegrini managed his last game in 2016 he was City's oldest ever manager at the age of 62 years and 241 days. The previous oldest was Sven-Göran Eriksson who was 60 and almost 4 months. Sven eclipsed the previous record holder Ernest Mangnall by two years.

Joe Mercer was 57 years and 2 months when he handed over the role of team manager to Malcolm Allison. Mercer was 57 years and 10 months when his spell as general manager came to an end in 1972.

Left: Age before beauty, as City's oldest ever manager, Manuel Pellegrini, hooks evergreen Frank Lampard.

Feed the Goat

There are some players who are destined to become cult figures from the moment they arrive, while others develop into cult figures over their career. Sometimes the reasons are obvious – a great performance, a promotion-winning goal, a rare talent – while at other times the vital elements are not so obvious to neutrals. Fans always know what constitutes a cult figure, although it has to be stressed that supporters themselves will sometimes disagree on the importance of a player to the club's history.

There have been countless cult figures over the years, so the aim here is simply to highlight a selection of fans' heroes from each period of the club's history.

Pre-War

The earliest cult figure of them all was Billy Gillespie, a man who stood out head and shoulders as a hero to the supporters of the period. Bustling Billy was a determined

City man from the start. A key member of the 1904 FA Cup-winning team, he had a great rapport with fans, and this was strengthened a year or so after the final when he walked out on English football as a protest against the FA for sanctions imposed on City. When he stubbornly refused to pay his FA fine, his rapport with fans increased further. He was very much a man of the people.

Another pre-World War II cult hero was Tommy Johnson, City's record scorer who in March 1930 was transferred to Everton against the wishes of the vast majority of supporters. Demonstrations and a boycott followed, and the average attendance dropped by 8,000 as a direct result of his departure.

Other cult heroes included the great Billy Meredith, of course, and '30s stars Fred Tilson, Ernie Toseland, Sam Cowan and Frank Swift.

The '50s and '60s

The 1950s saw most of City's Cup final players of 1955 and '56 – Ken Barnes, Roy Clarke, Bert Trautmann – achieve tremendous popularity, but it's fair to say that Bobby Johnstone was idolised by many as a man of the people. He was a great player, but fans also loved the stories of his life, contracting diphtheria as a child before being shot to fame as a member of Hibs' 'Famous Five' forward line.

In 1962, Scottish forward Alex Harley arrived From Third Lanark and netted 23 goals in 40 League appearances during a period when the Blues desperately needed a hero. He is recognised as the first player ever to have his name chanted at the ground, although it is recorded that stars of the '20s and '30s often appeared in 'shouts' of the period – "Keep chasing the pigeons, Tosie!" was a favourite shout by Ernie Toseland supporters, for some bizarre reason.

Harley only managed one season with City which, in many ways, guaranteed his status as a cult figure.

The '70s and '80s

By the '70s, the very nature of football meant that media hype would often create a 'hero' and expect supporters to agree, but fans would still make up their own minds.

Dave Watson was a true cult figure. Tough, determined and dedicated, Watson was City and England's no-nonsense central defender. One of his most popular moments was a wonder goal against fellow title-challengers Ipswich on 2 April 1977. He had a spell as captain and for at least two decades after his departure City struggled to replace him.

The '80s in particular saw some of the most unlikely players became idolised. The biggest cult figure of the late '80s was Ian Bishop. Lazy journalists believed

GILLESPIE'S SECOND GOAL

he became a hero because of his role in City's 5-1 win over United, but that isn't entirely accurate as Bishop had already become a favourite before the derby. Supporters recognised his determination right from the start of his Maine Road career. When he left after only 19 League games, his cult status was cemented. His return in the late '90s reduced that status a little but he remains a legendary cult hero.

A surprise '80s hero, for a brief period, was John Gidman. It was very unusual for any former United player to be accepted but Gidman was determined to win over the fans. Before he left United he stated publicly that City were the only side he would leave Old Trafford for – that went down well with Reds! – then in his first

Alex Harley (left); John Gidman, Imre Varadi & Tony Grealish (below).

game, a derby with United, he 'got stuck in'. His combative style ensured he was perceived as a true Blue. It helped that he arrived around the same time as Imre Varadi – another popular Blue – and the battling Tony Grealish.

Other '70s and '80s heroes include Paul 'Goalden' Moulden, Trevor Morley, Tommy Caton, Nicky Reid, Peter Barnes, Gary Owen, and virtually every member of the 1986 Youth team. Another was Mark Lillis. Lillis was not the greatest player but he typified the spirit of the mid '80s. He was a Blue through and through and it was obvious to all that he shared the same passion for the club as the supporters on the Kippax. In fact, he had been a Kippax regular himself. His first match as a player for City at Maine Road saw him score a goal and then perform a bizarre celebration with his arm to the Kippax – it later became his trademark celebration.

The '90s

The biggest cult figures of the '90s were undoubtedly Niall Quinn (although his TV punditry has lessened his status with some fans), Uwe Rosler, Georgi Kinkladze, Paul Dickov, Shaun Goater and Andy Morrison. Dickov is often remembered for

his last-gasp goal in the 1999 Play-off final but he had already achieved cult status after saving the club in the first leg of the Play-off semi at Springfield Park. He had equalised – a crucial goal – and his spirit and fighting qualities helped to change a number of League games during his time at City.

Clearly with Quinn, Rosler, Goater and Dickov, their attacking qualities helped strengthen their claims; but Quinn's role on the final day of the 1995-96 relegation season also helped enormously. After he was substituted, he urged the players to push for another goal while others were claiming City were safe, and then he appeared on television that night to apologise for City's failure. He wasn't to blame, but he stood up to be counted.

Andy Morrison was a cult hero in the Billy Gillespie mould. He was a bustling player with a determined attitude, and became a huge hero simply because he was the perfect captain at a time when true leaders were needed. He was also the last City captain to lift a trophy at Wembley.

Undoubtedly, the biggest cult figure of the period was Shaun Goater. 'The Goat' achieved so much during the '90s and the early years of this century that he will be remembered for a very long time.

The Modern Era

Shaun Wright-Phillips, Micah Richards and Richard Dunne remain cult heroes amongst fans for their loyalty and dedication to the Blues' cause. Dunne, in particular, demonstrated that a fighting spirit and determined approach was appropriate for the period when fans needed players to demonstrate their pride in battle. Wright-Phillips and Richards represented the success of City's Academy system and, as such, were loved by fans.

Since the success returned in 2011, many players have become legends but some have also become cult heroes. Mario Balotelli, with his nonchalant way of taking penalties and myriad stories of events in his private life, fitted the bill perfectly. He may not have been the greatest player, or the longest serving, but the stories of his time in Manchester

Our heroes Paul Lake and Ian Bishop back in September 1989.

kept us enthralled. One minute we're told he had popped into a women's prison because he was interested to see what it looked like from the inside; the next he's handing out money in central Manchester. The stories became incredible but they undoubtedly added to his iconic status.

And so to Pablo Zabaleta. No matter what he does or where he goes, fans will always picture him as a warrior for their cause. He would have been a cult hero no matter what the era or the situation City faced. Like Billy Gillespie right at the start of the club's history, Pablo was hero-worshipped by fans. Often, he would return to the pitch with his head bandaged ready to give his all. Best of all, after leaving City he was spotted wearing a City scarf while training at West Ham. Once a Blue, always a Blue!

Stand By Me

When looking at City's record crowds it is clear that the Blues have always been one of football's biggest draws. Like most clubs there have been some lows but, taking an overview of the club's history, City have consistently been one of football's most attractive prospects, generation after generation. And the proof lies in the bald statistics.

• City's record attendance is higher than any other English record on a club ground, and remains the highest domestic crowd other than a final or a game at Wembley.

• The Blues have attracted the largest individual divisional crowd for at least one season in every decade since records began. No other side has achieved this feat, although with a smaller capacity stadium than many of our rivals it is unlikely the

2010s will see this continue.

• Unlike the majority of clubs, City have never attracted the lowest crowd for their division in a season – it may be worth noting that Newcastle (7,986 in 1977-78), Chelsea (8,171 in 1973-74 & 8,473 in 1955-56),

Chronological Progression of City's Record Home Crowd

Attendance	Date	Opposition	Competition	Venue
4,000	04/10/1890	Liverpool Stanley	FA Cup	Hyde Road
6,000	03/09/1892	Bootle	Alliance League	Hyde Road
11,000	14/11/1891	Nottm Forest	Alliance League	Hyde Road
12,000	28/11/1891	Lincoln City	Alliance League	Hyde Road
13,000	25/12/1891	Grimsby Town	Alliance League	Hyde Road
14,000	03/11/1894	Newton Heath	Division Two	Hyde Road
20,000	07/12/1895	Newton Heath	Division Two	Hyde Road
30,000	03/04/1896	Liverpool	Division Two	Hyde Road
35,000	05/03/1904	Middlesbrough	FA Cup	Hyde Road
40,000	28/01/1905	Newcastle	Division One	Hyde Road
41,709	01/02/1913	Sunderland	FA Cup	Hyde Road
55,000 c	26/03/1921	Burnley	Division One	Hyde Road
58,159	25/08/1923	Sheffield United	Division One	Maine Road
76,166	08/03/1924	Cardiff City	FA Cup	Maine Road
84,569	03/03/1934	Stoke City	FA Cup	Maine Road
79,491	23/021935	Arsenal	League	Maine Road

All figures before 1925 are based on unofficial figures recorded in the media.

Chronological Progression of Away Attendance Record

Attendance	Date	Opposition	Competition	Venue
2,000	19/09/1891	Lincoln City	Alliance	John O'Gaunt's
10,000	03/10/1891	Newton Heath	FA Cup	North Road
12,000	26/12/1891	The Wednesday	Alliance	Olive Grove
20,000	01/01/1896	Liverpool	Div Two	Anfield
25,000	21/10/1899	Aston Villa	Div One	Villa Park
40,000	25/12/1902	Manchester Utd	Div Two	Bank Street
53,000	19/03/1904	The Wednesday	FAC s/f	Goodison Park
60,000	17/09/1910	Manchester Utd	Div One	Old Trafford
63,000	20/11/1921	Manchester Utd	Div One	Old Trafford
66,442	28/01/1922	Bolton W	FA Cup	Burnden Park
69,920	18/02/1933	Bolton W	FA Cup	Burnden Park
72,841	17/02/1934	Sheffield Wed	FA Cup	Hillsborough
75,540	05/03/1938	Aston Villa	FA Cup	Villa Park
100,000	10/03/1971	Gornik Zabrze	ECWC	Gornik

in the top division.

• City's old ground, Maine Road, has housed more 80,000-plus crowds than any other English club stadium.

• Prior to 2006-07, Maine Road had housed more 70,000-plus crowds than any other English club stadium. (Old Trafford's increased capacity now means that it holds that record, with Maine Road second).

• The attendance for the 1935 game with Arsenal was, at the time, Maine Road's second highest crowd, but has been listed here as it was the record crowd for any

Arsenal (4,554 in 1965-66) and United (3,679 in 1930-31) are among those who have suffered this mark of dishonour

Ask a policeman: The Platt Lane turnstiles, September 1967.

Etihad Stadium Chronological Progression of Record

Attendance	Date	Opposition	Competition
34,103	14/08/2003	TNS	UEFA Cup
46,287	23/08/2003	Portsmouth	Premier League
46,436	31/08/2003	Arsenal	Premier League
46,687	14/09/2003	Aston Villa	Premier League
46,842	28/09/2003	Tottenham H	Premier League
47,101	18/10/2003	Bolton W	Premier League
47,126	22/12/2003	Leeds United	Premier League
47,201	28/12/2003	Liverpool	Premier League
47,304	28/02/2004	Chelsea	Premier League
47,321	30/12/2007	Liverpool	Premier League
47,331	13/09/2008	Chelsea	Premier League
47,339	12/09/2009	Arsenal	Premier League
47,348	05/12/2009	Chelsea	Premier League
47,370	05/05/2010	Tottenham H	Premier League
47,393	24/10/2010	Arsenal	Premier League
47,408	19/11/2011	Newcastle U	Premier League
47,422	22/01/2012	Tottenham H	Premier League
47,435	13/05/2012	QPR	Premier League
54,331	16/08/2015	Chelsea	Premier League
54,502	17/10/2015	Bournemouth	Premier League
54,523	26/12/2015	Sunderland	Premier League
54,693	06/02/2016	Leicester C	Premier League

largest League crowd and largest provincial crowd (84,569).

• The attendances v League game at the time. This was surpassed in 1935 when Chelsea v Arsenal attracted 82,905, and in 1948 by a game between Arsenal and Manchester United played at City's Maine Road ground (recorded as 83,260 by Arsenal and City, but 81,962 by United).

• Crucially, this means that Maine Road still holds the record for

Season's Divisional Best Since 1925

Attendance	Season	Opposition	Division
62,994	1925-26	Manchester Utd	One
49,384	1926-27	Bradford City	Two
59,500	1927-28	Preston NE	Two
68,704	1929-30	Aston Villa	One
79,491	1934-35	Arsenal	One
74,918	1936-37	Arsenal	One
69,463	1946-47	Burnley	Two
63,925	1955-56	Blackpool	One
47,171	1965-66	Huddersfield T	Two
63,013	1969-70	Manchester Utd	One
63,326	1971-72	Manchester Utd	One
41,862	1983-84	Sheffield Wed	Two
47,285	1984-85	Charlton Athletic	Two
40,070	1988-89	Chelsea	Two
30,729	1996-97	Oldham Athletic	One (2)
32,471	1998-99	York City	Two (3)
33,027	1999-00	Blackburn R	One (2)
34,657	2001-02	Portsmouth	One (2)

City's 30 Highest Home Crowds of All Time

Attendance	Date/Score	Opposition	Competition
84,569	03/03/1934 1-0	Stoke City	FA Cup
79,491	23/03/1935 1-1	Arsenal	Div 1 (Old)
78,000	20/09/1947 0-0	Manchester United	Div 1 (Old)
76,166	08/03/1924 0-0	Cardiff City	FA Cup
76,129	03/03/1956 2-1	Everton	FA Cup
74,918	10/04/1937 2-0	Arsenal	Div 1 (Old)
74,799	30/01/1926 4-0	Huddersfield Town	FA Cup
74,723	29/01/1955 2-0	Manchester United	FA Cup
73,668	18/02/1928 0-1	Stoke City	FA Cup
71,937	22/01/1938 3-1	Bury	FA Cup
70,640	18/02/1956 0-0	Liverpool	FA Cup
70,493	28/12/1957 2-2	Manchester United	Div 1 (Old)
69,463	10/05/1947 1-0	Burnley	Div 2 (Old)
68,704	26/12/1929 1-2	Aston Villa	Div 1 (Old)
68,614	21/02/1934 2-0	Sheffield Wed	FA Cup
67,782	23/08/1947 4-3	Wolverhampton W	Div 1 (Old)
67,616	11/09/1948 0-0	Manchester United	Div 1 (Old)
67,494	07/02/1948 0-1	Preston North End	FA Cup
65,981	02/05/1960 1-2	Burnley	Div 1 (Old)
65,978	25/01/1936 2-1	Luton Town	FA Cup
64,862	09/01/1937 1-0	Manchester United	Div 1 (Old)
64,472	08/02/1930 0-1	Manchester United	Div 1 (Old)
63,925	24/09/1955 2-0	Blackpool	Div 1 (Old)
63,872	02/02/1957 2-4	Manchester United	Div 1 (Old)
63,704	31/12/1949 1-2	Manchester United	Div 1 (Old)
63,326	06/11/1971 3-3	Manchester United	Div 1 (Old)
63,052	17/08/1968 0-0	Manchester United	Div 1 (Old)
63,034	26/03/1966 0-0	Everton	FA Cup
63,013	15/11/1969 4-0	Manchester United	Div 1 (Old)
62,994	12/09/1925 1-1	Manchester United	Div 1 (Old)

of this magnitude during this period.

Season's Divisional Best

The following figures show the seasons since 1925 (when attendance records were formalised by the Football League) when City's highest home attendance of the season was also the division's highest.

Those seasons in italics are ones in which City's highest crowd was the highest for every division of the League.

To put these figures in to context, here are the record crowds of some of our major rivals over the years. Note that all these attendances are greater than the highest ever recorded by Liverpool and many other clubs. It's worth noting that if we exclude games at Wembley and other clubs' games at our own Maine Road stadium, City's fifth highest

Bolton in 1933 and Sheffield Wednesday in 1934 remain record attendances for those venues. The Gornik crowd in 1971 has been variously reported as anything from 100,000 to 110,000. Other Gornik European home ties were played in front of crowds

Record Crowds of City's Major Rivals

Club	Attendance	Year/Stadium
Arsenal	73,707	1998 at Wembley
Arsenal	73,295	1935 at Highbury
Aston Villa	76,688	1946 at Villa Park
Birmingham City	66,844	1939 at St Andrew's
Blackburn Rovers	62,522	1929 at Ewood Park
Bolton Wanderers	69,912	1933 at Burnden Park (v MCFC)
Burnley	54,775	1924 at Turf Moor
Charlton Athletic	75,031	1938 at The Valley
Chelsea	82,905	1935 at Stamford Bridge
Coventry City	51,455	1967 at Highfield Road
Crystal Palace	51,482	1979 at Selhurst Park
Derby County	41,826	1969 at the Baseball Ground
Everton	78,299	1948 at Goodison Park
Fulham	49,335	1938 at Craven Cottage
Huddersfield Town	67,037	1932 at Leeds Road
Leeds United	57,892	1967 at Elland Road
Leicester City	47,298	1928 at Filbert Street
Liverpool	61,905	1952 at Anfield
Manchester United	83,260 *	1948 at Maine Road
Manchester United	76,098	2007 at Old Trafford
Middlesbrough	53,536	1949 at Ayresome Park
Newcastle United	68,386	1930 at St James' Park
Nottingham Forest	49,946	1967 at the City Ground
Notts County	47,310	1955 at Meadow Lane
Oldham Athletic	46,471	1930 at Boundary Park
Sheffield United	68,287	1936 at Bramall Lane
Sheffield Wednesday	72,841	1934 at Hillsborough (v MCFC)
Stoke City	51,380	1937 at the Victoria Ground
Sunderland	75,118	1933 at Roker Park
Tottenham Hotspur	85,512	2016 at Wembley
Tottenham Hotspur	75,038	1938 at White Hart Lane
West Bromwich Albion	64,815	1937 at The Hawthorns
West Ham United	56,996	2017 at the London Stadium
Wolverhampton W	61,315	1939 at Molineux

* (recorded as 81,962 by MUFC),

attendance is greater than all the other clubs apart from Aston Villa, Chelsea and Everton. That is an incredible record, and one that those who criticise City's support and history should be made aware of.

... For Ever More

The previous pages have featured City's record crowds and highlighted the strength of City's support for individual games. However, to establish the true nature of the club's fanbase it is essential that we also look at average attendances. Consistency of support is one area where supporters of the Blues can feel justifiably proud.

It is a fact that the Blues have, generation after generation, been one of the English game's top attractions. Like all – and I do mean all – English clubs, there have been some average attendance lows over the years, but when the entire history of our club is reviewed and City's figures are compared with the national average, it is clear that the Blues have consistently been one of football's most attractive draws.

Consider the following:

In chronological order of their first appearance at the top of the average table they are: Everton (1888-89), Villa (1898-99), Newcastle (1904-05), Chelsea (1907-08), Tottenham (1909-10), City (1910-11), Liverpool (1922-23), Arsenal (1929-30) & Manchester United (1956-57).

• As early as 1895-96, City were the third best supported side in the entire League despite being a Second Division side. Only First Division sides Everton and Aston Villa could better the Blues. Modern-day giants Arsenal were 10th; Liverpool were 19th; United were 21st and Chelsea had yet to exist!

• In 1900-01, City was the second best supported side in the entire League, only 400 people behind Aston Villa (1st).

• The 1910-11 season saw the Blues top the attendance charts for the first time with an average of 26,000. This was the 8th highest average of all time at that point.

• The Blues were regularly amongst the best supported sides throughout the inter-war period. Our average exceeded 37,000 for the first time in 1927-28 when we established a record average crowd for the Second Division. This was also the entire League's highest.

• Since the beginning of the Football League in 1888 only nine sides have topped the table for average attendances.

• In 1947-48 City's average crowd exceeded 42,000 for the first time. Prior to that season only Chelsea (1919-20 &

Chronological Progression of City's Record Average Attendance

Average Attendance	Season	League	Highest	Lowest
6,800	1891-92	Alliance	Unavailable	
10,000 (3)	1895-96	Div Two	16,000 (Everton)	1,775
16,000 (3)	1899-1900	Div Two	19,825 (Aston Villa)	4,000
18,300 (2)	1900-01	Div One	18,700 (Aston Villa)	5,850
20,000 (2)	1903-04	Div One	20,350 (Aston Villa)	6,675
22,150 (3)	1906-07	Div One	33,650 (Newcastle U)	5,375
23,000 (3)	1907-08	Div One	30,850 (Chelsea)	10,525
26,000 (1)	1910-11	Div One	26,000 (City)	8,550
27,000 (3)	1913-14	Div One	37,900 (Chelsea)	9,950
31,020 (12)	1920-21	Div One	41,100 (Newcatle U)	16,250
32,000 (2)	1925-26	Div One	32,355 (Chelsea)	15,728
37,468 (1)	1927-28	Div Two	37,468 (City)	5,361
39,283 (8)	1946-47	Div Two	49,379 (Newcastle U)	12,505
42,725 (8)	1947-48	Div Two	56,283 (Newcastle U)	15,372
46,834 (3)	2003-04	Premier	67,641 (Manchester Utd)	16,240
47,044 (4)	2011-12	Premier	75,387 (Manchester Utd)	17,295
47,080 (4)	2013-14	Premier	75,207 (Manchester Utd)	20,407
54,041 (3)	2015-16	Premier	75,279 (Manchester Utd)	11,189
54,070 (5)	2017-18	Premier	74,975 (Manchester Utd)	10,640

All figures before 1925 are based on unofficial figures recorded in the media.

1946-7), Arsenal (1934-5, 1936-7, 1937-8 & 1946-7), Newcastle (1946-7), Liverpool (1946-7), United (1946-47) and Wolves (1946-47) had exceeded that figure.

• From 1975 to relegation in 1983 City were always one of the top four best supported sides.

• Since the '80s, whenever City have played outside of the top division, they have tended to be the best supported side in that division.

• Since moving to their current home in 2003, the increased capacity has allowed City to re-establish itself as one of the best supported sides in the country.

In general, many people believe success increases support, and while that is undoubtedly true to some extent, for City it is often periods of adversity that prove the loyalty of the club's fans. It is highly significant, for example, that the first time City were the best supported side in the entire League (1910-11), Manchester United (6th best supported side) won the League title for the second time in three seasons.

Similarly in 1925-26, when City were the best supported side in Division One and had established a new record average, the Blues were actually relegated. This, coupled with significant poverty and hardship in Manchester at the time,

should have reduced support but loyalty increased! In my book, *Manchester: A Football History*, I explore the relationship between attendances and Manchester's major sides and it is fair to say that City fans can feel immensely proud of their loyalty throughout the history of the game. Something that cannot be said by all of the League's biggest names.

It is worth underlining that City have never been the worst supported side in their division but, of today's so-called giants, Arsenal (1912-13 average = 9,100) and Manchester United (1930-31 average = 11,685) have. Our worst average of the 20th century came in the desperate 1964-65 season and was 14,753 (half our average of 1960-61 and a third of our 1957-58 figure). However, it is significant that for every League season our average has always been above the divisional average and, apart from 17 seasons, has always been in the top 11 nationally. Again, few of today's giants can say that – United's 20th-century low stands at 4,650 and Chelsea averaged 15,731 as recently as 1988-89.

For fans, average attendances are often used as an indicator of size of club and so a number of people over the years have tried to produce a definitive 'all-time' attendance table. Several years ago, around the time of City's move to their current home, analysis by a member of the Association of Football Statisticians claimed that if stadium capacity were not an issue for any club, City would be the fourth biggest club in terms of attendance. That analysis compared post-war attendance details with performance on the pitch. Since 2003 or whenever City's capacity increased, so did the club's average attendance – which would have a positive impact on the club's standing if that analysis were to be repeated today. As would the level of success achieved.

Figures can be manipulated in many different ways, but City can feel proud that they have many attendance firsts that can never be matched by many of today's perceived biggest clubs.

Chronological Progression of Record
This table (p117) shows the progression of City's record average attendance. It is fair to say that many of the figures pre-war are estimated based on newspaper reports,

etc. – and that the figures here are those widely accepted using similar methods of calculation for all football clubs.

When City published attendances for League games prior to the '50s they often published those who paid on the day with season and other ticket holders excluded. This frustrating practice obscures exact attendance figures and ensures that many crowds were under-reported.

The official crowd for Maine Road's opening game was often published as 56,993 but research of contemporary newspapers in the late '90s identified that the actual figure was 58,159 and that the lower figure excluded season ticket holders. The club had taken the unusual step of publishing the full attendance a few days after the inaugural game as they wanted to celebrate what was an impressive first attendance. The figures suggest that City had 1,166 season-ticket holders in 1923-24 and potentially all other home League attendances reported that season were short by this number.

To give an indication of the magnitude of City's support in comparison with other clubs, the highest average in the entire League and lowest average for the corresponding division are included. Also, the figure in brackets after City's average attendance denotes the position within the League that City's average held.

Top of the Chart

The following figures show the seasons when City were the best supported side in their division, along with the club's highest individual crowd that season.

Those crowds marked in italics were also the highest individual crowds for the entire division that season (crowds pre-1925 are inconsistently recorded and so have not been highlighted).

It is fair to say that when an average crowd is within 4,000 of the highest then the stadium is likely to have been full for the majority of games with the size of away support varying.

Seasons City Have Topped the Divisional Charts		
Average	Season	Highest Crowd
10,000	1895-96	30,000 (Liverpool)
10,000	1898-99	25,000 (N. Heath)
16,000	1902-03	30,000 (United)
18,275	1909-10	40,000 (Oldham)
26,000	1910-11	40,000 (Liverpool)
21,000	1914-15	40,000 (Oldham)
32,000	1925-26	*62,994 (United)*
30,848	1926-27	*49,384 (Bradford C)*
37,468	1927-28	*59,500 (Preston)*
31,715	1928-29	61,007 (United)
35,016	1950-51	45,842 (Hull)
27,739	1965-66	47,171 *(Huddersfield)*
24,220	1984-85	47,285 *(Charlton)*
23,500	1988-89	40,070 *(Chelsea)*
26,753	1996-97	30,729 *(Oldham)*
28,273	1998-99	32,471 *(York)*
32,001	1999-00	33,027 *(Blackburn)*
33,059	2001-02	34,657 *(Portsmouth)*

Half the World Away

Much has been written about City's overseas players over the last decade or so. Sometimes this has been positive and occasionally negative. It is therefore appropriate to take the time to look back at City's history of overseas players and their records.

The first player born outside of the British Isles to appear for the Blues was Canadian defender Walter Bowman, who had come to England as part of a Canadian touring party and while over here joined Accrington Stanley in January 1892. He made five appearances for them and scored three

goals, before joining Ardwick (City) the following season. He made his debut on 18 February 1893 and scored as the Blues beat Crewe 3-1.

Bowman was not only our first overseas player

and goalscorer but also the first to have played for his country. He stayed at City until 1900, but mystery surrounds his later life. Recent research has identified that he eventually settled in Butte, Montana, where it is believed he was married to a teacher. For trivia buffs, it is worth noting that Butte was the birthplace of daredevil stuntman Evil Knievel!

After Bowman, it was 45 years before another overseas-born player appeared for our first team (note: for this feature, overseas includes every country other than those of the British Isles). That player was Les McDowall – and before anyone raises their hand to point out that McDowall was British, it's true. He was a British national. However, McDowall was actually born in Ganga Pur, India in 1912, the son of a Scottish missionary.

The first non-British national after Bowman to play for the club was perhaps the most famous of them all – Bert Trautmann. A former Luftwaffe paratrooper and Prisoner of War, Trautmann joined City after the war, making his debut around 70 years ago in 1949.

Apart from American-born Gerry Baker in 1960, City did not sign any other overseas-born players until the late '70s when South African Colin Viljoen arrived at the club via a marginally less exotic stop-off at Ipswich Town.

CHURCHMAN'S CIGARETTES

L. J. McDOWALL (MANCHESTER CITY)

First Overseas Player to be Capped

The first player to be capped for a country outside of the British Isles while still on City's books was Norwegian Aage Hareide. Hareide made nine international appearances during the early '80s while a City player, including one game against England. In 2018 he managed the Danish national side at the World Cup.

Most Appearances by Overseas Player

Bert Trautmann has made more City appearances than any other non-UK-born player. He appeared in 545 first-team games and when this was set he was City's appearance record holder. Since that time only Englishmen Alan Oakes, Joe Corrigan and Mike Doyle have appeared in more.

Bert represented the Football League in two games and became the first German to appear in the FA Cup final (1955).

In recent seasons, Pablo Zabaleta (Argentina), Vincent Kompany (Belgium), David Silva (Spain) and Yaya Touré (Ivory Coast) have all made over 300 appearances for the club. At the end of 2017-18, Sergio Agüero (Argentina) was on 292 appearances.

First Player from Behind Iron Curtain

When City signed World Cup star Kaziu Deyna in 1978 he was the first player to join City from Communist eastern Europe. Deyna came from Poland and City chairman Peter Swales and secretary Bernard Halford had to negotiate with the Polish Army for the release of Deyna. It was a highly complicated transaction with the Blues paying part of the fee in medical equipment and other goods.

Continental Drift

City have signed a player from every continent, apart from Antarctica. The first arrivals from each continent were:
North America – Walter Bowman.
Europe – Bert Trautmann.
Australasia – David Oldfield (British)/ Jason Van Blerk.

KAZIMIERZ
DEYNA
MANCHESTER CITY

UWE ROSLER

than any other overseas player. A decade ago that record was held by Shaun Goater (Bermuda) who netted 103 first-team goals in 212 appearances.

The previous record holder was Uwe Rösler, who scored 64 in 177 appearances.

By the end of the 2017-18 season, David Silva (Spain) had scored 61 goals in 346 appearances, while Yaya Touré ended his City career with 81 goals from 316 appearances.

Africa – Jim Whitley (British)/Dixon Etuhu.
Asia – Les McDowall (British)/Jihai Sun.
Central/South America – Paulo Wanchope.

Most Goals

Sergio Agüero (Argentina) has of course scored more first-team goals for the Blues

Villa and Ardiles

Although City did not sign '70s stars Ricky Villa or Ossie Ardiles (both Argentinians),

the Blues did show an interest. The two men had yet to arrive in England when City made enquiries. Ultimately, the Blues pulled out of negotiations, however stories circulating at the time of Villa's arrival at Tottenham suggested the player was convinced he had signed for City and not Spurs!

First Overseas Manager
Sven-Goran Eriksson was the first non-British national to manage the Blues, however Les McDowall was the first not to have been born within the UK.

First Brazilian Player
Attacking midfielder Geovanni arrived at City on a one-year Bosman deal in July 2007, becoming the first Brazilian to sign for the Blues.

Bojinov
Valeri Bojinov was the first Bulgarian to play for City. He also entered the record books in Italy when he became the youngest overseas player ever to make his debut in Serie A. He made his first appearance for Lecce he was aged just 15 years and 11 months.

Irish Republic
The first City player to appear for the Republic of Ireland following the creation of its own FA was defender Leo Dunne. He was capped twice (Switzerland & Germany) in 1935 while on City's books, but the player only made three first-team appearances for the Blues.

Billy Walsh
Between 1924 and 1950 players from the Republic of Ireland could either elect to play for Northern Ireland or the Republic. Northern Ireland competed in the British Home International Championship as

Ireland, and in 1947 and 1948 Dublin-born Billy Walsh won five caps. Both before and after these appearances he also played nine times for the Republic – this besides having appeared for England schoolboys!

The First Team
Not exactly an overseas story, but certainly one that may surprise. Most people probably assume that the first team for our inaugural League game (in 1892, playing as Ardwick AFC) was mostly made up of English players; however the truth is that only three, possibly four, members of that opening side were English. The English players were Bill Hopkins, Harry Middleton and David Weir, while the nationality of another player, John McVickers, remains unclear. His name suggests he was Scottish, but he may have been English.

ALFIE
HAALAND

Of the other players, five were Scottish (goalkeeper Billy Douglas, Bill Angus, David Robson, David Russell, and Bob Milarvie) and two were Welsh (Joe Davies & Hugh Morris). There was an Englishman on the pitch for every one of our League games that season (Middleton only missed one game).

Our First 50 Overseas-born Players
The following table lists the first 50 overseas-born players to appear for City. Where these have taken British citizenship or appeared for British international sides, the word 'British' appears in brackets after their birth nation.

It is clear from this record that the arrival of one player from a country often leads to others from that same country being signed up by City. This is most obvious with the Georgian players and those from Germany – during one 22-month period, five German nationals were signed.

Name	Born
Walter Bowman	Canada
Les McDowall	India (British)
Gerry Baker	USA
Colin Viljoen	South Africa
Kazimierz Deyna	Poland
Dragoslav Stepanovic	Yugoslavia
Aage Hareide	Norway
Ivan Golac	Yugoslavia
Tony Cunningham	Jamaica (British)
David Phillips	Germany
David Oldfield	Australia (British)
Steve Lomas	Germany (British)
Danny Hoekman	Netherlands
Michel Vonk	Netherlands
Kare Ingebigtsen	Norway
Alfons Groenendijk	Netherlands
Uwe Rosler	Germany
Steffan Karl	Germany
Jim Whitley	Zambia (British)
Maurizio Gaudino	Germany
Eike Immel	Germany
Georgiou Kinkladze	Georgia
Ronnie Ekelund	Denmark
Michael Frontzeck	Germany
Jeff Whitley	Zambia (British)
Mikhail Kavelashvili	Geogia
Giuseppe Mazzarelli	Switzerland
Gerard Wiekens	Netherlands
Jason Van Blerk	Australia
Murtaz Shelia	Georgia
Kakhaber Tskhadadze	Georgia
Shaun Goater	Bermuda
Danny Tiatto	Australia
Danny Allsop	Australia
Chris Killen	New Zealand
Terry Dunfield	Canada
Dixon Etuhu	Nigeria
Alf-Inge Haaland	Norway
Paulo Wanchope	Costa Rica
George Weah	Liberia
Laurent Charvet	France
Andrei Kanchelskis	Ukraine
Egil Ostenstad	Norway
Eyal Berkovic	Israel
Simon Colosimo	Australia
Ali Benarbia	Algeria
Lucien Mettomo	Cambodia
Christian Negouai	Martinique (French)
Niclas Jensen	Denmark

Where the Heart Is

For those who attended games there, Maine Road will always be regarded as the spiritual home of Manchester City. The stadium opened in 1923 and was the leading League ground in the country. Constructed at the same time as Wembley Stadium by the same builders, Sir Robert McAlpine, with the aim of developing an 'English Hampden' – people often incorrectly think it was designed as the 'Wembley of the North' but that simply isn't true. The architect and builders based their ideas on Hampden Park, perceived at the time as the greatest stadium in the world. Maine Road opened in August 1923.

Wembley opened a few months earlier than Maine Road, and because of crowd control issues at the first FA Cup final, it did not have a good reputation in 1923. Some reports suggested City adjusted their plans as a result of chaos at Wembley – "The lessons of Wembley have been taken to heart, and a feature of the ground will be six tunnels communicating with the terraces, giving easy access to all parts."

The first Mancunians heard of the new stadium came on 9 May 1922 when the Blues announced incredible plans to develop what they believed would be the greatest stadium in England. The 16.25 acre site was purchased for £5,550 and the original plans outlined that Maine Road would be developed in two phases with the first seeing the construction of an 85,000-capacity ground with one huge seated grand stand and terracing on the other three sides. The second phase was to see the terracing extended and then roofed to provide covered accommodation for a remarkable 120,000.

The sensible capacity of Maine Road at the time of opening was probably around 80,000, though City's management felt it could hold 90,000, and the *Topical Times Sporting Annual* for 1934-5 stated a figure of 86,000. The crowd for the first game was revealed to be 58,159 but film of the match claims there were 80,000 there and, when the footage is compared to crowds known to be 70,000 or more, it does suggest the opening game attracted a figure closer to 75,000 than 58,000.

In the main, newspaper reports of

the opening match - a 2-1 victory over Sheffield United on 25th August 1923 - focussed on the stadium rather than the game with the Manchester *Guardian* particularly impressed. The newspaper provided a whole range of statistics on the venue, making note of the size of the tunnels and of the terracing, especially the ground's Popular Side (latterly the Kippax) where there were 110 tiers of steps at its highest point. It seemed the most fantastic venue: "Come in and take your ease but here, inside these barriers, you stay and by these great pits and tunnels, quietly and quickly you depart. This scheme in its simplicity and great scale suggests power and force in the way that a pyramid does, or a Babylonian tower, and there could scarcely be a better scheme to represent the passionate concentration of fifty or eighty thousand men and women on the fortunes of the field below."

Referring to the Main Stand, the article added: "The Grand Stand by itself is an elaborate mechanism only to be afforded by the rich town club. For long after the match was over curious crowds explored its many staircases by which the holders of all sorts of tickets are conducted without fail or confusion to their various seats. The topmost section sits aloof and remote at an incredible distance from the field. Like a squall falling suddenly from the hills, its clapping came at times in sudden gusts from far away."

The *Guardian* reporter was particularly impressed with his initial view of the venue: "This ground is the last word in the provision of comfort and security for (and against) the explosive force of the great crowds that follow the League teams. There is something almost barbaric in the impression which, when it is full, it makes on the observer. As one comes on it suddenly from Claremont Road, a great rounded embankment towers up in front, and over it at one side looms the highly arched roof of a stand whose dim recesses cannot be discerned at all except from the ground level. Only the fresh green paint on the front of it, picked out with gold, detracts from the broad impression of size and power, giving a rather incongruous air of neatness and modernity."

The actual credit for the move to Maine Road must go to chairman Lawrence Furniss and manager Ernest Mangnall. At the time of opening it was suggested that the stadium should be named after Furniss, but the chairman clearly felt that no venue should bear the name of a living member of the club. Instead the first time the name Maine Road appeared in print as the ground's name came on the morning of the game: "The main entrances will be in Maine Road, by which name the ground will be known, for the time being at all events."

During its first season the stadium demonstrated its worth as on 8 March

1924 a crowd of 76,166 – the highest crowd yet assembled at a football venue in Manchester – watched the legendary Billy Meredith play for the Blues against Cardiff in the FA Cup.

A decade later the capacity was tested again when, for the first time in the history of the stadium, the gates were closed before the game. The official attendance figure was 84,569 – it remains the largest provincial attendance.

Originally only one side was roofed – the 10,000 seater Main Stand – but in 1931 the first stage of the club's development plan saw additional seating and a roof built in the Platt Lane/Main Stand corner. Four years later the second phase of the plan saw the roof extended over the rest of the Platt Lane Stand. The developments surrounding this

Kippax away turnstiles

stand actually increased the capacity of the venue as the

North Stand and Main Stand

Platt Lane Stand was extended at the back with

North Stand

wooden planks to square off the terracing. Assuming the record crowd of 84,569 had

Sky Blue Heaven: Maine Road viewed from the air in the late 1940s.

127

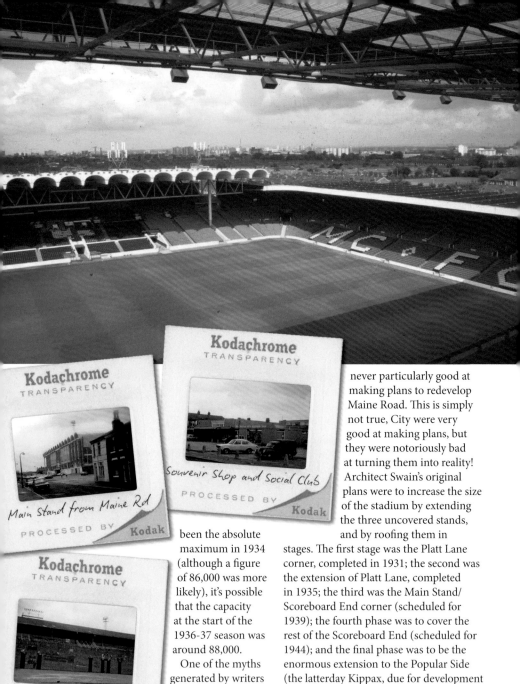

Kodachrome TRANSPARENCY

Main Stand from Maine Rd

PROCESSED BY Kodak

Kodachrome TRANSPARENCY

Souvenir Shop and Social Club

PROCESSED BY Kodak

Kodachrome TRANSPARENCY

Kippax Turnstiles

PROCESSED BY Kodak

been the absolute maximum in 1934 (although a figure of 86,000 was more likely), it's possible that the capacity at the start of the 1936-37 season was around 88,000.

One of the myths generated by writers over the years is that Manchester City were never particularly good at making plans to redevelop Maine Road. This is simply not true, City were very good at making plans, but they were notoriously bad at turning them into reality! Architect Swain's original plans were to increase the size of the stadium by extending the three uncovered stands, and by roofing them in stages. The first stage was the Platt Lane corner, completed in 1931; the second was the extension of Platt Lane, completed in 1935; the third was the Main Stand/ Scoreboard End corner (scheduled for 1939); the fourth phase was to cover the rest of the Scoreboard End (scheduled for 1944); and the final phase was to be the enormous extension to the Popular Side (the latterday Kippax, due for development by 1950).

The plans were put on hold with

Maine Rd from Claremont Rd

Platt Lane Main Stand corner

relegation in 1938 and then stopped altogether with the outbreak of war.

By the beginning of the '50s Maine Road was still a major venue and continued to attract internationals and semi-finals, but the club recognised that covered accommodation and other facilities had to improve. The ground remained much the same as it had been in 1935, and then in 1953 floodlights were added.

In 1957 the Popular Side was extended slightly, roofed, and renamed the Kippax Street Stand. The extension was not as great as the one planned when the stadium first opened, but at least the roof meant the stadium provided covered accommodation for over 50,000 fans. No other Manchester venue had ever been able to match that, and few League grounds could compare.

In 1963 the Platt Lane Stand was seated with row after row of wooden benches. This meant that Maine Road housed more seats than any other British club – around 18,500 – something that continued throughout the '70s and early '80s with the development of the 8,120 capacity North Stand. Then in 1964 the floodlights were replaced with much higher and more powerful floodlight towers, and this was followed in 1967 by improvements to the Main Stand roof. The middle section of the roof was replaced by a rather odd looking construction which allowed an unhindered view for the directors and those in the most expensive seats, but it did nothing to improve the look of the stadium.

In 1971 the original Scoreboard End was demolished and replaced by a new cantilever stand. Initially the stand was terracing, but after a year the management decided to turn it into a seated stand, and the North Stand was born. At the same time amazing plans were made to demolish the Kippax Stand and replace it with an incredible structure that would allow vehicles on to the roof, where drivers would be able to watch the game from their own cars! Former chairman Eric Alexander later revealed: "The plans were aimed at creating a sort of private viewing area, while also improving facilities for Kippax regulars. The two big issues in the early '70s were the increasing shortage of good car-parking spaces and the lack of good quality facilities at the Kippax side of the ground. The plan would have improved both situations considerably."

The plan was abandoned when Peter Swales became Chairman in 1973. From then on Maine Road's development seemed to be piecemeal. Apart from security features such as the installation of perimeter fencing, little of note changed until in 1981 Swales announced a £6 million redevelopment of the stadium. The first phase saw the Main Stand roof replaced again, this time with a distinctive cream-coloured barrel affair.

This roof, held up by two enormous stanchions, was erected at a cost of £1 million. Relegation in 1983 caused the other redevelopment plans to be halted. This was a major shame as the second phase was due to see a much needed

new roof placed over the Kippax Stand, followed by the redevelopment of the Platt Lane Stand.

The next significant development was the replacement of seats in the front section of the North Stand as part of £500,000 worth of alterations during the summer of 1991. The following year, the 1935 Platt Lane Stand was demolished and the rather smaller Umbro Stand was erected in its place at a reported cost of £6 million, including 48 executive boxes on two tiers. It was opened in March 1993 and during the summer of 1997 was renamed the Platt Lane Stand.

With the government and football's governing bodies insisting that terracing be removed at the top stadia, the Kippax Stand's days were numbered. By this time Francis Lee was chairman and he hastily set plans in place to build a new three-tier stand, housing the best facilities at any football ground in the north-west.

In April 1994, an emotional day commemorated the end of the old Kippax Stand, and immediately afterwards City demolished and started construction of its replacement. The new stand was completed in stages over the course of the following 18 months and Maine Road once again felt like a major venue; however the capacity of the ground was significantly lower than at any other point in its history,

and was the lowest for a City venue since 1899.

The new 10,000-seater stand was officially opened by Bert Trautmann, while Francis Lee's consortium made dramatic and impressive plans to reconstruct the rest of Maine Road. His idea was to extend the other three sides of the ground to allow for a construction similar to the new Kippax, and a capacity of around 50,000. However, as the '90s progressed, Lee also became keen to negotiate with Manchester City Council and other bodies for City to become tenants of the new stadium being proposed as part of Manchester's bid to stage the Olympic Games. Three successive bids ultimately failed, but the city was awarded the 2002 Commonwealth Games.

While the bids and planning of first the Olympics and then the Commonwealth Games was occurring, Maine Road's capacity had to increase, and so a temporary stand – nicknamed the 'Gene Kelly Stand' as fans became accustomed to 'singing in the rain' – was erected in the corner between the Kippax and the North Stand during 1997/98. In an attempt to satisfy the huge demand for tickets, additional temporary seating was then added in stages, including a stand between the Kippax and Platt Lane Stand dubbed 'The Alan Ball Stand' by one of the fanzines as it 'was small and didn't make much noise'.

In May 2003 Maine Road staged its last game, and so a mere eight years after the official opening of the new Kippax, and ten after the Platt Lane Stand was built, Maine Road was redundant. During 2003-04 the stadium was demolished.

Maine Road was always a passionate

home for City fans, but it was also a significant venue from a national perspective. As well as City's games, the stadium hosted international matches (including the first World Cup qualifying match held in England); FA Cup semi-finals; a League Cup Final; the first European game played in England; concerts by the likes of Queen, the Rolling Stones and Oasis; religious festivals; Rugby finals, and even an international tennis tournament.

The Main Stand
Erected in 1923 when, at the time of construction, it had the largest roof span of any stand at any football ground in the country.
Final capacity: 8,466.
Original capacity: 10,000.

The Platt Lane Stand
Roofed and extended in two phases during 1931 and 1935. Seated 1963 (wooden benches).
Final capacity: 4,548.
Seated capacity of old stand (c.1986): 9,702.

Highest standing capacity: c.20,000.

The North Stand
Original 'Scoreboard End' terracing until demolition commenced in 1970. New terraced stand opened in 1971 and became seated in 1972.
Final capacity: 8,527.
Seated capacity in 1972: 8,120.
Original standing capacity: c.18,000.
Standing capacity 1971/2 season: 22,000.

The Kippax Stand
Roofed and extended in 1957. Demolished during the 1994 close season, with the new stand opening in stages during 1994 and 1995.

In 2019 it will be a quarter of a century since we said goodbye to terracing, and for those of us old enough to remember those days there was one standing area which, above all else, represented the passion fans had for their club.

Unlike most other grounds City's main terracing ran the full length of the pitch and wasn't tucked away behind a goal. Because of its positioning the Kippax breathed life into every area of the stadium

You're benched: Looking towards the Platt Lane Stand, circa 1980.

and was huge. Originally, it held in excess of 35,000, but even in its final days it still gave the impression of power and passion.

The Kippax was originally known as the Popular Side, matching a similarly dominant feature of the Blues' Hyde Road ground, when it opened in 1923. That first season it held an estimated 35,000 in a crowd of 76,166 – then a national record attendance for a club ground. In 1934 when 84,569 packed into the stadium City's vast stand may well have held almost 40,000.

Throughout the period up to the mid-50s the Popular Side developed its reputation but it was when it was roofed in 1957 that it became the true heart of the club. The club announced it would be known as The Kippax Street Stand and that is what it officially remained until 1994 although most of us knew it simply as The Kippax. Its capacity by this time was about 32,000, reducing to 26,155 by the end of the '70s.

Kippax Fax

• Originally, four vast tunnels (one in each corner and two built into the stand) and two significant stairways allowed fans to move onto the Popular Side.

• A flagpole, positioned at the back of the terracing up to 1957, allowed a blue and white flag emblazoned with the words City FC to proudly fly.

• Chanters' Corner, also known as 'the Sways,' was the area where the more vocal members of City's support gathered. Packed above a tunnel and next to the segregation fence, fans here often generated the main chants.

• The '60s saw The Kippax's reputation grow. Fans sang their way through success after success as Joe Mercer's Aces won the European Cup Winners' Cup and every domestic trophy possible.

• The final capacity of The Kippax was 18,300 – making this the largest terraced area at a League ground on its final day (The Kop held its final game on the same day but had a smaller capacity).

• The Kippax was used for the last time on 30 April 1994, for the visit of Chelsea.

• The *Blue Print* fanzine's flag was a popular presence on many matchdays from the late '80s until 1994, making its last appearance at The Kippax's final game. The flag had been reduced in size by then. But it still covered much of the terracing.

• Segregation was unnecessary for most of the stand's existence, but by the end of the '60s a rope would often be used to separate City and United fans on derby day. This was replaced by permanent barriers in the mid '70s which were increased over the years to keep home and away fans apart.

• In 1985, when City defeated Charlton 5-1 in a promotion decider on the final day of the season, the Kippax was so packed that supporters remain convinced that its official capacity of 26,155 was significantly exceeded. Those of us on the terraces that day will never forget the shock we all experienced when the official crowd of 47,285 was announced – some 5,000 short of full capacity!

The Kippax is no more, but those of us who experienced the stand will never forget its power, passion and presence. Its spirit lives on with thousands of Blues who stood there now bringing their own children and grandchildren to the Etihad.

Maine Road Facts & Figures

Highest attendance: 84,569 v Stoke City, FA Cup Sixth Round on 3 March 1934 (this remains a record for games outside of London & Glasgow).

Highest League Attendance: 79,491. v Arsenal, 23 February 1935 (the record Football League attendance at the time).

Highest Average Attendance: 42,725, 1947-48.

Highest non-City Attendance: 83,260 Manchester United v Arsenal, 17 January 1948 (remains the record Football League attendance of all time)

First Football League game: v Sheffield United, 25 August 1923.

Last League Game: v Southampton, 11 May 2003.

Other events: Maine Road has hosted many non-football events over the years from religious meetings to pop concerts. From 1939 to 1956 the ground hosted the Rugby League Championship Play-off finals, with one attendance reaching the staggering figure of 75,194 (14 May 1949), and during the '80s and '90s Maine Road regularly held pop concerts.

Maine Road – Progressive Capacity

1923 – 84,000	1931 – 86,000
1935 – 88,000	1946 – 84,000
1953 – 76,500	1957 – 77,000
1963 – 64,000	1972 – 54,500
1973 – 52,600	1989 – 48,500
1992 – 39,359	1994 – 19,150*
1995 – 31,458	1997 – 32,147
1999 – 34,026	2000 – 34,421
2002 – 35,150	

Note: 19,150 was the capacity for the first match of 1994-95 season; capacity increased after every game until 1995 close season figure was reached.

Mr City

One of City's least known and yet most important figures is Lawrence Furniss. During his lifetime's dedication to the Blues, Furniss held almost every position imaginable at the club. In the early 1880s he was a player, his first recorded game occurring during the 1884-85 season.

As a player, Furniss was said to be quite skilful and he is mentioned in a couple of the surviving reports from the mid 1880s. The *Gorton Reporter* mentioned him in the opening game of the 1885-86 season, played at the start of October 1885: "The Gorton AFC commenced the season this afternoon, when a match against Earlestown was played on the new home ground, Bull's Head, Reddish Lane, Gorton. Earlestown won the toss, and played with the wind and the sun at their backs during the first half, and scored the first goal after about twenty minutes play. Furniss equalised shortly after with a

splendid shot from half-back, the score at half-time being one goal each.

"The game was well fought, but nothing further was scored in the second half, and at the call of time, neither side held the advantage, the game

resulting in a draw of one goal each. The Gorton club has a good list of fixtures. The club is in a good position, and there is every prospect of a successful season."

According to one match report, Furniss was the Gorton captain during 1885-86, and he later became the Ardwick AFC secretary-manager in 1889 and remained in charge until 1893. This meant that the Blues won their first trophy successes (the Manchester Cup) under Furniss, and that his leadership guided Ardwick into first the Football Alliance and then into the Football League. During this period he remained active within St Mark's Church itself as a sidesman, and it could be argued that his involvement with Manchester City guaranteed that the church's link with the club continued through to Furniss's death in 1941.

When Manchester City was established in 1894 and Ardwick collapsed, it was Furniss who paid off many of Ardwick's old debts. He even put his wedding off for a couple of years as he raised the appropriate finance to ensure Manchester City could develop, free of any negative association with Ardwick's final days.

After his period as manager he remained an influential figure in the club. He became a director; was chairman at the time of City's move to Maine Road, and was President when the Blues won the League Championship for the first time in 1937.

In one newspaper during 1923 it was actually suggested Maine Road should have been named after Furniss. Whether this was ever discussed at Board level is debatable but it seems highly likely Furniss would have refused such an accolade. He was clearly of the opinion that the team was more important than any individual

City F.C. President dead

HE "DISCOVERED" BILLY MEREDITH

THE death was announced to-day of Mr. Lawrence Wain Furniss. president of Manchester City Football Club. and one of the pioneers of football in Manchester.

Mr. Furniss, who was 79, lived at the Old Hall, Marple. He had been in failing health for some time, but retained his close interest in the City Club, with which he had been associated from its infancy, and he paid visits to several matches last season.

Mr Furniss used to tell how

associated with the club. This action, in itself, is a major reason why the naming of stands and walkways around any stadium needs careful consideration. Had the stadium been named after Furniss, his name would undoubtedly have remained well known; however Furniss was right in the belief that no man is bigger than the club, even if it means his name has now been largely forgotten.

Sadly, Furniss passed away in 1941 after 60 years' active involvement with the club. Understandably, as his death came during a crucial period of World War II, it was largely ignored by the media and overlooked by supporters of the club. That was a great shame, but no doubt Furniss himself would not have objected. Manchester City was his legacy.

135

Franny Lee: Rock 'n' Roll Star

It was the final song played at the end of the 2018 League Cup triumph, and was used as the song the teams walked out to for over 20 years at Maine Road. Some 46 years after its recording, it's time to get the City anthem 'The Boys in Blue' up on your iPod/record player/PA system...

Over the years, City have produced a variety of official songs including 'Up the Blues' (recorded 1973), 'Blue City' (1974, based on 'Una Paloma Blanca') and 'We're Back' (1985); but it was the club's first proper venture into the music industry that became the club's anthem. 'The Boys in Blue' was recorded in March 1972 during a period when many leading football clubs were beginning to release vinyl records, such as Chelsea's memorable 'Blue Is the Colour.'

These records were occasionally connected to a club reaching a major final but often a club simply wanted to create something fans could sing along to.

'The Boys in Blue' was written by Kevin Godley, Graham Gouldman and Lol Creme, who became successful as the band 10CC, the song being was recorded at their Strawberry Studios in Stockport. Film of the recording is now contained within the collection of the North West Film Archive at Manchester Metropolitan University. Will McTaggart and I included it – in fact we named the show after it – in 'The Boys in Blue,' a film show of City-related films from the 1920s to 2003. We have staged the film show at a number of venues in recent years and have always ended the show with 'The Boys in Blue' footage, cueing audience members to often sing along. Film of the 1972 recording clearly shows all City's stars of the period singing, although some were more enthusiastic than others, and if you listen carefully to the actual song some voices, most notably Francis Lee's, stand out. Most of the players had achieved phenomenal success at City and many were international players. Some had won European and domestic trophies during the period 1967-72 and so their words have always had a particular significance to fans.

Not only that but they have inspired generations of City fans and players. Phrases such as 'the Boys in Blue will never give in' and 'together we will stand' are still relevant today and, when we think back to our 2012 League title success it was City's togetherness and determination to 'never give in' that proved vital.

The first proper airing of the song came on 1 April 1972 at 2.55pm before the Stoke League game. The club decided that they'd play it as the team came out and hoped fans would sing along. They published the words in the programme and the song was such a hit with fans that it became *the* City tune for the team to come out to for the following 25 years. Even now, all these years later, it remains popular with fans and the knowledge that Bell, Lee, Summerbee, Doyle, Book, Oakes, Donachie and the rest sang it gives the tune an added significance.

For those who may not quite remember all the words – all together, now...

City, Manchester City
We are the lads who are playing to win
City
The Boys in Blue will never give in

Football is the thing that we all live for
Saturday's the day we play the game
Everybody has to pull together
And together we'll remain

Even if we're playing down at Maine Road
Or if we play a million miles away
There'll always be our loyal fans behind us
To cheer us on our way

City, Manchester City

We are the lads who
are playing to win
City
The Boys in Blue never give in

Blue is forever the best team in the land
Playing together, together we will stand
City
Blue and White they go together
We will carry on forever more

Maybe in another generation
When other lads have come to take our place
They'll carry on the glory of the City
Keeping City in first place

City, Manchester City
We are the lads who are playing to win
City
The Boys in Blue never give in
The Boys in Blue never give in
The Boys in Blue never give in

The song has been part of City's DNA for nearly 50 years, longer than 'Blue Moon' and many other chants. Over the decades, the voices of our '70s idols captured our imagination and gave us hope that "maybe in another generation" future players would "carry on the glory of the City."

And then it actually happened.

It might not be one to always sing to, but it is one that always brings a reminder of the quality players of the 1970s, and the significance of today "when other lads have come to take [their] place."

The Boys in Blue will never give in!

E BOYS IN BLUE . . .

at of our supporters will know, the City team have made a record called
ys in Blue'. We thought that it would be nice if we played the record before
atch and all our fans could join in and have a 'jolly old sing-song'. So get
ocal chords ready for about 2.55, and we'll give it a try. Young and old
r female, everyone join in.

A Crowd and a Half

WILLS'S CIGARETTES

E. F. BROOK (MANCHESTER CITY)

It may have virtually slipped out of living memory but in March 1934 the largest footballing crowd ever assembled in Manchester witnessed a game that still, over 80 years later, remains etched in the record books. No less than 84,569 paid to watch City face Stoke in the FA Cup quarter-final at Maine Road – a crowd that surpassed Manchester's previous best by around 8,000 (set in 1924 when Cardiff faced City in another FA Cup quarter-final).

Both the 76,166 crowd that witnessed the Blues defeat Cardiff and the 84,569 who saw City beat Stoke in 1934 were national records for any game staged outside of London. In fact, excluding games at Wembley and FA Cup finals elsewhere in the capital, no other competitive club fixture has ever attracted more paying fans. For this to have happened in the Depression suggests a great deal about the passion and fervour City fans had for the FA Cup at the time.

Cup games against Stoke had attracted large crowds before – almost 74,000 watched the fifth round tie six years earlier – but no provincial crowd had ever approached this size. City had been developing as a good cup fighting side for several seasons. In 1932 they were semi-finalists and in 1933 finalists. Momentum and expectation was building, and the 1934 FA Cup was the number one obsession for Blues. This was the trophy they wanted, and in the fifth round thousands of Blues travelled to Sheffield Wednesday for a game that remains to this day Hillsborough's record crowd (72,841). That game went to a replay watched by an incredible midweek afternoon crowd of almost 69,000 at Maine Road.

The Potters had been promoted the previous season and were recognised as another entertaining side. Mancunians and Potters alike were excited by this tie. Thousands travelled up from the Potteries and the Manchester press focused on their activities in the city centre: "Waitresses ran distractedly from table to table, never quite catching up with the orders of the hungry visitors from the Potteries."

In the days when games were not all-ticket, it was important to get to the ground early. Four hours before kick-off, great queues had formed at Maine Road. According to one journalist, the turnstiles opened early, and a full two hours before kick-off the ground was packed: "Masses of people were standing outside the turnstiles waiting to enter and climb on banks that from all appearances were packed so tightly that no fish in a tin seemed an adequate comparison."

Twenty minutes before the game was due to commence the police ordered City to close the gates, locking thousands outside. Mancunian Joe Carley later wrote: "I remember a Stoke supporter expressing his apprehension before the match started, but I consoled him with my remarks on the modern ground and the strong iron barriers. The blighter nearly fainted five minutes later when an ominous crack behind us heralded the fact that a large section of the barrier had collapsed under the crowd's weight."

In 2003, attendee Alwyn Noden remembered the scene: "I was 14 at the time. The brass band played as youngsters were being passed over the crowd on the Popular Side to sit in front of the wall surrounding the pitch. There were only a small number of policemen inside the ground. If memory serves me there were only four – two sat in dugouts at each corner of the Popular Side. There was also a man walking around the touchline carrying a large sign which read 'A tale of two Cities on the Maine Road to Wembley.' This was greeted with terrific applause from both sets of fans."

Fans were sitting on the touchline and goalkeeper Frank Swift, in particular, was conscious of the large group of supporters sat around his goal. In his usual manner, he tried to joke with them, however his thoughts must surely have been on the problems experienced at Hillsborough when a dead supporter had been stretchered past the City team as they prepared to take to the field in the previous round.

Stoke looked for an early goal, with Tommy Sale and 19-year-old Stanley Matthews putting Frank Swift

under enormous pressure. Matthews' inexperience when facing the imposing Swift caused him to squander his first chance but the Manchester *Guardian* reported that a short while later he tried again: "Another chance fell to Matthews and, after Swift had beaten away the ball it rolled the full width of the goal, not two feet from the line, with no one able to master this excitement sufficiently to be able to kick it one way or the other."

Those missed opportunities set the tone for Stoke and gradually the Mancunians began to dominate. After 14 minutes, Eric Brook received a wide pass well out on the Kippax wing and raced for the Platt Lane corner flag. He was only feet away from the hundreds of supporters who had managed to climb over the white perimeter wall and sit on the touchline. He then made what was described as 'a speculative lob' from the wing, which seemed to change direction in mid-flight. The Stoke keeper Roy John appeared to have covered, jumped up but somehow missed it as it curled past him into the net.

Supporter Fran Parker saw enough of the goal to realise it was something special: "I saw Brooky on the wing and he kicked

SUNDAY GRAPHIC
and SUNDAY NEWS
SUNDAY, MARCH 4, 1934.

RECORD CROWD WATCH A CUP-TIE
HOW MANCHESTER CITY REACHED THE SEMI-FINAL

A record crowd of 84,569 at Maine-road—the biggest which has ever attended a game in England outside an F.A. Cup Final or an international—saw Manchester City win through to the Cup semi-final for the third season in succession by defeating Stoke City 1—0. The picture above shows the all-important goal being scored by Brook (centre, right), with John, the Stoke goalkeeper, attempting to save.

Arrow indicates the feet of the man who WOULD see the Cup-tie at Maine-road, Manchester.

LAST MAN IN!
A BACK VIEW OF THE 84,569

By R. A. PUGH

SATURDAY NIGHT.

THIS afternoon I was "Spectator 84,569" (or thereabouts) at the Cup-tie between Manchester City and Stoke City at the Maine-road football ground. Not for me the luxury of the five-and-sixpennies; mine was the humbler lot of one of the 70,000, or more, on the "bobs"—and with it was the obvious choice of watching the match—or having a shillingsworth of enjoyment watching the spectators!

Certainly, the greater number elected to watch the match. If they came early enough or had stamina and height above the ordinary, that was quite possible. I never saw the match.

I never had the slightest idea which side was winning, but —

I spent a very illuminating Cup-tie marvelling at the triumph of mind over matter as demonstrated by tardy Cup-tie fans.

Einstein himself would have gazed with jealous respect at the youth who had retrieved the rusty chassis of a whilom bashette, planted the pushing end in the ground, and stood on the other end.

THE LITTLE MORE—

Hardly less ingenious as an improvised solo-grandstand was the derelict frame of an ancient bone-shaker, on which was mounted a man of about 5ft 3in, who gloated over the heads of 6ft back-benchers who couldn't see a thing.

It was largely for their benefit that he constituted himself into a sort of running commentator. (All B.B.C. Inquiries care of this office.)

"There goes Brook . . . He's dribbling. . . . Come on, Eric. He's —"

Continued in Page 15

132 YEARS
AND STILL GOING STRONGER

TO-DAY'S *Sunday Dispatch* beats all the records of its 132 years of existence.

The revenue from its advertisements is greater than ever before.

This has made possible a newspaper of 32 large pages, including four pages in colour for the children.

BUSINESS IS BETTER

What does to-day's record mean? It means that business in Britain is better, and business men can go forward with courage to attract the growing market for their goods.

It means also that advertisers have a faith even more staunch in the greatest Sunday newspaper every week attracting more readers.

The dummy torpedo dropped by a naval aeroplane near Worthing Pier has now been recovered from the sea.

---

the ball and it seemed to twist. I don't know how, but it did, and when it went in I closed my eyes tight. It was a great feeling and I was so excited at seeing such an amazing goal!"

Afterwards, some claimed the goal was a fluke, but Fran disagreed: "He was a great player. He played for England, and was one of our biggest stars. He knew what he was doing. From where I sat on the edge of the pitch it was as clear as day that he had shot at goal. He may have been on the touchline himself, but goalscorers like that look for openings all the time. Most players probably wouldn't have been able to score it, but Brooky was different."

In 2003 Denis Houlston described this goal as one of the highlights of his entire City-supporting life. Houlston was 17 at the time of the goal: "It was a lovely warm day and Eric Brook's winning goal came from the area I stood. I was always a third of the way along the terracing from the Platt Lane corner, and about 20 yards from the wall. I think Brook played in every position for the Club – he certainly went in nets once – and was a very good player. When the goal went in it was marvellous. Nirvana."

Off the pitch the scene was not so pleasant, with around 100 people taken to Manchester Royal Infirmary. The *Guardian* claimed: "Men who had fainted, and there were scores in this corner of the ground alone, were passed roughly but efficiently over the heads of the crowd to the grass, where the ambulance squads laid them abut and splashed water in their faces."

On the terracing, BJ Walsh from Marple Bridge became concerned: "A body was passed down. I was upset, thinking he was dead. He looked so cold and lifeless and didn't come round until half-time. Once he'd gathered his thoughts he started talking to us. It transpired he was a Stoke City fan. He amazed us all by saying that Stoke had been the better side – he'd been unconscious!"

There were however a few moments of humour on the terraces. In the '90s Harry Hughes recalled: "I was behind a barrier with my chest being pushed in – not the best place to be in a huge crowd. So I decided to duck under the barrier and come up the other side. As I rose I discovered that I'd come up between a man and his wife and he looked at me in wonderment. Totally astonished that I should have appeared as if by magic between him and his wife. I managed to drop my cap over my eyes and move off before I got myself into trouble!"

With the terraces packed, it was difficult for some to know exactly what was happening on the pitch. Several ingenious solutions were found. As the *Guardian* reported: "An anonymous person at the front began to describe the game for them. This unofficial commentator stuck to his self-appointed task, and being something of an expert in the game, gradually won silence for his remarks. Thus it came about that several hundred people who might have got really bad tempered and made trouble were satisfied with hearing about a game instead of seeing it."

City were in control until the final minutes when Stoke piled on the pressure. Legendary keeper Frank Swift was forced into action. He later recalled the drama of the final minute: "Stoke forced a corner and everybody bar the goalkeeper crowded into our penalty area in an effort to force the equaliser. Over came the ball, and up went the heads of what seemed every other player on the field. Big Arthur Turner, the Stoke centre-half, got his head to the ball, and with me standing helpless – and with 84,000 hearts in a similar number of mouths – the ball curled slowly over the bar. Then the whistle..."

Houlston: "On the final whistle I didn't need to use my feet to leave. I was wedged in a solid wall of human flesh and swept through the exit gate like a surfboarder."

City went on to win the FA Cup that season and to re-establish themselves as

Dale (Manchester City) robs Matthews while Sale watches from the ground.—(" Sunday Graphic " pictures.)

GROSVENOR HOTEL
DEANSGATE · MANCHESTER

MANCHESTER CITY
F.C. LTD.

BLUE AND WHITE
OFFICIAL PROGRAMME

Vol. 28 No. 91.   March 3rd.   Twopence.

PLAY FOR SAFETY!

MANCHESTER & SALFORD SAVINGS BANK

a major force, but this oft-overlooked match had been highly significant. Stoke's young star Stanley Matthews was tipped as an England star of the future. The programme for the match accurately predicted that Matthews was "a player on the threshold of a great career."

Inevitably, Eric Brook was idolised for many goals in a wonderful City and England career, but his effort against Stoke was hugely important in the Blues quest to return to the big time.

Many fans from the '30s claimed this was the greatest City goal ever scored at Maine Road. It seems only fitting that the old stadium's record crowd should have witnessed it.

Match Statistics

3 March 1934. FA Cup quarter-final.

City 1-0 Stoke City.

Scorer: Eric Brook (14 mins).

Attendance: 84,569.

Gate receipts: £5,426.

City: Swift, Barnett, Dale, Busby, Cowan, Bray, Toseland, Marshall, Tilson, Herd, Brook.

Stoke: John, McGrory, Spencer, Tutin, Turner, Sellars, Matthews, Liddle, Sale, Davies, Johnson.

City Break Their Duck

By 1904 the Blues were developing rapidly. They had achieved promotion in 1899 as Champions of Division Two. This was the first national success of either Manchester side and allowed, for the first time, City to play in a division higher than the Heathens (United). Near neighbours Glossop had also been promoted.

The Blues finished their first season in the top flight in a respectable 7th place. Sadly, relegation followed in 1902, but City again won the Second Division title in 1903. They had played with style and conviction and when the 1903-04 season commenced they managed to maintain their wonderful form under ex-Celtic boss Tom Maley and his loyal Blues trainer, Jimmy Broad.

In the FA Cup the Blues eclipsed all previous seasons for either Manchester side by reaching the Cup final. They faced Bolton at the Crystal Palace in London and thousands of Mancunians journeyed to the capital to witness Manchester's progress. For many locals a visit to London was seen as a major excursion and the majority of City fans who travelled south had never previously visited the capital. They travelled overnight and early morning they took their first tentative steps around London looking at the sights. They seemed to congregate around places such as Trafalgar Square and St Paul's Cathedral, and many newspapers of the period focused on their time in the capital.

The game itself was fairly tight with the Blues winning 1-0 thanks to a disputed goal from captain Billy Meredith. Meredith was football's first true superstar and many neutrals had gone to the final simply to see the great man play.

This was a great moment in the history of Manchester and, incredibly, the Blues still had chance of further success that season. They had one remaining fixture and if results worked in their favour City would win the League Championship as well. The day after the final the Blues travelled to Merseyside. They stayed at New Brighton and then faced Everton on the following Monday evening. Sadly, the exploits of the previous few days limited their opportunities and they were defeated 1-0 at Goodison Park. Sheffield Wednesday, who had been one point ahead of the Blues, ended their season with a victory leaving City three points behind in second

As the population of Manchester began to make their feelings known the city council and the police realised that this was an achievement worth celebrating and they hurriedly organised additional police. At the same time City announced the route they would be taking from Central Station back to Ardwick – which included many backstreets, such as Dale Street, where the poorer inhabitants lived.

When the City side arrived back at Manchester around 9.30pm the city centre was packed. Reports made it clear that the entire population of the city had turned out to greet their heroes and share in the success. A horse-drawn carriage, driven by Albert Alexander senior – a man who would later be vice-chairman of the Blues – took the players on the first homecoming parade the city had known. Reports describe a wide range of people from different social classes taking to the streets while Billy Meredith lifted the trophy in celebration.

place. It was still Manchester's highest League position at the time.

Straight after their game at Everton, during which the FA Cup was on display, City travelled by train back to Manchester. Within the city, most Mancunians were keen to stage some form of celebration, however the city council and senior figures within the constabulary were not interested, arguing that it was time for Manchester to get back to work.

But this was a pivotal moment in the history of Manchester. The FA Cup success of City in 1904 was the first time the city had had reason to celebrate. Prior to City's success Lancashire CCC had won major honours, but cricket did not appeal to the greater part of Manchester's population. Other major activities included one-off events at the Manchester Racecourse, or festivals lasting several days. The FA Cup success had genuine mass appeal and brought with it national acclaim.

The Athletic News reported on the scenes: "As soon as they caught sight of the trophy trimmed with blue and white ribbons which Meredith now and then raised above his head, they gave vent to prodigious cheering. Most of the windows of the upper stories were packed with people whose plaudits, added to the blowing of a bugle here and there and the music of the band, made a deafening sound.

congestion meant the Blues had to play a vital match at Everton only two days after the final.

Who were City's Cup-run opponents?
All of the sides the Blues faced on their journey to the final were familiar names and recognised as good Cup fighters. Starting with Sunderland in round one (home, 3-2 home), City played Woolwich Arsenal (away, 2-0), Middlesbrough (home goalless draw; away win 3-1), Sheffield Wednesday (1903 & 1904 League Champions beaten 3-0 in the semi-final at Goodison Park), and Bolton Wanderers (won 1-0 at the Crystal Palace Ground).

How did the fans travel to the final?
The majority of fans set off the day before the final and travelled by railway excursion – the final became known to Londoners as 'The Lancastrian Invasion' as both City and Bolton fans filled stations across the capital. According to one report over 16,000 Lancastrians arrived at Euston during the night with nowhere to sleep. They amused themselves by drinking from 'nine-gallon barrels of beer' and stone jars of whisky, while shouting periodically 'Play Up City!' according to the Manchester Chronicle. Similar scenes occurred at St Pancras, King's Cross, and Marylebone before fans ventured out to try and take in the sights.

"To the accompaniment of incessant cheering, the procession made its way at walking pace down Dale Street where what might be called the welcome of the middle classes was exchanged for that of the proletariat. It came from rough working men and larrikins and beshawled women and children in arms and hand, and was hearty if not heartier than had gone before."

City's victory united in celebration all Mancunians regardless of background, and City's strong identity as Manchester's club was strengthened that day.

Why is 1904 important?
Winning the FA Cup in 1904 – only ten years after formation as Manchester City – proved that a city like Manchester could compete with the best. 1904 also saw the Blues finish second in the League – fixture

Does any footage of the final exist?
It may seem incredible as motion pictures were still in their infancy, but it is known

that several minutes of play were filmed, including the goal. The players were also filmed with the FA Cup at New Brighton. This footage was then shown in pubs in both Manchester and Bolton in the days that followed the final. Sadly, despite extensive research, no copies of this rare recording have yet been located.

What became of the players?

• Billy Meredith was not only captain and scorer of the final's only goal, he was also football's first true superstar. Despite a spell playing for United at Bank Street (roughly a quarter of a mile from City's stadium today), he returned to the Blues to continue playing until his 50th year.

• Jack Hillman – Tavistock-born goalkeeper who also had spells at Everton, Burnley and Millwall. In later life he managed a shop in Bolton, and at the time of the 1934 FA Cup final he had on display the 1904 ball in his shop window.

• John McMahon – Joined the Blues in 1902 from Preston. Worked with Meredith to create a third Manchester League side, Manchester Central FC.

• Herbert Burgess – Born in Openshaw, he joined the Blues from League side Glossop in 1903. In later life he coached a Hungarian side to League success and also had a spell in Italy.

• Sam Frost – Enjoyed trophy success at City and Millwall, but tragically committed suicide in 1926, aged 47, after his chain of shops failed.

• Tom Hynds – A Scottish centre-half who helped steady the Blues. He later played for Arsenal and coached in the USA, British Columbia and Italy.

• Sam Ashworth – An architect by profession. Sadly, the illegal payments scandal which rocked City in the years following the final meant he was stripped of his amateur status by the FA.

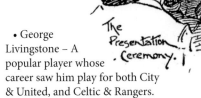

The Presentation Ceremony.

• George Livingstone – A popular player whose career saw him play for both City & United, and Celtic & Rangers.

• Billy Gillespie – The 'loveable rogue' of the team, he later emigrated to the States. After Gillespie's death his widow wore the 1904 medal on a chain around her neck. Sadly, it was stolen from her in a nursing home before her death a few years ago.

• Sandy Turnbull – Joined in 1902 from Preston and later became the first man to score a goal at Old Trafford. Turnbull was killed in action during World War I.

• Frank Booth – Born in Hyde, joined City after spells at Glossop and Stockport. He later played for Clyde in the Scottish Cup final before returning to the Blues shortly before the war. He became a coach at Hyde Road, but passed away in 1919 as a result of his wounds.

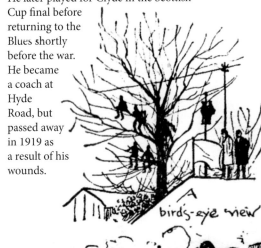

A birds-eye view

Tangled Up in Blue

Identity is important to any football team and City's use of pale blue stretches back to the 1880s with Ardwick AFC. It may well have been worn earlier, but unfortunately we do not know what kits were utilised by St Mark's when they played their first reported games in

1880. However, we do know that after the club reformed as Gorton AFC in 1884 they chose to wear a distinctive kit consisting of black shirts with a white cross pattée emblazoned across the left breast. This smart new kit set the tone for what the players hoped would be a successful period in the club's development. From the moment it was first worn in 1884 the club progressed and grew, becoming Ardwick in 1887, before re-launching as Manchester City in 1894.

The team had been established by the young cricketers of St Mark's Church in West Gorton, whose first reported football match came in November 1880. Little evidence exists of the clothing they wore for games back then. Only after many ground moves and name changes did a more professional and stylish team emerge in October 1884.

The black kit with a white cross is believed to have been selected by club official William Beastow, who had been a prominent figure at St Mark's Church and whose son had played in the earliest recorded St Mark's game against Macclesfield Baptist in 1880. So important was the launch of the club as Gorton AFC in 1884 that the earliest known photograph of the team was taken.

Local MP and businessman Sir Richard Peacock (founder of the great Gorton-based engineering firm Beyer-Peacock) donated money to the club and helped ensure its survival and growth. By 1886 he was recorded as its President. He appears on the photograph, which may well have been taken at his home at Gorton Hall. The names of the people on this photograph have been suggested in other publications however it must be stressed that we do not know the specific players who appear. Educated guesses can be made based on starting elevens, prominent figures and positional play but this was 1884 and the exact date of the photograph is not known, nor did the original contain the names of those who appear on it.

It is not known how long the kit was

worn or how many games were played wearing it, but we do know that Gorton played 16 matches during 1884-85, including two against Newton Heath (present-day Manchester United). The club's fiercest rivals at the time, however, were not Newton Heath but their near neighbours, Gorton Villa. The two sides met three times that season with Gorton beating Villa twice (4-0 and 3-0) and drawing the other (1-1).

In 1887 the club was renamed and re-launched as Ardwick, wearing a new kit consisting of royal blue and white striped shirts. The colour blue has remained important to the club ever since.

• It seems our first use of blue dates back to 1887 and the formation of Ardwick AFC in their royal blue and white stripes.

• In 1890 Ardwick's kit was known to be one of pale blue and white 'quartered' shirts. Back then, this meant a blue and white panel on the front with alternate panels on the back. In other words, what we might call blue and white halves!

• In 1894 City's kit was Cambridge blue with white shorts. One football annual recorded grey shorts but match reports and other evidence talk of white shorts.

• Joshua Parlby was City's secretary in 1894 and he would have had responsibility for the colour selected. He may have focused on the blue worn by Ardwick or

may well have been influenced by his earlier life. What is known is that the colour was unique. Other sides wore blue – Blackburn Rovers and Liverpool wore quartered shirts incorporating a pale blue while Everton wore a lighter shade than their current colours – but City were the only team to wear the shade they chose as a full colour shirt.

• In 1904 City's first major trophy, the FA Cup, was won in Cambridge blue shirts and white shorts.

• As time progressed, the shade of blue became a little darker, but remained a pale blue. It was often called sky blue by 1914.

• In the 1926 FA Cup final, City adopted

Left to right: Gorton AFC, 1884; Ardwick AFC, 1890; and FA Cup 'cornflower blue,' 1926.

a darker blue. Known as cornflower blue, it was a slightly darker blue than City currently wear.

• It is often said that in the early '60s Coventry City decided to adopt sky blue after a director had been impressed by Manchester City's colours and performances.

• City wore sky blue for their first European game (European Cup v Fenerbahce) in September 1968.

• The classic City Blue was worn during the Mercer-Allison years. Sometimes the numbers would be white, sometimes maroon, and when a badge was added at the start of the '70s it was placed in the centre of the front.

• During the late '70s the

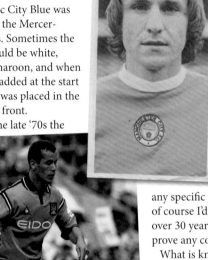

shade of blue darkened again (and the shorts also became blue) but a pale version was reintroduced in 1985 (with the return of white shorts).

• In 1997 a much darker 'Laser Blue'

appeared, but was ultimately short lived.

• Since the takeover by Sheikh Mansour the shade of blue has been more consistent with City's history.

There are lots of rumours but few hard facts relating to the reasons City chose blue back in 1894.

People often talk about a Masonic influence but, despite years of research, no evidence has been found that the Masons influenced the 1894 kit at all. The earlier black kit and white cross may well have been influenced by Freemasonry, after all William Beastow – who is believed to have presented the shirts – was a senior figure in the local Masonic community, though links to 1894 appear to be grossly exaggerated. If anyone has any specific contemporary evidence then of course I'd be delighted to see it, but over 30 years of intense research has yet to prove any connection whatsoever.

What is known is that the colour had already been used to an extent by Ardwick and so it wasn't simply established at City's formation in 1894, which those supporting the Masonic connection claim.

It should be stressed that City have been wearing their first-choice shirt colour longer than any other Premier League team, although Newcastle also adopted black-and-white stripes in 1894. Meanwhile, Everton wore a light blue shirt prior to adopting their current shade, and Arsenal wore all-red shirts. It is a fact that City are the only side to have worn light blue consistently throughout their long League history.

Penalty Prize

The award of a penalty-kick is often contentious, with attackers being accused of 'diving,' or defenders of cynically hacking down their opponents while pleading innocence. In 2017-18 alone several penalties should have been given for fouls on Raheem Sterling but, for whatever reason, the match officials decided to give the defenders the advantage. Penalties grab media attention unlike any other potential match-winning moment. So, with that in mind, let's look at City's penalty record – in particular at the 1971-72 season when Francis Lee established a controversial national record.

In 1971-72 City were awarded and scored 13 penalties in a 42-game League season, when Francis Lee took every penalty, creating a record that still stands.

Much has been said about whether Lee 'dived' or looked for decisions to be given his way, but before we examine the facts behind each penalty it is worth highlighting that the 1971-72 season saw referees cracking down on foul play. The

FA had instructed officials to adopt a stricter approach to negative play, leading to more positive decisions. It has to be stressed that it also caused referees to question the validity of every penalty appeal. Their goal was certainty, not to be duped by play-acting on a regular basis.

Looking specifically at Lee's record, it is clear that only five of the 13 League penalties were awarded for fouls on Lee himself. So the media nickname 'Lee Won Pen' seems inappropriate, while the City fans' version, 'Lee One Pen,' is spot-on.

The 1971-72 season started with a defeat against Leeds on 14 August, but four days later Lee scored twice (including his first penalty of the season) as Crystal Palace were defeated 4-0. Within the week, Lee had netted two further penalties, making his total three in three games. This immediately brought attention his way.

On New Year's Day his penalty in the 2-2 draw at

149

Lee's 1971-72 Penalty Record

Date	Opponents	Score	Attendance	Reason Given
18/08/71	Crystal Palace (h)	4-0	27,103	Lee Fouled
21/08/71	Chelsea (a)	2-2	38,425	Lee Fouled
24/08/71	Wolves (a)	1-2	26,683	Mellor Fouled
18/09/71	Nottm Forest (a)	2-2	21,488	Unclear
09/10/71	Everton (h)	1-0	33,538	Young Fouled
06/11/71	Manchester U (h)	3-3	63,326	Lee Fouled
20/11/71	West Ham U (a)	2-0	33,694	Davies Fouled
04/12/71	Derby County(a)	1-3	35,384	Summerbee Fouled
18/12/71	Leicester City (h)	1-1	29,524	Lee Fouled
01/01/72	Nottm Forest (h)	2-2	38,777	Lee Fouled
12/02/72	Sheff Utd (a)	3-3	38,184	Handball
04/03/72	Arsenal (h)	2-0	44,213	Handball
22/04/72	Derby County (h)	2-0	55,023	Marsh Fouled

Lee also scored penalties in the following cup competitions during 1971-72:

Date	Opponents	Score	Attendance	Reason Given
15/01/72	Middlesbrough (h, FAC)	1-1	42,620	Lee Fouled
08/09/72	Wolves (h, FL Cup)	4-3	29,156	Lee Fouled

Spot-on: Francis Lee delivers from 12 yards in the 1970 ECWC final.

penalty came on 12 February (v Sheffield United); but it does indicate that the pressure and attention on Lee was increasing. Every move he made in the penalty box was being analysed. So much so that many of the players involved in that season believe the Blues were awarded fewer penalties than they should have been. In the '90s Lee claimed: "The season I scored 13, I should have had

home to Nottingham Forest caused the *Manchester Evening News Pink* to declare that he had equalled the League's 40-year record. That was not factually accurate as the record stood at 11 League goals and was was not equalled until the next

a lot more. We had one shot palmed over against Arsenal, and against Ipswich Mick Mills committed the most blatant handball I have ever seen. Neither was given. I have always said that if I had been awarded the number of penalties I deserved, you could add a hundred goals to my career. I can't think of more than three or four dubious penalties I ever won."

Had City been awarded those penalties, it is possible the Blues could have won the League title during 1971-72 as they only missed out by a point, and the Ipswich game ended in a 2-1 defeat.

So what was Lee's penalty secret? Why was he such a great penalty taker? Lee: "Everyone said I blasted the ball, but I used to aim for the stanchion and hit the ball at three-quarter speed, pretending

I was passing the ball 50 or 60 yards. I would take a long run-up to give the keeper longer to think about it. It gave him less of an idea which side I was going to hit it."

Lee recognised the need for decisiveness: "Pick a corner, turn round, walk back, get totally focused, and then put it in the corner. I didn't worry about any keeper. I used to stay behind after training and take penalties against the City keepers. I used to take ten penalties when I told them where I was aiming, and ten where they didn't know. I knew if I could beat them when they knew which way the ball was going, I didn't have to worry about any goalkeeper."

Although Lee netted 15 penalties in 46 League and cup games during 1971-72, perhaps the best Lee penalty story concerns the following close-season tour. City were leading 2-0 against a Swedish side and were awarded a penalty. As Lee prepared himself, the Swedish goalie asked the City star if he could be the first to save a Lee penalty. Lee replied: "Okay. I'll put it to your right. I won't hit it too hard."

Lee ran up and sent the ball hurtling to the keeper's left as he dived right. Afterwards, Lee said to the disappointed keeper: "That's how you score 15 penalties without missing!"

• Will Lee's record ever be surpassed? In 1988-89 Graham Roberts scored 12 penalties for Chelsea as they won the old Second Division title but even that feat was in a 46-game season. So the odds are Franny's feat will prevail in the top flight.

• In 1971-72 City also converted a pen in the Texaco Cup on 15 September, but Mike Doyle took that as Francis Lee was not on the field at the time.

• Tony Coleman was City's regular penalty taker before Lee. Coleman's substitution meant that Lee's first City penalty was scored on 20 January 1968 v Sheffield United.

• Lee's most important penalty of all came in the 1970 ECWC final. His goal that night, awarded for a foul on Neil Young, gave City a 2-0 lead, the match ending 2-1.

• As for City's overall most important penalty prize? How about the 1999 Second Division Play-off final which was settled in City's favour via a penalty shoot-out?

• More recently, the 2016 League Cup final against Liverpool was another high-pressure shoot-out thriller at Wembley.

Wee Jim Tolmie smacks home a pen back in 1983-84.

All Around the World

For four decades Colin Bell was recognised as City's most-capped international player with 48 appearances for England; however in recent years several players have challenged his dominance, and David Silva has now held the record for over two years.

Here we examine City's greatest international appearance holders and how the record has developed through time. It tracks every City player who has held the record, highlighting how many caps they won and how long they held the record for. Naturally, only international appearances while registered as a City player count towards this record.

Joe Davies, 3 Welsh caps with City
Chirk-born Joe Davies joined Ardwick in 1891. He was the first scorer for City's predecessors, netting a hat-trick in their first League game, but was already an international before the club joined the League. In total he made three Welsh international appearances during two spells with Ardwick and City, finally leaving in 1896.
Held the record for five years.

Billy Meredith, 22 Welsh caps
Meredith knew Davies well as both men were from Chirk and played together at various

levels. Recognised as football's first true superstar, Meredith loved life at City and captained the club to Manchester's first major success in 1904. By that time he had already eclipsed Davies's record of three caps, and by the time he was suspended by the FA for his part in a payments scandal in 1905, Meredith had managed 22 Welsh international appearances with City.
Held the record for 59 years.

Roy Paul
24 Welsh caps
Several men came close to Meredith's record, including England forward Eric Brook (18 caps), goalkeeper Frank Swift (19) and Roy Clarke (22, though the record was already held by Paul by the time of Clarke's final cap) – but no one could surpass it until Roy Paul in the '50s. Swift was a shade unfortunate as he became an England regular during wartime, but those games do not count in official records.

Paul was another popular Welsh captain who drove City on to glory in the FA Cup in 1956. His inspirational attitude was remembered with affection by all those who knew him and, as he guided City to glory, his influence was often compared to that of Meredith. Paul surpassed Meredith's record during 1955 with appearances against England, Scotland and Austria, before his final international while with City against Northern Ireland.

Held the record for 15 years.

Francis Lee, 27 English caps
The first Englishman to hold the record was Francis Lee, who equalled Paul's record on 13 October 1971 when he appeared against Switzerland in Basle in a European Championship qualifier, and then beat it the following month in the return game at Wembley. Interestingly, Lee did not score in that return game but another Blue, Mike Summerbee, did find the net as England drew 1-1.

The following April Lee made his last England appearance in the 3-1 European qualifier defeat by West Germany. Lee scored in that match but was not selected again despite remaining one of the nation's top goalscoring talents. Many neutrals believed Lee should have been a permanent England fixture.

Remember, Lee's career was far from over at this point and many pundits believed Lee still had more to offer the England team, as demonstrated not only by his part in City's ongoing development, but also during his title-winning season at

Derby County in 1974-75.

Lee's last international was also Bell's 16th. Francis Lee also played for a UK XI against Wales in 1969 – presumably the side was a 'rest of the UK' team.

Lee held the record for two years.

Colin Bell, 48 English caps
Another member of the

highly successful City side of the late '60s and '70s, Colin Bell eclipsed Lee's England record on 27 May 1973 when he appeared in his 28th international. The opponents were Czechoslovakia in a 1-1 friendly at Prague. By this time Bell was a regular in the England team after making his first appearance in 1968 and travelling to the World Cup, alongside Lee, in 1970.

Bell's England debut had come in a friendly against Sweden at Wembley on 22 May 1968. That day England won 3-1 and Bell was the only Blue in the side. Ten days later he was joined by Mike Summerbee (making his third international appearance) as England lost out by the odd goal to West Germany in Hanover.

The first competitive international played by Bell came on 7 May 1969 when England beat Wales 2-1 in the Home International Championship. That was Bell's fifth England game and was noteworthy for the exploits of another Blue, Francis Lee. Lee scored his third goal in four appearances and was also an ever-present in the tournament that season as England ran out comfortable winners, winning all three games.

David Silva
8-1-1986
Manchester City FC (ENG) 1,70 m 67 kg

In the years that followed, Bell increased his tally to 48 England appearances, but a serious injury suffered in a Manchester derby meant that his career, especially his international career, was cut short by many years. Had the injury not occurred it is likely Bell would have been a regular international for the rest of the decade.

Colin Bell appeared in an unofficial international when a 'Full' England team played against a 'Young England' side in 1968-69. Eric Brook (five games) and Frank Swift (one game) both played in similar games but these have not been listed for any player.

It is worth noting that Colin Bell also played in the British team that faced the six other Common Market (modern-day EU) countries when the UK joined in 1973, while Frank Swift (1947) and Bobby Johnstone

(1955) also played in British sides against a combined European team.

Bell held the record for 41 years.

David Silva, 56 Spanish caps (by November 2015)

After Bell, Richard Dunne came close to beating Bell's record, but it took a World Cup-winning star to finally take the record. That man was David Silva, who joined City in 2010 and beat Bell's record when he appeared for Spain at Luxembourg in October 2014. Silva went on to make 56 appearances before another player surpassed his total.

Held the record for one year.

Joe Hart, 75 English caps

England goalkeeper Hart was only a few appearances behind Silva when he beat Bell's record, and with the varied nature of international selections and

Free Lions

THE ENGLAND FANZINE FROM THE FOOTBALL SUPPORTERS' FEDERATION

ISSUE 141

THE FOOTBALL SUPPORTERS' FEDERATION

SAN MARINO V ENGLAND
5TH SEPTEMBER 2015

injury concerns it was always possible that Hart would leapfrog Silva at some point. This actually happened in November 2015 when Hart made his 57th England appearance. The goalkeeper remained City's most capped player until March 2016 when he was overtaken by Silva. Hart since increased his total to 75 caps while with City but 12 of these have come during loan spells with other clubs.

Held the record for four months.

David Silva, 87 Spanish caps (including World Cup 2018)
David Silva regained the record in March 2016 and has now made 87 Spanish appearances while on City's books. In August 2018 Silva announced his international retirement after thrilling performances at the 2018 World Cup, despite Spain only reaching the Round of 16 where they lost to hosts Russia.

Silva had, of course, made international appearances before joining City, but only those while on City's books count towards this record.

Other modern-day City players have also recently eclipsed Bell's long-standing record. For example, Vincent Kompany reached 56 caps while with City during the 2018 World Cup and Agüero has totalled 58 international appearances since joining the Blues. It is also worth remembering that other City players have made more international appearances. Dave Watson, for example, made 65 England appearances, but only 30 were during his time at City. Claudio Reyna captained the USA national side for whom he made over 100 appearances.

Going back through time it should be recognised that our previous record holders had far fewer opportunities to make international appearances.

Inevitably, both World Wars prevented formal full internationals from taking place. England's refusal to enter the World Cup until the late '40s (the first England World Cup qualifier being staged at Maine Road in 1949) meant the Home International Championship and a modest scattering of friendly matches were all players could expect to appear in.

All four of Frank Roberts' England appearances, for example, came in consecutive internationals during one season. Looking back at the pattern and regularity of England fixtures, it becomes apparent that four or five internationals per year was fairly normal – whereas by the mid '50s even quiet seasons would see seven to nine England games.

Today, World Cup qualifiers and European Championships mean that some seasons could see in excess of 13 games in a year. In 1990 England played 15 internationals (and still didn't win the World Cup) while in 1966, when they did find success, they played a total of 17. Clearly any modern player who becomes an established international in a World Cup or European Championship-challenging side could quickly earn a dozen or more caps.

One final point of interest is that the first two record holders were both Welsh and both FA Cup winning City captains – Billy Meredith and Roy Paul. For the first 60 years or so of our League career, City attracted many great Welsh players.

The Buck Stops Here

The following table lists all trophy/promotion-winning City managers in order of success to the end of the 2017-18 season, rated in the following order – European trophy, League Championship, FA Cup, League Cup, second-tier championship, League runners-up, FAC final, League Cup final, second-tier promotion, and third-tier promotion. Charity/Community Shield winners have also been included – but not finalists.

Manager	Trophies won
Joe Mercer	ECWC, League, FAC, League Cup, 2nd tier Championship & Charity Shield
Manuel Pellegrini	League & two League Cups
Wilf Wild	League, FAC, FAC finalists & Charity Shield
Roberto Mancini	League, FAC, FAC finalists & Community Shield
Pep Guardiola	League & League Cup
Tom Maley	FAC, 2nd-tier Championship, League runners-up
Les McDowall	FAC, FAC finalists, 2nd-tier promotion
Tony Book	League Cup, League runners-up
Sam Ormerod	2nd-tier Championship
Harry Newbould	2nd-tier Championship
Peter Hodge	2nd-tier Championship
Sam Cowan	2nd-tier Championship
Kevin Keegan	2nd-tier Championship
Ernest Mangnall	League runners-up
Albert Alexander*	FAC finalists
John Bond	FAC finalists
Ron Saunders	League Cup finalists
Joe Royle	2nd-tier promotion & 3rd-tier promotion
Billy McNeill	2nd-tier promotion
Mel Machin	2nd-tier promotion
Malcolm Allison	Charity Shield

Alexander was vice-chairman but took on role of caretaker manager from Nov 1925 to the day after the 1926 Cup final.

Joe Mercer is without doubt our most successful manager and should be recognised forever more as a true great within the game. As well as a terrific managerial record – don't forget he also found success at Aston Villa prior to City (League Cup, Division 2 Championship & League Cup finalists) – he was also a highly successful footballer, winning three League titles and the FA Cup. He was also a great England captain and popular caretaker manager of England.

During Mercer's time at City he was supported by the forward-thinking coach Malcolm Allison. Allison worked extremely hard with the players and was responsible for much of City's development, however this should not downplay the role of Mercer. In recent years there has been a growing trend to apportion credit to one or other of the men, but the truth is that they worked together (also along with chairman Albert Alexander Jr) to help City develop significantly. Mercer was the perfect leader, but Allison was an equally powerful force within City.

Allison became team manager on 7 October 1971 but sadly trophy success, other than the 1972 Charity Shield, eluded him. Having said that, it is a myth that neither Allison nor Mercer were successful elsewhere. Mercer had success at Aston Villa, while Allison won the Portuguese title and cup with Sporting Lisbon.

City's second most successful manager to date is Manuel Pellegrini. He took over in June 2013 and guided us to a League and League Cup double in his first season, adding another League Cup in 2016.

Third equal are Roberto Mancini and Wilf Wild, both of whom brought the League and the FA Cup to City. Mancini replaced Mark Hughes in December 2009 and seemed to be the catalyst for a serious assault on the League. The FA Cup came first, as it did with Wild, and once that had been won confidence grew. While Mancini was an important and high-profile managerial change, Wild's appointment came more as a result of circumstance than an absolute desire to manage. Wild had been a member of City's administration staff from 1920, working closely with the secretary-manager of the club. In those days the secretary and manager role were very much the same thing and the person holding the position was expected to perform all player-related activities and all administrative duties such as paying the wages, organising ground developments and the like. In March 1932 manager Peter Hodge resigned and Wild took on all responsibility for team matters as well as all administrative duties. In his first full season he guided City to the 1933 FA Cup final, and then in 1934 the Blues won the Cup. In 1937 Wild's side won the League for the first time.

As well as playing success, Wild also had responsibility for the development of the Platt Lane Stand at Maine Road and was in overall charge when Maine Road staged its record attendance of 84,569 – that day he had to spend most of his time worrying about crowd safety instead of playing matters!

When Wild stood down as manager in 1946 he was recognised as City's greatest manager up to that point. He reverted to purely secretarial duties, but sadly passed away in December 1950 while still performing that role.

Trophies per Season

Runners-up and finalists are not included in this seasonal average breakdown.

Manager	Cups	Seasons	Ave
Manuel Pellegrini	3	3	1
Pep Guardiola	2	2	1
Sam Cowan	1	1	1
Joe Mercer	5	6	0.83
Roberto Mancini	2	4	0.5
Tom Maley	2	4	0.5
Wilf Wild	2	7	0.29
Kevin Keegan	1	4	0.25
Tony Book	1	5	0.2
Harry Newbould	1	6	0.17
Peter Hodge	1	6	0.17
Sam Ormerod	1	7	0.14
Les McDowall	1	13	0.08

Relegation Managers

The following men were in the hot seat on the day relegation was confirmed. It must be noted that in certain cases, the manager came in to salvage the season following the disastrous performance of their predecessor's team. In fact Joe Royle's place both here and in the Most Successful Managers table needs to be explained.

Royle achieved a significant amount during his three years as manager. He arrived when the Blues seemed destined to be relegated and narrowly failed in his bid to keep them out of the third tier. Morale was low, quality poor, and Royle's gargantuan task was to try to bring the Blues back to life.

A tough but amazing promotion season followed, with enough momentum to achieve a second consecutive step up. In retrospect it was a step too far, and the 2000-01 Premiership campaign ended in relegation, but all fans recognised the Royle-inspired rebirth, without which we could have remained in a desperate state for many years.

Manager	Relegations
Sam Ormerod	1 (from 1st to 2nd)

Previously guided City to first ever promotion.

Harry Newbould	1 (from 1st to 2nd)

Went on to win Div 2 title.

Peter Hodge   1 (from 1st to 2nd)
Arrived with 2 games left to play, but defeat on last day of season meant Blues were relegated by 1 point.
Wilf Wild   1 (from 1st to 2nd)
Won League title previous season!
Jock Thomson   1 (from 1st to 2nd)
Replaced successful and popular Sam Cowan.
Les McDowall   1 (from 1st to 2nd)
Previously guided City to FA Cup.
John Benson   1 (from 1st to 2nd)
Replaced John Bond with 17 games to go.
Jimmy Frizzell   1 (from 1st to 2nd)
Took over in Sept of relegation season.
Alan Ball   1 (from Prem to One)
Replaced Brian Horton the past summer after two seasons of exciting football.
Joe Royle   2 (from One to Two & Prem to One)
Arrived with 14 games left; but missed survival by 1 point.

Sam's Season
By the end of the 2017-18 season, three managers averaged one trophy per season, including City's two most recent bosses. But there is one man who

actually managed for less than a season and brought a title success. That was Sam Cowan, the former City captain, who became boss in December 1946 with the *Sunday People* claiming: "Cowan was the most popular player ever at Maine Road. If the City followers give him the same support now he will be a happy and successful manager."

Cowan was an inspirational leader and only four of the 30 League and Cup games he managed ended in defeat. City won the Second Division title comfortably but Cowan mysteriously resigned in the close season. For years people suggested commuting had been an issue – Cowan had been living in Brighton with his young family and travelling to Manchester for only part of the week – but the truth appears to be that interference from a director meant Cowan was not able to carry out plans he felt necessary for the new season. Cowan was a good friend of former Blue and new United manager Matt Busby and it is known that Cowan wanted the same sort of regime that Busby was being allowed to develop at United.

Everton Player, City Manager
Seven former Everton players have become City managers. They are: Jock Thomson, Joe Mercer, Howard Kendall, Peter Reid, Alan Ball, Joe Royle and Mark Hughes. In addition former Everton player Asa Hartford was City caretaker manager August to October 1996. Reid, Royle and Hartford are also former City players.

League was Lawrence Furniss. Furniss, a former player, was in charge as the Blues joined the League in 1892 (when still named Ardwick AFC). Previously he had twice led to the club to Manchester Cup success and had established the side as Manchester's biggest and most progressive during the early 1890s. Ardwick finished fifth in Division Two (his only League season), but Furniss went on to become a director of the Club when it reformed as Manchester City in 1894.

International Managers

City managers Joe Mercer (England), Malcolm Allison (Kuwait), Peter Reid (Thailand), Kevin Keegan (England), Sven Goran-Eriksson (England), Mark Hughes (Wales) and Roberto Mancini (Italy) have all managed at an international level. Stuart Pearce was caretaker manager of England in 2012 and also managed the Great Britain Olympic football team.

Longest-serving Managers

While Wilf Wild remains the longest-serving City manager, Les McDowall actually managed more seasons of League football, due to the intervention of war. Wilf Wild (14y 8 months), 7 full peacetime seasons & 7 wartime seasons.
Les McDowall (12y 11 months), 13 seasons.
Ernest Mangnall (11y 10 months) 8 peacetime seasons & 4 wartime seasons.
Sam Ormerod (7y) 7 seasons.
Joe Mercer (6y 3m plus 8m as General Manager) 6 full seasons.
Harry Newbould (6y) 6 seasons.
Peter Hodge (5y 11m) 6 seasons.
Tony Book (5y 3m plus 14m as General Manager) 5 full seasons.

Furniss the First

The first man to take on the role of secretary-manager for the Blues in the

FA Cup Success

Five men have guided the Blues to FA Cup success. The first was Scotsman Tom Maley who brought home Manchester's first trophy in 1904 when City defeated Bolton 1-0 at the Crystal Palace. Maley's brother, Willie, was the Celtic manager at the time and his success in the 1904 Scottish Cup final made unique history.

Maley also guided City to the Second Division Championship (1902) and in the FA Cup-winning season his City side narrowly missed out on the Double, finishing second to Sheffield Wednesday.

The other FA Cup-winning City managers are Wilf Wild, Les McDowall, Joe Mercer and Roberto Mancini.

League Champions

City have won the top division of English football on five occasions. The three most recent managers – Pep Guardiola, Manuel Pellegrini and Roberto Mancini – have each won it; Joe Mercer was manager in 1967-68, and Wilf Wild was the leader for City's first Championship in 1936-37.

Fewest Seasons

The following guided City for less than two full seasons as permanent managers: Sam Cowan, Johnny Hart, Ron Saunders, John Benson, Jimmy Frizzell, Howard Kendall,

Alan Ball, Steve Coppell and Frank Clark.

Ex-player Johnny Hart left the manager's chair for health reasons after less than six months. During this time he brought Denis Law back to the Blues. Former Red Steve Coppell claimed health was the reason he left Maine Road after his extremely brief spell in charge between 7 October and 8 November 1996.

Alan Ball	1995-96
Steve Coppell	1996
Frank Clark	1996-98
Joe Royle	1998-2001
Kevin Keegan	2001-2005
Stuart Pearce	2005-2007
Sven Goran Eriksson	2007-2008
Mark Hughes	2008-2009
Roberto Mancini	2009-2013
Manuel Pellegrini	2013-2016
Pep Guardiola	2016-

League Managers

Here is the complete record of City's managers in the League:

Lawrence Furniss	1889-1893
Joshua Parlby	1893-95
Sam Ormerod	1895-1902
Tom Maley	1902-1906
Harry Newbould	1906 -12
Ernest Mangnall	1912-24
David Ashworth	1924—25
Albert Alexander	1925-26
Peter Hodge	1926-32
Wilf Wild	1932-46
Sam Cowan	1946-47
Jock Thomson	1947-50
Les McDowall	1950-63
George Poyser	1963-65
Joe Mercer	1965-1972

(general manager from 1971)

Malcolm Allison	1972-73

(team manager from 1971, with Mercer as general manager until 1972)

Johnny Hart	1973
Ron Saunders	1973-74
Tony Book	1974-79
Malcolm Allison	1979-80
John Bond	1980-83
John Benson	1983
Billy McNeill	1983-86
Jimmy Frizzell	1986-87

(continued as general manager)

Mel Machin	1987-89
Howard Kendall	1989-90
Peter Reid	1990-93
Brian Horton	1993-95

Former Players

Nine out of the total of 39 men who have managed the Blues on a permanent basis were also former City players. They were: Lawrence Furniss, Sam Cowan, Les McDowall, Johnny Hart, Tony Book, John Benson, Peter Reid, Joe Royle and Stuart Pearce.

In addition, former Blues Ken Barnes, Fred Tilson, and Asa Hartford have had spells as caretaker manager.

Don't Look Back in Anger

The 1990s started with a great deal of optimism. Howard Kendall, recognised as one of the greatest managers of the era, was City's boss and, with a mix of talented young players and seasoned professionals, his team seemed capable of finding major success. Sadly it didn't quite work out like that as, before the year was out, Kendall returned to his first love, Everton. Despite a few exciting top-flight seasons, the decade was to see the club drop to its lowest ever League position. Often painted these days as a decade of failure, it is actually worth re-examining the period to see whether it was truly as disastrous as the modern-day media claim.

Focusing solely on the decade between 1990 and 1999, City:

• Kicked off as a top-flight team and soon became founder members of the Premier League in 1992. In fact, City spent the majority of the decade in the top tier!

• The Blues finished both 1990-91 and 1991-92 in fifth place. For most years between 1968 and 2018 this would have brought European football, however a ban on English clubs playing in UEFA competitions had recently been lifted and the nation's allocation was still restricted. The ban had followed major crowd disturbances at the European Cup Final when Liverpool fans were held responsible for widespread violence which resulted in the death of 39 people.

• The dismissal of manager Peter Reid after only three games of the 1993-94 season led to demonstrations against chairman Peter Swales. As in previous years, the chairman expected the

against Gillingham. Those goals dragged City back into the match at 2-2 and, after extra time, promotion was won via a penalty shoot-out.

• The decade tested the loyalty of fans and while City were never higher than the sixth best supported League side, Maine Road was typically full for games. Capacity dropped as low as 19,000 in the early '90s and stabilised at 30,000 later in the decade.

demonstrations to die down after a while but former player Francis Lee announced he wanted to launch a takeover. This ensured the demonstrations continued and, after a bitter battle, Swales stood down around Christmas 1993. By the season's end Lee and his consortium had gained control of the club.

• Lee improved activities off the pitch considerably but on the pitch his appointment of Alan Ball in 1995 was not well received. The club struggled under Ball and suffered relegation at the end of his first season. Further struggles followed at the start of 1996-97, leading to Ball's dismissal.

• A crazy period of managerial change in 1996-97 was worrying enough, but then in 1998 another relegation came. This meant that City would be playing the 1998-99 season in the third tier of English football for the first time. Changes at board level followed again, after demonstrations against Lee during the 1997-98 season.

• 1999 saw City climb out of the third tier thanks to late goals from Kevin Horlock and Paul Dickov in the famous Wembley Play-off final

• There was a massive turnaround in playing staff during the decade as each managerial change prompted the new boss to bring in players he wanted, casting aside those of his predecessors.

• In 1994 the famous Kippax Stand staged its last game before the terracing was demolished. On its final day, it was the largest capacity terracing still in use. The Kop at Anfield had its final day at the same time, but it was smaller.

• The appointment of Joe Royle in 1998

Niall Quinn shoots and misses (left).
A nail-biting day out at Wembley, 1999 (below).

came too late to prevent relegation, but it was absolutely the right appointment for the time. Royle knew City and was dedicated to returning the Blues to the Premier League.

• Stars of the decade include Georgi Kinkladze, Shaun Goater, Paul Dickov,

Niall Quinn, Uwe Rosler, Tony Coton, Gerard Wiekens, Ian Brightwell, Michel Vonk, Keith Curle, Colin Hendry and Terry Phelan.

The '90s is often perceived as a desperate decade for City, and it did see the club drop to its lowest ever League position. But focusing on the failures ignores some great successes and moments along the way. The first five years saw some excellent football, particularly under Brian Horton (1993-95), and the mood amongst fans was usually positive. The board issues became too much of a distraction but, putting that to one side, it should be remembered that as fans we felt there

was a great opportunity to become the team of the 1990s. By 1991 Liverpool had started to lose their way and there was no team, not even Arsenal, who seemed capable of dominating football. City had as great a chance as any but a combination of bad luck and poor judgement – plenty of the latter! – meant the club slowly started to self-destruct. At the same time a neighbouring team began once again to find success.

Nowadays we look back and think of the loyalty of fans – and that was extremely strong – but the '90s was really a decade of two halves. The first saw an ambitious club make a challenge and consider itself a contender. The second half was one of failure, followed by the first signs of recovery.

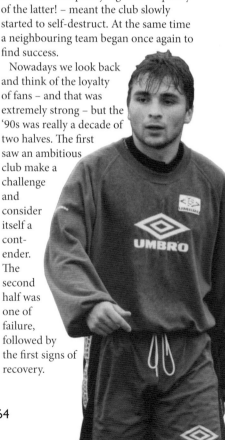

Starter Home

In 1887 Gorton AFC moved to a new ground. As this was outside of the Gorton district the club was relaunched as Ardwick AFC, establishing the foundations for the club's later move into League football.

It was actually Kenneth McKenzie, the club captain, who first discovered the potential of wasteland located close to his workplace. This land was a decent size, but wasn't used for any kind of positive recreational activity, although it was a gathering spot for local youths and had seen a number of bare-knuckle bouts take place there. McKenzie felt it offered potential as a football ground and he immediately told the leading football committee members of the find. It is believed they took some convincing as the land was uneven and riddled with polluted streams; however, with few other options, the Gortonians decided it did have potential. In addition, Lawrence Furniss and Walter Chew were both aware that this land lay close to the club's spiritual home of St Mark's Church.

Furniss identified that the land belonged to the Manchester, Sheffield & Lincolnshire Railway, and after some negotiation Gorton were able to rent the land for £10 for a period of seven months. Furniss, Chew and company spent a few weeks trying to level an area suitable for a pitch and by late August the ground was ready. It was still relatively basic but it was deemed suitable for a relaunch of the club. The move to this ground caused the committee to consider changing the name of the club. As the new ground was based in the district of Ardwick, rather than Gorton, Ardwick AFC was duly born. A circular was issued on 23 August 1887 and the inaugural meeting was held at the Hyde Road Hotel on 30 August.

The Hyde Road Hotel became the headquarters of the club and was also used

as dressing rooms for several years.

Within a decade the Hyde Road ground, as it became known, had grown into a major venue. In some ways the ground developed at a similar rate to the club. In 1892 Ardwick were founder members of Division Two, then two years later Manchester City was established, and in 1896

the Blues were the League's third best supported side behind Everton and Villa.

In 1904 a major refurbishment occurred following the FA Cup success, and in 1905 the venue was selected for an inter-league game between Ireland and England. The FA Cup semi-final between Newcastle and Sheffield Wednesday was also staged there. The inter-league match was filmed and the footage is now believed to be the oldest showing a professional football venue in Manchester. The camera was positioned in front of the Main Stand at the Galloway corner, and film clearly shows the Popular Side, part of the Galloway End, the Main Stand and the players' tunnel.

By this time, crowds of 40,000 could be housed, and although the stadium was often packed to bursting, the club appear to have downplayed the number that were actually present for financial and safety reasons. A few games,

most notably a Cup tie with Sunderland in 1913 and a League game with Burnley in 1921, caused local journalists to question the club's organisation, safety record and reporting of attendances at Hyde Road.

At regular intervals suggestions were made that the Blues would have to move, and options were sought out; but there was a feeling amongst the senior committee men that City would only move if a significantly better venue could be found. There were even audacious plans to redevelop the Hyde Road ground itself and renowned architect Archibald Leitch was given an office at the ground. He developed plans to turn the pitch 45 degrees and erect a stadium capable of holding 80,000. Unfortunately, World War I scuppered those grand plans and other potential moves.

In March 1920 Hyde Road became the first provincial ground to be visited by a reigning monarch when King George V attended City's victory over Liverpool. He did this because he knew

City v Oldham, 1913, in front of Hyde Road's Popular Side.

it would be a great way to meet a large number of Mancunians as City remained Manchester's number one club despite United's move to Old Trafford in 1910.

Actually, United's development of Old Trafford caused the Blues to improve Hyde Road considerably in 1910. City decided to improve facilities for all supporters and set plans in place to provide shelter for a total of 35,000 spectators. This was achieved by erecting multi-span roofs on the three remaining open sides, a source of great pride to Mancunians.

Although no other Manchester football venue would match this record for all-round cover until the '70s, Hyde Road's 40,000 capacity remained far too small. The close proximity of railway lines, factories and housing limited expansion. By 1920 City were publicly planning a move to a site at Belle Vue, but in November of that year fire destroyed the club's 1890s Main Stand. The rest of the stadium survived, but a move became absolutely vital if the Blues were to capitalise on their popularity.

City should have moved immediately but decided to soldier on at Hyde Road after negotiations with United to share Old Trafford proved difficult. Rather than pay exorbitant rental to United the Blues patched up the ground and found enough breathing space to create magnificent plans for the future. Interestingly, City's attempts to patch up Hyde Road brought the club national attention, with journalists travelling to Manchester to check on City's progress. The *Glasgow Evening Times* was particularly impressed: "Manchester City must have some good friends. They are of course the popular club in Manchester. It was surprising to find a fine new stand, estimated to hold 6,000 spectators, rising to the height of 25 tiers on the site of the old structure. In addition, extensive new

A railway loop line ran in front of City's Boys Stand at Hyde Road!

terracing had been carried out, and new dressing rooms for both teams and offices had been erected. Talk about the building of an American city!"

Inevitably, Hyde Road was unable to cope with City's continuing growth and the management realised a move was absolutely vital. During the 1921-22 season they planned to develop a new stadium at Moss Side, and managed to prolong the life of Hyde Road until the start of the 1923-24 season. The last game at Hyde Road was a public practice match in August 1923. Afterwards it was dismantled and within a decade or so all trace had disappeared for ever, or so everyone believed. In the late '90s metalwork from one of the club's multi-span roofs was rediscovered as the roof of a factory in Sale. The building has since been demolished, but another section of roof still survives today as a football stand at Halifax Town's Shay Stadium. City sold the stand and a few turnstiles to Halifax for £1,000, and this stand remains a key feature of the Shay even today.

The site occupied by the Hyde Road ground is currently used as a storage yard for containers and lorries, after several years use as a skid pan for the Hyde Road bus depot. In the main, the site has not housed any form of building and so when travelling past by railway towards Piccadilly train station, it is still possible to visualise how the venue would have looked when first found in the 1880s.

The Main Stand

Erected in 1899 after being purchased from the Fulham Pageant for approximately £1,500. Extended in 1904. Destroyed by fire, November 1920. The Main Stand had replaced an earlier 1,000-seater stand, built in 1888 by Chester's Brewery.

Capacity: usually stated as 4,000, although this may in fact be the seated capacity. The stand was divided into two sections with the upper tier all seated. In front of this was a paddock which may have held up to a further 4,000. After the 1920 fire the replacement stand was reported as having 25 terraced steps and holding 6,000 by several newspapers.

The Galloway End

Roofed during the 1910 close season as part of a £3,000 refurbishment plan (an incredible sum; Huddersfield spent fractionally more

than this on the creation of their state-of-art Main Stand the following year). At the other corner, where the Galloway End met the Popular Side, the terracing was oddly shaped because terraced houses on Bennett Street cut into the terracing. Footage of the 1905 inter-league match between the English and Irish Leagues show that large wooden screens had been erected at this end to stop those living in the houses from viewing the game.

A plan of 1894 shows an earlier stand at this end of the ground, but no trace appears on any photos or plans post 1897.
Capacity: c.8,000

The Boys' Stand

The corner between the Galloway End and the Main Stand was split from the rest of the ground by a railway loop line that ran into Galloway's boiler works. The area behind the line housed an area of terracing known as the Boys' Stand. Young supporters stood in this section free of parental influence and this was often known as a rowdy and raucous part of the football ground.

It provided many supporters with their first experience of football and, due to its unique atmosphere, was immensely popular and perhaps led to young fans developing a close affinity with the club. It is worth noting that City's support grew in the decades that followed the move to Maine Road despite the Depression and other financial hardships. This was a time when Boys' Stand regulars of the 1900s and 1910s became adults and parents.

Likewise, City's loyal support in the '80s and '90s is often attributed to the efforts of those who established the Junior Blues in the '70s, and it seems logical that the Boys' Stand helped encourage young fans to feel that City was their club.
Capacity: c.2,000

The magic days of old puffing Billy!

By JOHN BEAVAN
Political advisor to the
Daily Mirror

IF you are born in Manchester, you are either a City man or a United man and all through life you never change.

I am a City man because I lived in Ardwick, and Manchester City's original name in the year when Queen Victoria celebrated her golden jubilee was Ardwick F.C.

There must still be a number of grey-haired regulars at Maine Road who, like me, first saw City from the boys' corner of the old Hyde Road ground.

My parents let me go there because they thought I would be safe from the crush and the coarse language.

Little did they know. The factory lads were very rough. They would put a lighted cigarette butt on the hat of an unsuspecting boy in the row before them and sing: "It's burning. It's burning. A bloody big 'ole in yer 'at."

The Stone Yard Stand

(aka the Hotel End or Hyde Road Stand) Roofed 1910. A large section of this irregular-shaped stand was seated with a paddock in front, and the rest was basic terracing. The seated section (closest to the Main Stand) was used to house the directors, press and season ticket holders following the 1920 Main Stand fire. Despite its importance, the club were unable to erect any turnstiles at this end of the ground.

Capacity:
c.2,000 seats;
4,000 standing.

Popular Side

Roofed in 1910. This terracing was the home to City's most passionate supporters, and was usually the area where crushing occurred during big matches. Many important games saw supporters climb up on to the roof for a better view. The roof at this side only covered three quarters of the stand's length due to the proximity of terraced houses which stood on Bennett Street.

Capacity: c.17,000

Turnstiles

The first pay box was erected around 1888 for a cost of £5 15s. Due to the close proximity of a stone yard, the railway and Galloway's works, Bennett Street and a small area next to Galloway's Works were the only areas available for placing turnstiles and entrances. This caused serious problems both before and after all major games, as the street was simply unable to cope with the large volume of people attending City's matches.

At the time of Maine Road's demolition in 2003, at least 13 turnstiles were identified as being from Hyde Road, with four known to have been in place at Hyde Road in 1896, possibly earlier.

Hyde Road Facts & Figures

Highest official attendance: 41,709 v Sunderland, FA Cup Second Round on 1 February 1913.

Probable highest: v Burnley, First Division game on 26 March 1921. Attendance was probably somewhere in the region of 50-55,000, after fans smashed down gates and filled the Pop Side roof!

First Game: Ardwick v Hooley Hill (Denton) 17 September 1887.

First Football League game: 3 September 1892 v Bootle.

Last Football League game: 28 April 1923 v Newcastle United.

Highest Average Attendance: c.31,020 1920-2.

Hyde Road Progressive Capacity

1887 – 4,000	1888 – 7,000
1891 – 10,000	1892 – 20,000
1896 – 25,000	1899 – 30,000
1904 – 40,000	1910 – 40,000 *
1920 – 45,000	1921 – 40,000

* Covered accommodation for 35,000.

Welcome to Manchester

It can be a bitter rivalry at times but City have always demonstrated that they are supportive neighbours to United. Whenever United has been in a desperate state or in need of support – whether financial or looking for facilities – City have offered to help. Here is a quick review of some of the neighbourly acts the Blues have made over the years.

In the Beginning
Both clubs' earliest-known football games were in November 1880, although there had been sporting activity at the Newton Heath L&Y Railway (United) and at St Mark's Church (City) in the 1870s. In their

first recorded games, St Mark's lost 2-1 to Macclesfield Baptist on 13 November and the Heathens were defeated 6-0 by Bolton Wanderers A-team a week later. During those formative years the clubs met frequently, and in 1889 Ardwick's (City's) Walter Chew organised a floodlit friendly with Newton Heath in aid of the Hyde

Coal Mine Disaster where 23 people had died. Other charitable derby matches have occurred over the years.

Financial Support
By the early 1900s, City was a popular and growing First Division side while the Heathens struggled financially in Division Two. A series of fundraising initiatives sought to stabilise the club with City's management making several significant donations in 1901 to keep the Heathens afloat. These included directors John Allison, John Chapman (City chairman) and Edward Hulton. City also donated a significant sum of £10 while Chapman contributed £1 1s in 1901. Further support followed in 1902.

Meredith & Co.
The great City captain Billy Meredith led the Blues to FA Cup glory in 1904, when City also narrowly missed out on the League. A little over a year later, FA investigations into the club showed that the Blues had been paying some players more than the maximum wage allowed. The FA punishment meant that, more or less, the entire squad was banned and forced to leave the club. Not wanting their star man to leave Manchester, the club and City supporters encouraged Meredith and some of the other stars, such as Sandy Turnbull, to join the Reds.

Further Success
In 1909, United won the FA Cup for the first time and the Blues director Albert Alexander senior provided the carriages for the Reds' homecoming. United had asked him to lead the procession carrying the players and the Cup. The idea was

that the success, with Turnbull and Meredith starring, was a continuation of City's 1904 FA Cup glory and the Reds and the Blues wanted all of Manchester to celebrate together.

Lack of Support!

During the summer of 1920 City's management considered moving temporarily from Hyde Road to Old Trafford as it was deemed the City ground's 40,000 capacity was too small. Games had become difficult to manage there with the police frequently insisting that turnstiles be closed early despite the ground not always being full and thousands locked out. The layout of the venue made it difficult to manage entrances effectively and the ground's capacity was often challenged. United and City negotiated but, in the end, the Blues decided to remain at Hyde Road until they could move to their own new stadium.

The following November, fire destroyed the Hyde Road main stand and City had no choice but to ask United if they could move to Old Trafford on the terms suggested in the summer. Amazingly, United said their terms had changed, and City were now expected to pay a guaranteed income plus all gate receipts in excess of the corresponding fixture from the previous season. At this

City, it was United who suffered most. With Old Trafford crowds falling to an average of 11,685 in 1930-31, Second Division United were in serious danger. Ultimately, City and United appealed to the Football League and Central's offer to become a League side was withdrawn. Central, who had attracted several prominent non-League crowds, soon decided to throw in the towel.

time City knew they would be able to attract at least 60,000 for high-profile games, meaning that United would gain a guaranteed rental *plus* the entire income from as many as 20,000 spectators. That was more than United received for many of their own games, as their 1920 average was only 27,140. Understandably, City patched up Hyde Road. Widespread media criticism of United was severe.

Manchester Central

By the beginning of the '30s, with City at Maine Road and United at Old Trafford, the rivalry had developed; however, the management of the clubs remained extremely close. So when a third Manchester team, Manchester Central – established as an alternative MCFC playing at Belle Vue – was accepted as a member of the Third Division (North), the Blues and Reds worked together to kill off the threat. Originally set up to provide east Manchester with a replacement for

Groundsharing

In 1941, despite the issues faced in 1920 when they were in need, the Blues offered to help when Old Trafford had suffered bomb damage. There were several prominent Manchester venues at the time with sufficient capacities and facilities – the rugby clubs and Belle Vue – but the relationship between the Blues and Reds was such that sharing Maine Road was always the preferred option. United offered to pay the Blues roughly 10% of gate receipts (less tax). During their Maine Road exile, United's support reached new levels and the club made record profits.

European Nights

When United became the first English team to enter the European Cup, their first games in the competition were staged at City's Maine Road during 1956-57. Midweek European football meant that floodlighting was preferred to ensure suitable kick-off times. As City had installed theirs in 1953, United chose to move their games from Old Trafford. At Maine Road United generated their highest home European crowd of all time – 75,598 for the 1956 clash with Borussia Dortmund.

Disaster Strikes

No Mancunian needs reminding that the city suffered a major tragedy in 1958 when an aeroplane carrying the United team, officials and journalists back from their European tie in Belgrade crashed at Munich Airport. The death of 23 touched all Mancunians and, in the days that followed, the city came together to support those involved and pay their respects to the deceased. City offered United whatever assistance they needed. Bert Trautmann offered to act as translator and to provide other support to United. City invited United chairman Harold Hardman and new secretary Les Olive to be guests of honour at the first game played in the city after the tragedy – City v Birmingham (15 February 1958). The mood that night was sombre with hymns such as 'Abide With Me,' with soloist Sylvia Farmer, played pre-match as fans stood bareheaded and silent. Symbolically, the match was abandoned due to torrential rain in the 40th minute.

Fifty years after the disaster, of course, City and United fans came together at Old Trafford to commemorate the anniversary. They demonstrated to the world that Mancunian allegiances can be put to one side at appropriate moments.

Here's an extract from a letter that was written by a 79-year-old City fan in 1957, which remains relevant today:

"I have always regarded it as a highlight of the year to watch two fine teams from the same city in action... Sometimes City are on top of the world, sometimes United. Which is just as it should be. Nobody with the interests of the game at heart could honestly wish for one side to win everything all the time. I'd just like to say 'all the best' to both teams for the future, and I hope the name Manchester will long remain at the top of the football world."

City pay their respects to friends and opponents killed at Munich. Spurs v City, 8 February 1958.

City of the Future

It has been City's home since 2003 and for many fans will be the only home venue ever experienced. Fifteen years is a long time in football but, believe it or not, the story of the Blues' current home goes back over 30 years!

The first suggestion that City would move to a new stadium came in the late '80s. At that time Bob Scott – a key figure behind the resurgence of the Palace and Opera House theatres – outlined an amazing plan for Manchester to stage the 1992 Olympics. Many Mancunians thought it was a crazy idea, however the *Manchester Evening News* focused on the story and eventually a front page headline – '£100m site for Blues?' – made the plan feel achievable. Within the article City chairman Peter Swales stated: "If it all happens and the stadium is built, it is

pretty special to make us move.

"The Olympic Bid committee have explained what they are trying to do and I think it is a very bold, adventurous plan to bring the Games to Manchester."

Club officials from that period have since stated that the plan was nothing more than a brief discussion, however as time moved on and Manchester's Olympic dreams grew, the idea to move became much more serious, the only drawback being that Manchester first had to get the Olympics.

Manchester's bid may have ultimately failed, but it did bring the fantastic consolation prize of the Commonwealth Games. Francis Lee pushed to ensure City played their part in all matters relating to the stadium and, once he resigned as chairman, new chairman David Bernstein, Chief Operating Officer Chris Bird and

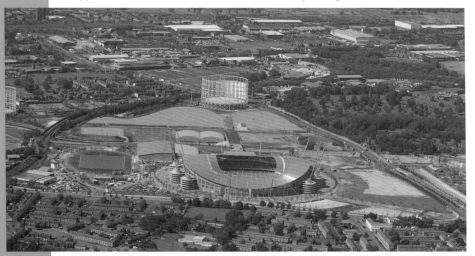

something we have got to be interested in. It is at a very early stage. We have spent a lot of money at Maine Road and the new stadium would have to be something

director Alistair Mackintosh focused on the stadium development and the move.

In August 1999 David Bernstein signed the legal documentation agreeing to

largely dismantled to leave a more modest athletics stadium as a legacy.

This means that the 1999 Play-off win was even more crucial than simply improving the fortunes of Manchester City. Whereas the 2012 Olympic Stadium was built without a permanent tenant in place, Manchester's stadium had to have the certainty that the venue would have a life beyond the Commonwealth Games, otherwise it would not have been built.

By summer 2002 the stadium had been built as a 35,000-seater athletics venue, and once the Games ended in August 2002, work commenced on reconfiguring the stadium into a football venue as planned from the start.

Initially the stadium had consisted of a couple of two-tier stands at the east and west sides, and a single-tier South Stand. The temporary stand at the northern end was dismantled within days of the end of the Games, and work commenced on lowering the pitch by around six metres, with tons of earth removed. The lower tier was then constructed and the North Stand erected. The capacity was raised to approximately 48,000.

Even though the Blues had only spent two of the previous seven seasons in the Premier League (City's worst ever spell on the pitch) Bernstein and Bird had committed the Blues to the stadium move and to the expense necessary to make this the leading footballing venue in the country. Meanwhile, behind the scenes,

the move and the following December Prime Minister Tony Blair laid the first stone of what was to become the City of Manchester Stadium.

Prior to City's promotion in 1999 there were real fears that the club could potentially be marooned in the third tier, so building a 48,000-capacity stadium would have been a major gamble. City had to be moving forwards if a permanent move were to be made. In addition, the funders would not contribute to a permanent stadium without an anchor tenant. Had City not been in a position to move, the Commonwealth Games would have been staged in a more temporary structure. A permanent stand would have been built housing approximately 10,000 with temporary seated stands creating a 35,000 venue, which would then have been

City contemplate move to new Games stadium

MANCHESTER City could move to a new 70,000-capacity stadium being built for the 2002 Commonwealth

By John Ley

the reasons and Dave Jones, the Southampton manager.

sionals — and most speak pretty good English.''
Aarsheim, a Norway Under-21 midfield

Bernstein and Bird had resigned. Deputy chairman John Wardle replaced Bernstein and Alistair Mackintosh ultimately became the club's Chief Executive.

The stadium was opened as a footballing venue on Sunday 10 August 2003 when the Blues defeated Barcelona 2-1. Nicolas Anelka scored the stadium's first goal in the 34th minute at the North Stand end, and four days later the first competitive match saw City defeat Welsh side Total Network Solutions 5-0 in the UEFA Cup Qualifying Round.

The stadium continued to evolve in the years that followed. The directors' box was reduced in size. A TV commentary box was erected, and a second TV gantry created at the front of the third tier of the West Stand as the main gantry was too high for football action. Other developments included a groundbreaking Memorial Garden which contained stonework from the Hyde Road Hotel, a mosaic from Maine Road and a tribute to Marc-Vivien Foe. Next came the City Superstore, the City Social and the club's award-winning museum and tour, 'The Manchester City Experience.'

Since the 2008 takeover there have been many significant developments at the stadium. Almost immediately the new owners appointed Jon Stemp to manage infrastructure developments and he set about building a new office block, City@home, while also planning significant changes to the club's existing training facilities at Carrington and developing new ones at the Etihad site. Around the pitch, reprofiling of the area enabled the club to install additional seating pitchside. This was all part of a wider expansion plan which has seen the South Stand extended (2014-2015) with a third tier and a rebuilt Legends Lounge. The 'Tunnel Club' executive area has also been developed. The capacity has increased to 55,097, although segregation needs mean that is unlikely ever to be reached.

The stadium move has allowed the Blues to achieve their highest average attendance of all time, and in its first three years following the Games, the stadium staged international football; a UEFA Women's Championship game; a Rugby League international and concerts by the Red Hot Chilli Peppers, U2, Oasis, Take That and Bon Jovi. The Oasis concerts brought the largest crowds to the stadium as the volume of people allowed on the playing area enabled the stadium to house around 60,000. Oasis were also the first non-City organisation to play to sell-outs at both Maine Road and the new stadium.

Further concerts, internationals and high-profile events have been staged at the stadium since, such as the 2008 UEFA Cup final between Rangers and Zenit. The stadium has also won various architectural awards and is now the centrepiece of the Etihad Campus development which includes the City Football Academy.

Looking to the future it seems the North Stand will be extended at some point to bring a capacity of over 60,000 to City for the first time since the early '70s.

The Colin Bell Stand
Erected in 2002 as a two-tier stand for the Commonwealth Games. Basement area and dressing rooms were included in the original build below ground level. After the Games the pitch area was excavated and the tunnel was opened up and lower tier constructed in 2003. Originally known as the West Stand.

The North Stand
Built during 2002-03 following the Commonwealth Games. Unlike the South Stand, this end contains executive boxes and the family stand.

The South Stand
Converted into a two-tier stand after the Games, and then extended with a third tier in 2014-15, this end houses the Legends Lounge, away supporters and City's more vocal fans.

The East Stand
A similar construction to the Colin Bell Stand, from the perspective of spectators. Dubbed 'The Kippax Stand' by nostalgic supporters. Also includes corporate facilities.

Etihad Facts & Figures
First Game: v Barcelona, 10 August 2003.
First Competitive Game: v Total Network Solutions, UEFA Cup, 14 August 2003
First League Game: v Portsmouth, 23 August 2003.

Etihad Progressive Capacity
2002 – 38,000	2003 – 47,726
2011 – 47,405	2014 – 46,708
2015 – 55,097	

Redevelopment work between 2010 to 2015 meant the capacity varied at time, depending on building needs and safety requirements.

Noughtie but Nice

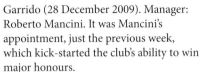

The period from 2000 to 2009 saw many changes at City. The decade began with Joe Royle's Blues hopeful of promotion back to the Premier League and ended with the club being perceived as the richest on the planet. The club was never the richest but its owner, Sheikh Mansour of Abu Dhabi, is one of the wealthiest individuals connected with global sport.

The decade also saw City move from their home of 80 years to the new City of Manchester Stadium, now renamed the Etihad, and a total of six managers guide the Blues on a permanent basis. It was a transitional decade in many ways, so here is a reminder of some of the key changes experienced as the club paved the way for the successes that have followed.

Focusing exclusively on the decade from the start of the millennium to 2009, City:

• Drew the first League game of the decade 1-1 at Crewe Alexandra in the second tier. Attendance 10,066. Scorer: Lee Crooks (3 January 2000). Manager: Joe Royle.

• The last League game of the decade was a 3-0 Premier League win at Wolverhampton Wanderers with goals from Tevez (2) and

Garrido (28 December 2009). Manager: Roberto Mancini. It was Mancini's appointment, just the previous week, which kick-started the club's ability to win major honours.

• City were managed by the following men: Joe Royle (until May 2001), Kevin Keegan (May 2001-March 2005), Stuart Pearce (March 2005-May 2007), Sven Goran Erikkson (July 2007-June 2008), Mark Hughes (June 2008-December 2009) and Roberto Mancini (December 2009-May 2013).

• City started the decade in Division One (second tier) but only spent the rest of that season and the 2001-02 season outside of the Premier League. The best Premier League finish of the decade was eighth in 2004-05, although the 2009-10 season saw the Blues finish fifth.

• City won the First Division title in 2002 and were presented with the traditional Football League Championship trophy they had held in 1936-37 and 1967-68, though this was now the second tier's title-winning prize and not the top flight's.

• After 80 years, City left Maine Road in 2003 and moved to their current home.

• The decade saw City return to European football for the first time since 1979. In 2003-04 the Blues reached the second round proper of the UEFA Cup, losing to Groclin on the away goals rule and then in 2008-09 they reached the quarter-finals of the same competition. They lost 4-3 on aggregate, but the home leg proved to be one of the greatest atmospheres the new stadium has ever experienced as fans urged the team on.

• In 2007 the club was taken over by Thaksin Shinawatra, the former Thai Prime Minister. At first his ownership

football match played! That day the news broke that a takeover was about to happen, and the day ended with the signing of Robinho. The takeover wasn't actually completed until 23 September 2008 – the anniversary of a memorable derby victory in 1989 – but it was the start of the transformation of the Blues.

• The Blues won the FA Youth Cup in 2008 with a 4-2 aggregate victory over Chelsea.

• Stars of the decade included those that had helped lift City back into the Premier League; those that stabilised the club, and those who began the search for major

suggested the club could achieve a great deal and exciting plans for the future were developed, particularly once he had appointed Garry Cook as the club's CEO. However, Shinawatra's financial situation worsened as investigations were made into his political life. Ultimately, he sold the club on to the Abu Dhabi United Group.

• Transfer deadline day 2008 will always be remembered as one of the most exciting days the club has ever experienced – and there was not even a

honours. These include Vincent Kompany, Pablo Zabaleta, Carlos Tevez, Elano, Richard Dunne, Joe Hart, Shaun Wright-Phillips, Nicolas Anelka, Shaun Goater, Gerard Wiekens, Danny Tiatto, Kevin Horlock, Sylvain Distin, Shaun Goater, Eyal Berkovic, Ali Benarbia, Marc-Vivien Foe, Trevor Sinclair and David James.

The 2000s were transformational years that saw City finally return to a position of strength after a dismal late '90s. The foundations were laid for all that followed. At the decade's start we lagged behind our traditional rivals but by the end we were ready to challenge them consistently in a manner unknown since the '70s.

Football League Division One Champions, 2002 (above); Sylvain Distin leads City out v Everton, September 2004 (right).

Hello, Goodbye

Back in 2008, City's headline-grabbing purchase of Robinho on transfer deadline day raised a few eyebrows and highlighted the Blues intention of returning once more to a position of strength in English and European football. At the time, some suggested this was something out of the ordinary, so here's a nice reminder of what City had achieved in terms of transfer records before Robinho's purchase.

Although City's transfer record between the late '80s and 2008 suggested the Blues rarely competed for the highest value transfers, the truth is somewhat different. In fact, many would argue that City's history dictates that the club should always compete for the biggest stars. If anyone tells you City have no place to challenge, then remind them that it was the period 1983 to 2008 that was out of character with City's entire history, not the period since 2008. Consider these facts:

• The Robinho transfer meant that City had beaten or equalled the British transfer record in five separate decades.

• City were the first British side to buy two £1 million players.

• In 1981 the Blues purchased their third million-pound man, Trevor Francis. This equalled Nottingham Forest's record, although the feat was not matched by any other club until Manchester United bought Mark Hughes from Barcelona in 1988.

• City's own transfer record had been smashed twice within a few months on four occasions prior to 2009 and again

in 2015 with the arrival of first Raheem Sterling and then Kevin De Bruyne

• As early as 1904 the Blues were regarded as matching the British record, and in that same year they also broke the record for winger.

Amazingly, alongside City's record of high-value purchases, we have also managed to develop a significant number of home-grown players, generation after generation.

Prior to Robinho, the last time City held the British record was back in 1979 when the Blues purchased Steve Daley for £1,450,277. It became fashionable to criticise this purchase as, ultimately, it was not a success (and Daley was replaced at Wolves by the slightly

Gallaher's Cigarettes.

JAMES McMULLAN
MANCHESTER CITY

more expensive but successful Andy Gray). However, it has to be remembered that at the time Daley was wanted by several high-profile clubs and everyone from fan to manager to chairman publicly

expressed delight at the news that he had come to Maine Road. And, as Peter Swales later put it, the £1,450,277 fee wasn't too bad, as it also included tax!

Before the 1979-80 season was out, Daley was joined by Kevin Reeves (£1.25m) and a year later Trevor Francis made the second million-pound move of his career (reported as £1.2m at the time), joining the Blues from Forest. City fans were delighted with the activity, and

Chairman Peter Swales appeared on a variety of debate shows after being accused of sending the transfer market crazy. He was accused of ruining football, but the truth was that he simply ruined City's ability to compete as the debts City then faced crippled the club for a generation – or even two! While City stagnated, other clubs continued to spend and raise the transfer record higher and higher.

After the transfer of Francis, City did not write another £1 million cheque until Clive Allen arrived in July 1989, but once we moved into the '90s the Blues started spending again. Keith Curle became the first Blue to cost more than £2 million when he was bought from Wimbledon for £2.5 million in 1991, and a year later we paid the same club the same amount again for Terry Phelan. Some Wimbledon fans claimed their existence owed much

Ivor Broadis shows off his silky skills (above);
Aymeric Laporte signs on the dotted line (right).

to the £5 million City had contributed in that period.

Further increases followed during the '90s with Kevin Keegan inflating our own record to £5 million in February 2002 when he purchased Jon Macken. Only three months later, he doubled the record by signing Nicolas Anelka for a fee reported as £10-13 million, according to sources.

Then in 2008 City managed to smash their own record twice, and the Robinho transfer took it to ten times the record figure of only a decade ago. It was also the British record.

My sincere thanks to all the fans who gave me such a warm welcome for my first game.

Steve Daley

G. DORSETT, Manchester City.

I've searched back through a variety or articles, records and cuttings to try to identify the full history of City's transfer record. It is clear that there are some periods when little is known about the precise amounts the club spent on players, so it is possible that some of the earlier figures detailed here were eclipsed by other City signings. However, I believe this can be used as a guide to show the development of our transfer record.

The first actual fee I've been able to identify to date was £30 back in 1896 for the purchase of forward John Gunn from Bolton. Gunn went on to score four goals in 22 appearances, so whether he was worth the fee is open to debate.

In 1904 the arrival of Irvine Thornley from local rivals Glossop was said, at the time, to have been a British record of around £800 (the record had been set at £700 by Newcastle in January 1904). However, the official transfer fee was later claimed to be only £450 when FA auditors started to look into City's books. The following October, auditors found discrepancies in the transfer and the Blues were ordered to pay a fine of £250 while Thornley was suspended for the rest of the season. Ultimately, the transfer cost at least £1,050 in hard cash.

City's first actual £1,000-plus transfer saw David Ross arrive for £1,200 in 1907. The transfer fee was quite complicated for the period as £1,000 went to the selling club (Norwich), £200 went to his earlier club (Bury) and City also played a friendly game against Norwich in which all proceeds went to Norwich. It also set the record for highest transfer involving a Southern League club.

Almost 30 years later our first £10,000 arrival was Irish international Peter Doherty. Regarded by those that saw him play as the greatest Irish player of all time,

DON REVIE

Doherty was only £890 cheaper than the British record at the time. He went on to help City to the League title in his first complete season, scoring 30 goals from 41 appearances.

The next record holder was Roy Paul, who went on to become a tremendous City captain, guiding the Blues to successive FA Cup finals in the '50s. There is a little confusion about the actual amount paid, as the arrival of Ivor Broadis the following year was said to have cost a couple of thousand more. All efforts to identify which amount is correct have so far failed.

From the early '60s onwards, City's record transfer has typically been broken whenever the Blues have sought to add a bit more glamour or style to the side. Well-known stars such as Denis Law, Francis Lee, Rodney Marsh and Dennis Tueart were typically popular record signings, but there were also several other big-name players who arrived for fees only slightly below our record. Occasionally these were record holders in other ways, for example Bobby Kennedy arrived for £45,000 in 1961 – a British record for a wing-half.

It is also worth pointing out that Dennis Tueart's signing was the second highest British transfer at the time. Only Bob Latchford's arrival at Everton cost more, however Latchford joined Everton in a complicated player exchange and so his precise personal value was open to interpretation.

Since Robinho's arrival City have of course smashed their own record by a significant margin. As with the purchases of the '70s and '80s the club has been criticised for spending, but this time the difference is that the players brought in have actually tended to deliver considerably more than the earliest £1 million players. Success and investment have helped establish the club as a profitable top-flight club, whereas the spending of the '70s and '80s placed the club in debt and struggling.

Chronological Progression of Record

Player	Reported Fee
John Gunn	£30 (Oct 1896)

The earliest identified transfer fee.

Joe Cassidy	£250 (April 1900)

Signed from Newton Heath (United).

Irvine Thornley	£450 (April 1904)

Regarded as British record at the time.

George Dorsett	£450 (Dec 1904)

A British record for a winger.

David Ross	£1,200 (Feb 1907)

Record transfer from Southern League.

Tommy Browell	£1,780 (Oct 1913)
Horace Barnes	£2,500 (May 1914)

Regarded at the time as equalling the British record.

Frank Roberts	£3,400 (Oct 1922)
Jimmy McMullan	£4,700 (Feb 1926)
Eric Brook &	
Fred Tilson	£6,000 (Mar 1928)

This was a combined fee and some records suggest Brook was valued at c.£4,750 though that seems unlikely.

Sam Barkas	£5,000 (Apr 1934)
Peter Doherty	£10,000 (Feb 1936)

Roy Paul	£25,000 (July 1950)
Ivor Broadis	£25,000 (Oct 1951)
Don Revie	£25,000 (Oct 1951)
Denis Law	£55,000 (Mar 1960)

Record between British clubs (surpassed previous by 10k)

Francis Lee	£60,000 (Oct 1967)
Rodney Marsh	£200,000 (Mar '72)
Dennis Tueart	£275,000 (Mar '74)
Paul Futcher	£350,000 (Jun '78)
Michael Robinson	£765,000 (Jun '79)
Steve Daley	£1,450,277 (Sep 1979)

British transfer record

Keith Curle	£2.5m (Aug 1991)
Terry Phelan	£2.5m (Sep 1992)
Lee Bradbury	£3m (July 1997)
Paulo Wanchope	£3.65m (Aug 2000)
Jon Macken	£5m (Feb 2002)
Nicolas Anelka	£10m (May 2002)

Often reported as £13m

Jo	£18m (July 2008)
Robinho	£32.5m (Sep 2008)

British transfer record.

Sergio Aguero	£38m (July 2011)
Raheem Sterling	£44m (July 2015)
Kevin De Bruyne	£55m (Aug 2015)
Aymeric Laporte	£57m (Jan 2018)
Riyad Mahrez	£60m (July 2018)

Note: Transfer amounts are rarely accurately reported and can contain a number of options, etc. The figures here are those that were generally reported at the time and may not necessarily be the official or final figure once appearances, options and other conditions are applied.

Marsh move tops £500,000 spree

By JOHN PARSONS

RODNEY MARSH flew from London last night to sign for Manchester City after leading a dazzling £500,000 parade of beat-the-deadline transfer moves.

Similar excitement before the market shuts at 5 p.m. today could carry the year's dealings close to £6 million. Chief developments yesterday were :

Queen's Park Rangers agreed to sell Marsh to Manchester City for £200,000 ; Aston Villa planned a £100,000 swoop for Luton's Chris Nicholl ; Wolves manager Bill McGarry lined up two £80,000 deals involving Hugh Curran and Jimmy Robertson ; and Leicester's Alistair Brown joined West Bromwich for £60,000.

stands between Manchester City and Marsh, the brilliant extrovert striker they have chased for four years. And the fact that City were pushed to £200,000 to get him will worry neither club nor player.

As he breezed into Manchester Airport Marsh said : 'Yes. I would rate myself at £200,000. At today's prices that figure is realistic.'

Agreed City team boss Malcolm Allison: 'This player is really outstanding, well worth the money. He's the sort of player you buy every five years. I'm sure he will help us win the championship. He's a flamboyant character. He'll bring more flair to the side—and a few more goals.'

Marsh, 27, admitted he had wanted to join a top club 'for a few seasons now.' He added : 'Perhaps Rangers decided to let me go because they have lost

a decision by the committee to make me cuts in playing staff and expenses.

Manager Roy Bentley said the team we unanimously in disagreement with the decision. He was running the present side in the Southern League at considerably less cost than when the club was in the Western League 12 years ago.

'To try to run a side with further cuts would be ridiculous,' he said.

The FA's Scapegoats

City's development during the early years of the 20th century caused some to believe that their rapid rise could not have been achieved without some form of illegal activity. There was a view amongst FA officials that City was a young, typically working-class northern club without a care for history, tradition or the rules of the game. This was not entirely true, however City was certainly an organisation unafraid of challenging the establishment.

Just as in the modern era, the Blues at the turn of the 20th century were setting out their stall for success – and, perhaps inevitably, raising concerns among rival clubs.

Promotion in 1899 as Second Division champions had given the club a great deal of satisfaction; then winning the FA Cup and finishing as League runners-up in 1904 was a major triumph. Some of City's players – most notably Billy Meredith, Sandy Turnbull and Billy Gillespie – were hugely popular. They were major stars and yet were also often at odds with the establishment. Gillespie was seen by some as a rather rough forward – his party piece was to barge into the goalkeeper (a technique still legal at the time but not necessarily in the spirit of the game) – while Turnbull was a strong-willed player with little regard for tradition. He played for enjoyment and the chance to succeed. Meredith was a national figure who was outspoken.

The media and public enjoyed Meredith's outbursts and his approach, but the FA was always uncertain.

After the 1904 Cup success the FA were keen to investigate to find out exactly how City had risen from no-hopers in 1894 to Cup winners and League contenders ten years later. Officials arrived at City's Hyde Road ground with a belief the Blues were making illegal payments. They left after finding some minor book-keeping irregularities but nothing too serious, that they would not have discovered at any other club at the time.

Sadly, a year after the FA Cup triumph, City's world fell apart when the FA took their opportunity to investigate again. The 1904-05 season saw the Blues challenging for the title again and on the very last day of the season City could have snatched the title from eventual winners Newcastle. The Blues' final match saw them needing a victory at Aston Villa. They lost 3-2 and ended the season third, two points behind Newcastle. Had they won they could potentially have taken the title on goal average.

The Villa game was full of incident and, unfortunately, gave the FA cause the excuse they needed to reopen their investigations. England international Alec Leake, the Villa captain, was allegedly offered £10 by Meredith to throw the game. Initially, Leake laughed at the suggestion when the FA approached him; but after another man from Birmingham came forward, Leake then claimed it was true – perhaps bearing in mind that it was the FA who picked the England side.

Strangely, however, the FA chose to selectively ignore certain other questionable aspects of the match. For example, City's Turnbull was, according to neutral journalists, dragged into the Villa dressing room after the game and was later thrown out with cuts and bruises.

Earlier, Villa's Leake had found Turnbull such a difficult player that he threw a handful of mud at him. Turnbull responded with a two-fingered gesture (highly controversial at the time!) and Leake then gave Turnbull a 'back-hander'. Yet the FA chose to focus on Turnbull's role and not Leake's.

City, along with other forward-looking northern sides, felt the FA's investigations were biased in favour of a side perceived as one of football's aristocratic clubs. The Football League supported City's attempts to gain justice. And, considering the alleged bribery and other incidents occurred during a League game, it seems strange that the League was not the body in control of the investigation.

Unfortunately, the FA arrived at Hyde Road shortly after the incident and studied City's accounts and other records like never before. Meredith was initially banned for the alleged bribe, but this was eclipsed when the full FA investigations were complete. The FA found that City had been making additional payments to their players for some time, and as a result they imposed sanctions which almost killed the club. Strangely, the FA had not noticed these issues in 1904 despite the problems allegedly predating that investigation. The manager, Tom Maley, and the City chairman were suspended from football *sine die;* two further directors were suspended for seven months, but the most

THE FOREST: Many thanks, old chap; by beating Bury you've kept me in first class company. You deserve the "pot." NEWCASTLE and EVERTON: We acknowledge your greatness. You can do us a good turn by beating Manchester City.

serious impact was on the playing squad. Seventeen players were suspended and fined. The entire squad that had finished as FA Cup winners in 1904 and narrowly missed out on the League championship two years running were banned.

Worse was to follow when significant pressure was placed on the Blues to transfer these players once their bans finished. Meredith, Turnbull and all the other stars were encouraged to join the then-poor relations at Manchester United. Mancunians argued that if Meredith and Co. had to quit City it was much better for them to join the Reds than to leave the area. Those players ultimately helped United to their first FA Cup win in 1909 and to the League Championship, while City were left to start again.

There is no doubt that the southern-based FA's investigations were totally unfair as far as Manchester was concerned. No other League side had ever suffered to such an extent regardless of tragedy or bans. How City managed to re-establish itself in the years that followed is amazing; but somehow they pulled it off. They also continued to be a hugely popular club and remained Manchester's best supported side, despite United's successes with our former players.

Definitely Maybe

For years it has been a release valve for City fans. Whenever the club failed to achieve what was expected, fans would walk away from the ground muttering, 'Typical City'. It prevented us from getting too frustrated with our players and managers. Over the years, some have suggested that the attitude has held the club back; but 'Typical City' encompasses our ability to expect the unexpected and actually works both ways: many times, the club has delivered far more than it ought have.

Games such as Bradford in 1989, Gillingham in 1999 and QPR in 2012 demonstrate both aspects of 'Typical City'. What should have been relatively simple games became incredibly difficult. And then, when all appeared lost, a miracle seemed to occur. Achieving promotion and League titles in this manner was 'Typical City', but then so was the 2017-18 season.

We all tend to remember the 'Typical City' defeats, but in 2017-18 the Blues' ability to break so many records and perform at such a high level was definitely 'Typical City'. Many media personalities had written City off as title contenders before the season started, so winning the Premier League in itself was perceived as being unlikely. Of course, Pep and most associated with City knew differently. But what more 'Typical City' way of winning the League is there than to break almost every record known, ensuring that those who had laughed at suggestions that City could dominate the League were left to eat their words?

Immediately after winning the League, I would have liked City to produce T-shirts detailing all the records with the final tag line, 'Typical City'. I think it is something we should now turn into a positive. Instead of focusing on our traditional cock-ups, let's focus on our greatest over-achievements.

Dropping to the third tier in the manner we did – a 5-2 win at Stoke in 1998 – was of course 'Typical City', but then so was achieving promotion two years in succession. Appointing a manager, Mercer, who had suffered a stroke and was still ill – especially with an assistant, Allison, who tended to 'go missing' for a few days – was 'Typical City'. But then so was winning the League title away at Newcastle on the last day of the season in 1968 when the trophy and the BBC were at Old Trafford expecting United to retain it.

Sacking a manager in November 1925 and not replacing him until the season was almost over was 'Typical City', but what followed was also unexpected – the

Blues clinch it in a blaze of glory

NEWCASTLE UTD... 3   MANCHESTER CITY 4

WHAT a magnificent match to decide a title! What a tremendous climax to a magnificent season as Manchester City waged a thrilling battle with Newcastle United in a game fit to grace Wembley

We're going up! Promotion celebrations at Bradford, 1989.

vice-chairman Albert Alexander took on managerial duties, guided City to a Wembley cup final via a thrilling FA Cup run that included a semi-final victory over United, and was responsible for one of the greatest derby performances when the Blues won a League game 6-1 at Old Trafford.

Finding the club without a fit goalkeeper for the 1949-50 season was a bit of a cock-up – and signing a Prisoner of War so soon after the hostilities was a major gamble. For that 'enemy' then to become a hero within weeks of his arrival was so 'Typical City'.

For me 'Typical City' will always be about expecting the unexpected. This approach stretches back almost to the beginning of the club. Many of the events surrounding the club's first successes can be seen as 'Typical City' in both its positive and negative contexts. Take for example the illegal payments scandal of 1905. City were no worse than many other major clubs but, in 'Typical City' style, they made it easy for the FA to uncover illegal payments above the maximum wage of £4. The bans imposed robbed City of a highly successful team, and many clubs would have crumbled. However, within 18 months of the bans being imposed and the club being ripped apart, those that were left plus their new manager and players were challenging for the title.

In 1959, *The Listener* magazine carried an article focusing on Manchester United, and claimed their fans "expected too much... It is out of this kind of expectation and certainty that there comes aggressive criticism, really vicious attacks on players." He added that United "often had to play against their own supporters, who become unwitting enemies."

In contrast, the author recognised that the Blues' ability to "win by a big margin, then lose the next by an equally big margin" created a different kind of fan at Maine Road. He claimed that City's crowd "is always hoping for victory but never really expecting to get it." He commented that supporters did not get angry in the way United fans of the period did, instead becoming 'resigned' to setbacks.

Obviously, a lot has changed since 1959 and the transition from struggling club in the late '90s to major European power by 2018 has seen a mood change. The humour and humility of fans may also change as time moves on.

However, we should never forget that 'Typical City' – or 'City-itis,' as Joe Royle termed it – has both negative and positive outcomes. It's part of our DNA, so let's hope the 2020s and beyond show the positive version of 'Typical City' more than the version we saw most in the '80s and late '90s.

Let's reclaim 'Typical City' as a positive comment every time we achieve major success or break a record!

Right Here, Right Now

This has been a record-breaking decade for the Blues, providing supporters born since 1976 with their first taste of major success and Champions League football. It has been an incredible period of top-flight, title-challenging stability and is, without doubt, the most successful decade in the club's long history – and it's not over yet!

In terms of trophy success, since the Blues won the FA Cup in 2011 no other English team has bettered City's haul. Chelsea have won as many major trophies and enjoyed trophy success as well, but since the start of 2010-11 the following are the most successful English League clubs:

Major Trophy Winners
7 – Manchester City (3 Premier League, 1 FA Cup & 3 League Cup) & Chelsea (1 Champions League, 1 Europa, 2 PL, 2 FAC & 1 LC).
5 – Manchester United (1 Europa, 2 PL 1 FAC & 1 LC).
3 – Arsenal (3 FAC).
1 – Leicester City (1 PL),

Wigan Athletic (1 FAC), Birmingham City (1 LC) & Liverpool (1 LC).

City have also finished every season (2009-10 to 2017-18) in the top three, apart from one (2015-16, when they finished fourth). No other team can match that record.

This decade forced the clock banner at Old Trafford, recording the years since City's last major success, to be taken down, and brought confidence that the Blues were a force to stay. It brought incredible success on the field but also saw great investment into the club's facilities to ensure that the Blues are a sustainable football club. The 2020s could see City reach new heights of success now that the foundations are in place.

Focusing exclusively on the years 2010 to 2018, City:
• Returned to trophy-winning ways at the 2011 FA Cup final, which had followed a tense but successful Manchester FA Cup semi-final derby at Wembley.
• Were managed by the following: Roberto Mancini (December 2009 to May 2013),

Manuel Pellegrini (June 2013 to June 2016) and Pep Guardiola (July 2016 to date).

• Ended the first season of the decade (2009-10) fifth in the Premier League and as League Cup semi-finalists.

• Finished 2010-11, Mancini's first full season, in third place, guaranteeing Champions League football. City also won the FA Cup at Wembley, beating Stoke City in the final.

• In 2011-12 City won the League for the first time since 1968 with a memorable final-day last-gasp goal from Sergio Agüero.

• The decade saw the building of the City Football Academy and other major investment in the region by the club's owner.

• Sister clubs were developed around the globe, including Melbourne City and New York City.

• A new badge was launched after the most in-depth consultation with supporters any club has ever experienced.

• City's average attendance exceeded 50,000 for the first time, following the expansion of the Etihad Stadium.

• In July 2018 City took their transfer record to a reported £60 million with the signing of Leicester City's Riyad Mahrez

• The 2017-18 season brought a multitude of records City's way. Many had been long-standing historical ones, while others were all-time Premier League landmarks. No other club had ever broken so many records in one season, or thrilled in this manner.

• Stars of the decade were plentiful. They include Vincent Kompany, Pablo Zabaleta, Carlos Tevez, Sergio Agüero, Yaya Touré, Edin Džeko, Nigel De Jong, Kevin De Bruyne, David Silva and Leroy Sané.

The 2010s was finally a decade which brought City back to a level of power within the game. No longer did people focus on City as a failing former giant. The Blues were once more recognised as a hugely successful club.

Blue Genes

Ever since the first reported St Mark's match, the parent-child relationship has been significant to the life of this football club. Support has passed through the generations with fathers and mothers encouraging their sons and daughters to support the Blues, and families can trace their 'City' family tree of support right back to the 1880s.

From a playing perspective, whenever a son of a famous father joins the club, the younger man is usually put under closer scrutiny than had his parents occupied any other occupation. Here at City there are many father-son connections, and three in particular that deserve remembering.

Sha-La-La-La Summerbee

England international Mike Summerbee remains one of City's biggest heroes. A star

side and was also the son of a professional footballer. Popular with fans and a great entertainer, he remains a City legend. By the early '90s much was being made of the third-generation Summerbee, Nicky. With his early career following a similar pattern to Mike's at Swindon Town, comparisons were being made prior to Nicky arriving at Maine Road in June 1994 for £1.5 million. The fee was considered high for the period, and inevitably Nicky was under closer scrutiny than perhaps he deserved.

An early indication came in a humorous moment at a pre-season friendly against Feyenoord at Maine Road shortly after his arrival in 1994. A City supporter wearing the most up-to-date home shirt sneaked on to the pitch while play was in progress.

during the '60s and '70s, Mike was a key member of our greatest

Nicky had the ball but had not noticed the fan who, by this point was calling for the ball with his hand up. Nicky then saw the blue shirt, made a move to pass but stopped when he realised it was a pitch

invader. At that point play stopped, fans had a laugh, and then a voice called out from the Main Stand: "His dad would have passed it to the fan and turned it into a bit of a show!"

Although the comment was humorous and perhaps true – you can imagine Mike involving the fan, after all it was only a meaningless friendly – but it did indicate that Nicky would only ever be compared to one of City's most popular players.

Nicky went on to impress, but it was difficult at times. Ultimately he moved on to Sunderland after 119 League appearances. Looking back on his time, Nick told me in 2015 about his move to Maine Road: "There were other clubs interested in me, but once I knew City were keen then there was only one place I wanted to go. Regardless of how it went, I'd do it all again if I had my time again. I loved City and wanted to play there. It was a major honour and some of those players like Niall Quinn and Georgi Kinkladze were phenomenal. If ever I was criticised, I used that to spur myself on."

Barnes Storming

Twenty years before Nicky's arrival at City, another son of a FA Cup-winning City player was under the spotlight. Peter Barnes, together with his brothers Keith and Michael, appeared to be exciting young talent. Peter had been watched by the club since boyhood. His father Ken was one of the stars of the '50s. A hugely popular player, like Mike Summerbee, Ken was a major hero and truly great player. After Ken's playing career came to an end he ultimately became a member of Joe Mercer's backroom staff and, by the time his son Peter was ready to sign for a League team, Ken was in a position where he could influence the decision. However – and this is a very significant

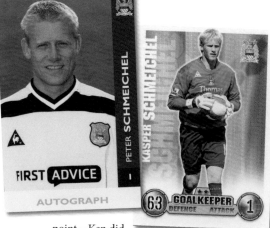

point – Ken did not want anyone, let alone his son, to be given preferential treatment. They had to be good enough, so Ken never pushed. Instead Peter went for trials at Leeds United (managed by another '50s City star, Don Revie), and almost signed. Fortunately for the Blues, other members of City's staff, most notably Johnny Hart, recognised the dilemma. Peter was ultimately signed on not because of family influence, but because he was 'more than' good enough. He had to prove himself more than others.

Within a short period of time, Peter proved he was another star, and in 1976 at the age of 18 he scored the first goal in the League Cup final. That season he became the first City youngster to collect the PFA Young Player of the Year award. In fact it wasn't until 2018 before another City player – Leroy Sané – equalled the feat, demonstrating the quality of Peter during his Maine Road days.

Peter went on to play 22 games

for England and score four international goals; but only three years after his League Cup final success he was sold to West Bromwich Albion. Supporters hated his departure and it is clear that Peter himself never wanted to leave. I interviewed him a few years ago, and he commented: "I remember a few months earlier thinking how great the club was. We'd beaten AC Milan and were doing well in Europe. We had a great side containing internationals Corrigan, Watson, Channon, Kidd, Hartford, Donachie, Bell, Deyna and me, and then all of a sudden it changed. One day I walked into the main entrance at the ground and saw Ron Atkinson waiting. I couldn't understand why he was there. 'Surely, we're not selling a player,' I thought. Then I heard Gary Owen was off to West Brom. I was shocked. Six weeks later, I was on my way there as well. Regardless of how things went at West Brom, this was such a major disappointment. I couldn't work out why I wasn't wanted."

Barnes was still in the early stages of his career and had a lot to offer. He should not have been sold. After spells at various clubs, including Manchester United, Peter returned to City in 1987 and today remains a popular presence on matchday.

Peter and Ken are the only father and son to both win major honours at City.

Schmeichel & Son

The third father-and-son City players to consider are 2002-03 goalkeeper Peter Schmeichel and his son Kasper. Peter helped City achieve consistency during Maine Road's last season (incidentally, his last clean sheet was the City-Sunderland game on 21 April 2003 – Maine Road's last City victory), and his son Kasper also

started out on his career with City.

Peter was a hugely successful goalkeeper and inevitably Kasper drew comparisons. His League debut came for City against West Ham in August 2007, and later that month he kept a clean sheet as the Blues beat United, so closely associated with his father, 1-0. Loan spells dominated his time at City and, once Joe Hart became established as City's number one, it seemed Kasper's opportunities would be limited. The arrival of Shay Given caused him to drop down the pecking order and he eventually left in August 2009. Since then, he has became a Premier League winner with Leicester City, and played brilliantly for Denmark in the 2018 World Cup.

Family Matters

Inevitably, there have been other father-son connections at City:

Beastow – William was one of the founders of St Mark's Church side in 1880 and his two sons played in the first reported match.

Bond – John was manager between 1980 and 1983 and he signed his son Kevin in September 1981.

Broad – Jimmy was City's trainer from more or less the beginning of the club through to the 1920s, and his sons became players. The more famous son, Tommy, was a star between 1915-1921.

Docherty – Tommy was United's manager when his son Michael played in two Manchester derbies for City.

Hart – Hall of Fame Lifetime Achievement inductee Johnny was a great '50s star and '60s/'70s coach. His sons Nigel and Paul both became League players, and Paul went on to a managerial career, most notably at Nottingham Forest.

Herd – Alec was a City FA Cup winner in 1934, and a major force in our 1937

1937 League Championship victory. His son David found success at United, but spent his early life living on Maine Road in one of the club's houses. The pair played alongside each other for Stockport County.

Meredith – The first City superstar, Billy, became father-in-law to '20s City man Charlie Pringle. They first played alongside each other for City in 1922, and the following season Pringle played in 49-year-old Meredith's last game, the FA Cup semi-final v Newcastle.

Oakes – Alan is City's record appearance holder, and his son Michael was a goalkeeper with Aston Villa and Wolves. Alan is also the cousin of City's youngest ever player, Glyn Pardoe, who is in turn now related to another '60s/'70s hero Mike Doyle (whose son married Pardoe's daughter, and Pardoe and Doyle now have a grandson). Both Pardoe and Doyle were grandparents to City's Tommy Doyle.

Wright-Phillips – Bradley is the son of former England international Ian Wright, and also the brother of City hero, Shaun.

Son of My Father: City's Michael Docherty runs rings round his old man, United boss Tommy.

Year Zero Exclusive

It is a thorny and often incorrectly reported subject, but generations of fans have often wanted to pick a name to celebrate as the original founder of the club. If we are talking about Manchester City, we can clearly state that Joshua Parlby was the driving force back in 1894. He established its identity, its colours and its aims. Athough he may not have originated the name or the idea for the club, he established the Manchester City we know today.

Before 1894 the club underwent many changes and there is still a significant amount of information that we simply do not know. We may never know some of the key moves in the 1870s and 1880s simply because records may not contain that material. I have been searching since the mid '80s for information on the club's history

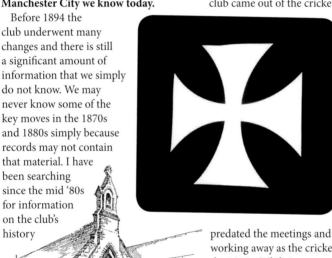

and have managed to identify a great deal, but the question of who formed the club as St Mark's (West Gorton) remains a mystery. In the mid 2000s it seemed the answer was the Rector's daughter, Anna Connell, but this now appears a complete red herring. Based on the knowledge that she created meetings for the Working Men of the parish in 1879, it was assumed that the church's cricket club evolved out of those meetings and that the football club came out of the cricket team. Early histories talk of the cricketers deciding to play football, and this was always important to the chronology. But research performed by 2010 proved that the cricket club predated the meetings and that Anna was working away as the cricket club grew in the 1870s. While it was an attractive story, the Anna Connell version appears to be no more than a myth.

Research I have performed in recent years is getting close to the answer and here, for the first time in a City publication, I have some information which adds to our understanding of how the club was established. This is based on contemporary material and interviews performed in the '20s and '40s with people who were there at the time of the club's formation as St Mark's.

A cricket team had been established by St Mark's during the 1860s, which by the late 1870s had proved relatively successful and possessed multiple teams. At some point during the late 1870s or early in 1880, someone suggested that the church develop footballing activities, establishing both association football and rugby teams. By the autumn of 1880 both sports had been so well received by the boys and young men of the parish that games were arranged. The first reported games for both sports occurred in November 1880, but it was only the football team that developed. Several players, most notably Walter Chew, remained active in the sport into the 1940s.

Hulme-born Chew, who was interviewed about the formation of the club by the BBC in the 1940s, has been regarded as the father of City in numerous books, tributes and records over the years, and has been perceived by some as the founder of St Mark's (West Gorton). However, Chew was only about 15 at the time.

In an interview discovered in 2017 but originally performed in 1922, Chew himself outlined that it was his older brother, William, along with some of his friends, who was the real founder of the club. He explained that the older boys founded the St Mark's team and that they played at Farmer's Field in West Gorton. One of the older boys, William Sumner, is believed to have been the club's first captain and his arrival in

Founding fathers. Well, brothers, at any rate. Walter (inset) and William Chew, pictured in later life.

Mr. W. Chew.

West Gorton around 1879 coincides with St Mark's move into both forms of football. He was an engineering student lodging in Gorton and was also a member of the St Mark's cricket club, though Walter did not name Sumner in his 1920s interview.

As Chew outlined, St Mark's first pitch was Farmer's Field, close to Thomas Street,

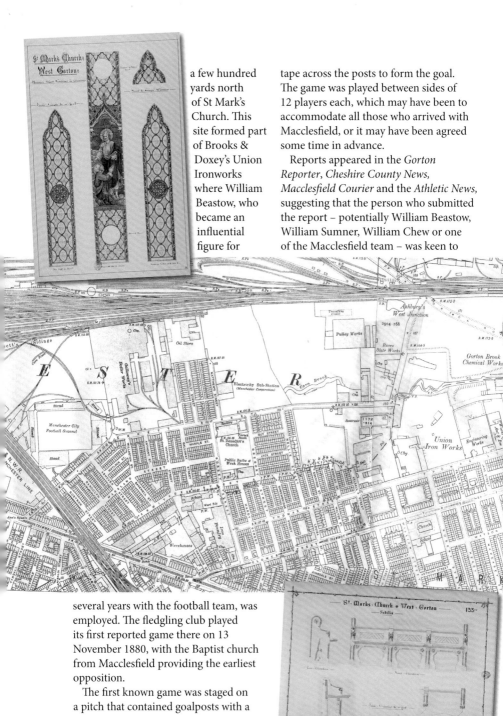

a few hundred yards north of St Mark's Church. This site formed part of Brooks & Doxey's Union Ironworks where William Beastow, who became an influential figure for

tape across the posts to form the goal. The game was played between sides of 12 players each, which may have been to accommodate all those who arrived with Macclesfield, or it may have been agreed some time in advance.

Reports appeared in the *Gorton Reporter*, *Cheshire County News*, *Macclesfield Courier* and the *Athletic News*, suggesting that the person who submitted the report – potentially William Beastow, William Sumner, William Chew or one of the Macclesfield team – was keen to

several years with the football team, was employed. The fledgling club played its first reported game there on 13 November 1880, with the Baptist church from Macclesfield providing the earliest opposition.

The first known game was staged on a pitch that contained goalposts with a highlight the game. At no point do the reports state this was the club's first game. It ended in a 2-1 defeat, staged at 3.15pm.

Those writing about City's birth have assumed Walter Chew was the more enthusiastic footballer in the household, but it appears he has often been credited with his brother's appearances. Contemporary reports only provide surnames and occasional initials. Reports of the earliest known game include W. Chew as a player and, if Walter's later comments on the club's formation are accurate, then this was most likely William Chew, his elder brother, who was aged 18 at the time.

The first known match report in existence showing both Chews in the line-up dates from October 1881. That may well have been Walter's first appearance for St Mark's as he admitted that his own role in Manchester City's history was limited to the later founding of another club, Belle Vue Rangers, in 1881-82.

Walter was the captain of that club, and some of their games were played at the same time that W. Chew appeared in St Mark's fixtures. This leads to the inevitable conclusion that mentions of W. Chew playing for St Mark's during its formative seasons, prior to its merger with Belle Vue, referred to William H. Chew and not Walter Chew.

In 1883, Belle Vue Rangers merged with West Gorton AFC (the successor to St Mark's) to establish a stronger West Gorton club. Walter had played for both clubs and is believed to have played a prominent role, going on to become a driving force behind the newly merged organisation.

So when the question of who founded the club is asked, it is important that we all recognise that without specific contemporary evidence, everything is educated guesswork. In the last 20 years the quest to find a 'founder' has led to inaccurate assumptions and reporting. The Anna Connell story blew up out of all proportion and it is highly possible that the same could occur with Walter Chew's view that it was William and his friends that started the club.

Given that Walter's testimony is the only evidence ever presented by someone who was there at the time, I personally think his story demonstrates it was the boys themselves who created the club. They may have been empowered by the Connells and by William Beastow – an influential figure across the parish and at the ironworks – but it seems it was actually them all along. This corresponds with early club histories and newspaper articles. As does the site of the first game, Farmer's Field, next door to the ironworks where many of the boys and young men worked.

Over the years, there have been calls by some to erect statues of the club's founder; but surely we would be foolish to erect anything connected with a specific name. If there were ever a monument to mark the club's foundation, it should simply be boys playing football, or even a football itself.

The formation of the club was never about an individual, but about building a team spirit.

After 140 years, it is great to see the same ideals still upheld by this great club of ours, continuing to serve and represent our modern-day community.

Mapping City's past: Farmer's Field was next to the Union Ironworks. Note St Mark's Church on Clowes Street.

the first half, and their opponents scored their three goals before ends were changed. It was not until near the end of the game that Great Lever were able to score their first and only goal. M'Quisk played splendidly for Hurst.

MACCLESFIELD BAPTISTS v. ST. MARK'S, WEST GORTON.—This Association football match was played on the ground of the latter, on Saturday, with the following result: Baptists, two goals; St. Mark's, one goal.

ST. PETER'S ATHLETIC (2nd) v. ST. PETER'S (Everton).—Played on Saturday last on the ground of the former, Stanley Park. After playing about twenty-five minutes the Athletic scored a goal, which the visitors disputed, and declined to play out the game, although the captain of the home team gave way.

ST. PETER'S ATHLETIC v. ST. MARY'S (Kirkdale). This Association match was played on Saturday last, on the ground of the latter (Stanley Park), and, after a fast and exciting game, ended in a draw, neither side being able to score. St. Peter's Team:—Nelson, goal; Robertson and Connolly, backs; Marr and Smith,

Ruining Football?

Back in 2009 I wrote *The Big Book of City,* and ended it with a final commentary on the reaction to City's owners. The book came out a year after the Abu Dhabi takeover had occurred, and I talked of the media comments and gave my own view as to what City was experiencing. I also commented on what I felt would happen in the years that would follow. We are now ten years on from the takeover and nine years after my 'final word,' so it is an appropriate time to review that piece.

I started by saying, "Some areas of the media and, indeed, many fans of today's so-called Big Four talked of these moves by the Blues as being bad for the game. They also claimed that City had 'no history.'"

I quoted the words of Stale Solbakken, the Copenhagen coach: "They are creating too big a mental distance between what we call reality and then Manchester City. The hardest part for City is that they, by tradition, are not a big club and therefore all the money in the world does not make a difference."

The piece also highlighted UEFA President Michel Platini's criticism: "One club, which had suddenly become very rich, made various astronomical bids in the transfer market. Of course, there was a tremendous outcry in the football family, people called it outrageous and scandalous."

This was all within a year of the takeover, and none of those involved had seen or heard the plans that were coming out of Manchester. I had, or at least, I'd seen and heard some of them. To me, it was fairly obvious that the purchasing of players was a necessity rather than a luxury and was a result of years of under-investment

in the club. City in 1970 was a major, profitable club and was achieving success on a European stage. Twenty years later the club was in debt and was downscaling year on year.

Back in 2009 I compared City's spending with that of Real Madrid, who had spent around £90 million on Cristiano Ronaldo that summer. I pointed out that Real Madrid were significantly more responsible for inflating fees than any other European club and recalled that, "in 2000 they paid a reported £37 million world record for Luis Figo; in 2001 they increased the record by around £9 million for Zidane; in 2009 they bought Kaka for another record fee of around £56 million before their purchase of Ronaldo."

I went on to consider trophy success which, to be truthful, is what Platini et al meant when they talked of 'no history'. I explained that while it was true that City had won fewer major trophies than the so-called Big Four, this had not always been the case. For example, Chelsea had only surpassed City's significant trophy haul in 2005. I added that City first found major success in 1904 by winning the FA Cup (and they also came close to making this a Double success by finishing runners-up in the League) – 51 years before Chelsea's first major success, 26 years before Arsenal's and four years before United's. I also highlighted that the Blues won a major

European trophy before Liverpool, Chelsea and Arsenal, and only two years after United (during a season, 1967-68, which also saw City win the League). It should be noted that City's European success came seven years before Platini's former team Juventus first found European glory.

My article talked of attendance comparisons, wages and much more, but I also commented that the supporters of many other clubs, outside the so-called Big Four of the period, had been supportive. That is beginning to change now, but there

spending power, experience and so on. Rather than City's transformation being bad for the game as a whole, it seemed more likely that the Blues' ability to challenge for the Premier League would open up the game for others.

are still many fans of clubs such as West Ham who understand how we feel and recognise we had a history to be proud of before the money. We were the lucky ones, but that was built on almost three decades of misery – or at least under-performance and under-investment.

2009 was still a time when City hadn't started to challenge, though clubs such as Liverpool, United, Chelsea and Arsenal must have been a little nervous. I said at the time that fans of sides outside of the so-called Big Four were keen to see the game change, wanting all teams to stand a chance of success; though they recognised that the game was no longer as open as perhaps it was in the '70s or '80s. I suggested that if City could challenge the so-called Big Four then it would be possible for others to gain along the way. I think this has happened with Tottenham being brought into the mix.

I added that City's investment could lead to five or six teams challenging for the top four places, and that it would be possible for those sides to each take points off the others, meaning that a seventh or eighth team could also be brought into contention simply by the fact that more points are lost by those with the larger squads, better

I suggested that greater competition for the top four places could increase the likelihood of a tighter finish to the season and, inevitably, more opportunity for other clubs to benefit. I didn't realise exactly how tight the 2012 season would be of, course, nor did I foresee the record-breaking achievements of 2017-18.

Ten years on from City's investment, it is clear that European qualification is no longer limited to the same four teams, while Leicester's Premier League success the other year is an indication that no longer can the same old four teams carve up the trophies between them. City's investment has proved good for football – look at the number of players improved by Pep and how some of them helped England during World Cup 2018 – while the figures paid during the early years of the takeover now look like absolute bargains. Football clubs can be accused of a lot of things but to suggest that City are 'ruining football' is ludicrous. The Blues did not start the spending – back in 1989 Ferguson's United was the most expensive team ever assembled in Britain – but because they have opened up the competition and limited the opportunities for ongoing success of those that grew to prominence in the '90s and 2000s, they have received criticism. English football is no longer dominated by four clubs.

It should also be remembered that much of the criticism City received back in 2008 and over the years that followed is based on the club having 'bought success'. Well, so has almost every team that has ever been successful! Way back in the 1880s, Preston North End became a prominent club due to the work of William Sudell who brought players to England from Scotland, offering them jobs at local employers among other inducements. His talented team of imports won the first League title and there are many similar examples that have followed.

The difference between City and some of the other clubs that have been successful after buying expensive players is that the club has also invested heavily into its Academy set-up. The investment the Blues have made into youth and community football dwarfs the rest. Ultimately, the City Football Academy will help young players progress and find success. That has been part of the vision since day one and, at some point in the future, anyone commenting on the development of football will recognise that City's 2008 strategy was simple:

• To buy players to enable the club to compete at the highest level as quickly as possible.
• To build facilities and invest in people to create a sustainable football club which produces its own talented young players.

A decade on, and City have achieved incredible success; but they have also established an enviable platform for long-term progress. The future looks bright.

MCFC Honours

Founded

Earliest Known Game: 13 November 1880. St Mark's (West Gorton) v Baptist Church (Macclesfield).

The specific formation date of St Mark's Football Club is unknown and it may be that the church played several unreported games before November 1880, possibly in the late 1870s. After a series of moves, a merger and various name changes the club became a more ambitious entity by 1884.

1884 – Founded as Gorton AFC.
1887 – Relaunched as Ardwick AFC.
1894 – Manchester City AFC established.

Europe

European Cup Winners' Cup Winners: 1970.
First European Cup game: 1968.
First European Cup Winners' Cup game: 1969.
First UEFA Cup game: 1972.

First League game: 1892 (As Ardwick) & 1894 (as City).
First top-flight game: 1899.

National Domestic Cups

FA Cup Winners: 1904, 1934, 1956, 1969. & 2011. Runners-up: 1926, 1933, 1955, 1981 & 2013.
League Cup Winners: 1970, 1976, 2014, 2016 & 2018. Runners-up: 1974.
Community Shield/Charity Shield Winners: 1937, 1968, 1972, 2012 & 2018.
Runners-up: 1934, 1956, 1969, 1970, 1973, 2011 & 2014.
Full Members' Cup Runners-up: 1986.

Women's Football

Founded

The women's team was established as an initiative via City in the Community.
1988 – Manchester City Ladies FC.
2014 – Relaunched as Manchester City Women FC.

Women's National Competition

Women's Super League Winners: 2016.
Runners-up: 2015 & 2018.
FA Women's Premier League Northern Division Winners: 2012.
FA Women's Cup Winners: 2017.
FA WSL Continental Cup Winners: 2014 & 2016.
Runners-up: 2018.

MANCHESTER CITY 1970 League Cup Winners

League

Premier League/League Championship Winners: 1937, 1968, 2012, 2014 & 2018.
Runners-up: 1904, 1921, 1977, 2013 & 2015.
Division One/'old' Second Division Winners: 1899, 1903, 1910, 1928, 1947, 1966 & 2002.

THE AUTHOR

Gary James has been researching and writing about the Blues for over 30 years, and has written several landmark publications on both City and on Manchester football in general. A City fan since birth, and a season-ticket holder since the age of 16, Gary cares deeply about ensuring City's history is given the recognition it deserves.

His first City book was published in 1989, with his highly acclaimed *Football With A Smile: The Authorised Biography of Joe Mercer, OBE* following in 1993 (updated 2010). His other works include: *Manchester – A Football History, Manchester The Greatest City, The Big Book of City, Farewell to Maine Road, The Pride of Manchester, Manchester City The Complete Record* and *Manchester The City Years.*

Gary has been a regular contributor to the City programme since 1994, and is now recognised as a leading expert on Mancunian football history. In recent years he has written for publications as diverse as the FA Cup final programme, the Women's FA Cup final programme, The Oxford Dictionary of National Biography, *The Times, The Author, When Saturday Comes* and the *Manchester Evening News.*

He is the founder and organiser of the International Football History Conference.

Follow Gary on twitter: @garyjameswriter or facebook.com/garyjames4

CREDITS & ACKNOWLEDGMENTS

Over the years, so many people have contributed to the success of my books that it would be difficult to recognise all here. So first of all a big 'thanks' to every City fan, writer, photographer and historian I've met and discussed the Blues with over the decades. In terms of this specific book I'd like to thank Derek Hammond and Gary Silke who have performed an excellent job on its design, layout, editing and all-round production. I've been impressed with their work over the years and so when the opportunity came to produce this book I leapt at the chance.

Next, thanks to all those who have provided photographs, memorabilia and other support including Noel Bayley, Frank Borson, Garry Cook, Alex Dowd, Edward Garvey, Phill Gatenby, Peter Godkin, Victoria Haydn, Brian Houghton, Anna James, Colin Johnson, Alan Jubb, Mike Kelly, Mark Kennedy, Vicky Kloss, Iain McCartney, Malcolm McAlpine, Will McTaggart, Brian Marwood, David Masey, Glen Midgley, David Miller, David Mooney, Tommy Muir, Kevin Parker, Geri Parlby, David Powter, James H Reeve, Stephanie Alder, Stuart Renshaw, Steve Rigby, Colin Savage, David Scally, Ken Smallwood, Tor Sønsteby, Jon Stemp, Graeme Thompson, Richard Tucker, Ric Turner, Dave & Sue Wallace, Cros Ward and Steve Worthington.

Special thanks also to all the journalists, photographers and officials who have helped chronicle the club over the years – plus, of course, a special thanks to Manchester City Football Club and its staff for their support.

TEAMWORK

Grateful thanks to everyone who subscribed to
Manchester City Folklore...

Sarah Scott, Rochdale
Chris O'Donnell, Chorlton
Halvor Hansen Hoevring, Norway
Mark Poyzer, Melton Mowbray
Anthony Preston, Stockport
Eric Heaton, Ilkley | Daniel Yates, Holmfirth
Brian Wainwright, Bury
Christopher Fallon, Stockport
Colin McNeillie, Durham
Steve Bowley, Cork | David Jones, Stockport
Ray Barlow, Blackpool
Tommy Davin, Galway
Pavlos Nousdilis, Drama, Greece
Steve Mee, Dublin
Michael Sorensen, London
David Millington, Manchester
Marie O'Rourke, Waterford
Mike Taylor, Bishop's Stortford
Jimmy McElroy, Galway
Andrew Wilson, Stockport
Michael Andersen, Copenhagen
Alan Richardson, Stockport
Tor Olav Lien, Oslo
David Glynn Hall, Chorley
Graham Anthony Hall, Chorley
Alfie Yates, Altrincham
Gary Weightman, Isle of Man
Bill Whistance, Southampton
Gary Sullivan, Framingham Earl
Kevin Duffy, Chadderton
Martin McNeil, New South Wales
Chris Morris, Castlefield | Ben King, Bolton
Dave Coop, Oldham
John Jepson, British Columbia
Graham & Siobhan Brine, Stockport
Tony Edgar, Isle of Man
River Starkey William Taylor, Rochdale

Rudolph Gatt, Malta
Michael Broome, South Australia
Nigel Rothband, Stanmore
Andrew Winterbotham, Dymock
Steve Nicklin, Romiley | Prodip Mitra, Ontario
John Stanhope, Chorlton
John McCarthy, Limerick
Ray Cosgrove, Rochdale
Alan Rainford, Marple | Paul Diggett, Cheadle
Terry Casey, Carnforth | Stephen Rigby, Sale
Paschal Ryan, Kilkenny
Jeremy Poynton, Mells
Mark Chidgey, Epsom
Mike Cooke, Harrogate
Mark Thompson, Hadfield
David Arthur, Chapeltown
Michael Linder, Alabama
Kalle Hållfast, Turku, Finland
Paul Hodkinson, Holmes Chapel
Robert Tyler, Weston-super-Mare
Roger Reade, Doncaster
Samuel Mulvaney, Leeds
Maxwell McLean, Shipley
Paul Roberts, Manchester
Steve Johnson, Heywood
Markus Lehikoinen, Turku, Finland
Adrian Love, Tonbridge
Tommy Muir, Cheadle Branch
Struan Malcolm, Stockholm
Shawn Siemens, Saskatchewan
Nurulamin Wan Hussin, Malaysia
Dario Iain Frith Alonso, Glossop
John Roughton, Hereford
Paul Renard, Laxey, Isle of Man
Dave Clapham, Ramsbottom
Brian Whitehouse, Shirley
Alan Arenson, New York - from South Africa
Joe Dodd, Cavan | David Butler, Pilling
Joe McAndrew, Lincoln
Helen Wiles, Boothstown
Rafael Alcaraz Barrera, Mexico

Christian Galdencio, Charlottesville

Charles Philip Taylor, Longeves, France

Robbie Meadows, Winsford

Phil Goldstone, Leeds

Stephen Jones, Bolton

Neil Keyworth, Mirfield

Michael Carty, Galway

Dorothy Burgoine, Hyde

Gabriel Ernest Danby, Timperley

Mark Kenyon, Abu Dhabi

Luke Lodge, Ossett

Jonah Greve de Lange, Oslo

Mike Jackson-Leafield, Hyde

Neil, Jennifer and Lily Mather, Cheadle Hulme

David Price, Rotherham

Robert Meehan, Stockport

Mark Swainson, Hyde

Simon Lyons, Woodford

Paul Lyons, Los Angeles

Charles Tate, Goostrey | Franklyn Tate

Andrew Booth, Dukinfield

Paul Hodge, Warrington | Charlie Hodge

Peter McNally, Littleborough

Damien Gillan, Newry | Tony Ostell, Oldham

Ray Stanley, Macclesfield

Karen Lee, Scunthorpe

Karl McClellan, Manchester

David Kilpatrick, Dobbs Ferry, New York

Martyn Hansen | Mike Carroll, Baguley

Colm Croughan, Athlone

David Coe | Michael Coe | George Coe

Sem Lima, Aalgaard, Norway

Ray Houldsworth, West Didsbury

Joseph Carroll, Cork | Syahminan Suut, Sale

Mark & Stephen Lunn, Northern Ireland

Chris Airey, Cheadle Hulme

Gary Moore, Rowley Regis

Mike Bagshaw, Skelmersdale

Donal McMullin, Donegal

John Fennell, Audenshaw

Kevin & Shirley Hughes, Rochdale

Mike Long, Seoul

Carl Waring, Bishops Stortford

Ben Corrie, Manchester

Mike Thomas, Newton Abbot

John 'Sacko' Saxon, Bolton

Petra Manker, Germany

Scott Wood, Belper | Paul Holt, Tameside

Tim Willitts, Lytham St Annes

Rik Clews, Trowbridge

Andrew Heydeman, Bury

Jonathan Lace, Leeds

Louis Lace | Martin Lace

Paul Andrew Cooper, Stockport

Paul Graham Cooper, Stockport

Léo Gaillard, Coulounieix-Chamiers, France

Jeff Wilton | Adam Purdue, Manchester

Stephen Barlow, Nunthorpe

Alex Barlow | Emma Barlow

The May Family Team, Clitheroe

Brendan Duffy | Phil Wilson, Stalybridge

Trevor Stavert, Preesall

David Moses Seitler, Oxford

Jonathan Seitler, London via Manchester

Michael Horrocks, Heywood

K Fairhurst, Altrincham

James Parkinson, London | Ian Parkinson

Simon, Becky, Jake & Ethan Atherton, London

Frank & Lynne Upton, Northampton

Andrew & Matthew Appleby, Manchester

Chris Hughes, Levenshulme

Mark Freeman, Salisbury

Pete Farrow, Blackpool

Lesley Ross, Stockport

Simon Wilkinson, Stoke-on-Trent

Nicola Butterworth, Prestatyn

Paul McConnell, Heywood

Zachary Bougen, Honiton

Gareth Williams, Nuneaton

Liz Megan Williams

Matt Bewley, Leeds | Paul Risby, Fitton Hill

Patrick Crooks, Church of MCFC, Leyland

John Baker, Warrington

Juha Birkman, Tampere, Finland

Michael Slade, Yeovil | Toivo Saksala, Helsinki

Chris Delaney, St Helens

Anthony Long, County Durham

Øystein Wolf, Nesoddtangen, Norway

Paul Hughes, Horsens, Denmark

Adam Howarth, Rochdale

Antony David Davies, Shrewsbury

Brian Lowndes, Irlam | Chloe Ryding, Preston

Sam Gibson, Huddersfield

Alan Booth, Stockport | Dave Halliwell

Justin Stade, Parker, Colorado

Peter Dillon, Stockport | Jessica Visco, Sale

Francis John Hoffman | Les McDonald, Bury

Chris Palmer, Tottington

Petri Riuttala, Nummi, Finland

Ken Crampton, Hythe | Mike Gill, Audenshaw

Lloyd Howson, Shermanbury

Stewart Scull, Ellesmere

Alice Newton-Galtress | Greg Heaton, Hitchin

Paul Jones, Littleborough

David Moore, Hollingworth

Daniel Donohue, East Didsbury

Tony Rowan - Never Forgotten

Gordon Hyslop, Cheadle

Howard Makin, Liverpool

In memory of Colin Wright

Tony MacManus, Bray | Mark Snow, Quebec

Steve McGill, Barnsley | Mark Pilling, Chester

Simon, Tina, Katie & Jess Mullock, Radcliffe

Mark Hewitt, Barnsley | Chris Bell, London

Peter Brophy, Altrincham

Matthew Lewis, Oldham | Phil Conway, Neath

Dr Richard Wild, Bournemouth

Mark Garrett, Dublin | David Nolan Whitefield

Howard McCarthy - aka Howie de Blue

Paul Wilson, Hadfield | Martin Kelly, Urmston

The Worthingtons - CTWD

Alan G Jackson, Failsworth

Ben Ward, Norton juxta Twycross

Paul Zamojskyj, Prestwich

Dave Miller, Stockport | Chris Thyer, York

Chris Shenton, Cheshire

Craig Atkinson, Preston | Jakob Lilia, Norway

Jess Trimble 2011 RIP

Nigel Gregory, Macclesfield

Russell Askew, Ashton-under-Lyne

Stephen Prescott, Atherton

Richard Mullen, Ellon | Dan Jenkins

Jill Scull, Cheadle | Joe Sunderland, Calne

Neil Eaves, Harpenden | Ian Carter, Hyde

Dan Eaves, Atlanta, GA

Johnny Doak, Newtownabbey

Akio Fernandes, Goa, India - die-hard Cityzen

Kevin Duffy, Buckingham

Kylie Duffy, Silverstone

Jo & Thierry de Magneval, France

Bill Chapman, New South Wales

Martin Cook, Rotherham

Nicola Williams, Didsbury

Andrew Zuill, Amesbury | Jacob Hyde, Bury

Ann & John Platt, Failsworth

Ron Heald, made his family blue

Ken Doodson, Rochdale

Archie Lockwood, Glossop

Graham Birch, Wainfleet

Alun Jones, Newtown | Cliff Nolan, Middleton

Donald Lowndes Sanderson, Doncaster

Daniel Burgess, Altrincham

Omar Jasper, Manchester | Jonathan Savage

Nick Kirkland, Macclesfield

Dave Stack, Wilmslow | Phil Mutch, Timperley

Alan (Eddie) Booth, Stockport

Mitch & Julie Booth, Buford, GA

Peter Wilson, Hereford

Jon Dyster, St Albans

Cathy Dyster | Peter Birbeck

Owen William Leaper

Steve Clough, Stalybridge

Mark Pemberton, Glasgow

John Weston, Blackpool

Phil Shields, Stockport

Mike Wilson, Stockport

Joe & Amy Gregory, Chadderton

Jacqui McOsker, Kansas City

Pete Higgins, Torquay | Andy Clarke, Gatley

Scott Game, Leighton Buzzard

Keith Gooch, Cranleigh

Peter Wilhelmsson, Vedevag, Sweden

Vivienne Roberts, Dublin

Martin Lawlor, Middleton | Mike Robertson

Sean Riley, Chadderton

Darren Clarke, Great Yarmouth

Mark Coles 'Colesy', Queensland

Gary Dickson, Sheffield | Dave Cathcart, Sale

Kevin Greaves, Barnard Castle

Harald Larsen, Aakrehamn, Norway

Tony Ostell, Chadderton | Alex Edwards

Wayne Sutherland, Denton

David Walker, Sharston

Carl Lane, Manchester | Joy Jones, Llanwrst

Kyle Lewis, Plymouth | Steven Cumbo, Bolton

Frank Fitzmaurice - a Reddish Blue

Lee Withington, Stockport

Neville Gardner, Rochdale

Chris Acheson, Thornton-Cleveleys

Matt Downen, Moline, IL

Stu Hargreaves, Stalybridge

Paul Manuel Bangor, Northern Ireland

Barry Maclennan, Inverness

Patrick Gormley, Tipperary

Gareth Hamer, Bury | Kyle Clarke, Newport

Pete Jordan, Hazel Grove

Alan Harmer, Worthing

Richard Donlan, Hazel Grove

Mark Taylor, Rochdale

Andy Taylor | Alan Dodd

Michael O'Meara - Not Really Here Since 1965

Brian Hardman, Cheadle Hulme

Michael Parker, Cheadle

Clive Gwilliam, Newquay

Louise Fort, Bolton

Stuart Frankland, Swinton

Tom Casey, Manchester | Rob Casey

Jens Bager Vang, Denmark

Garry Haines, Worcester

Mike Buckley, Ashton-on-Mersey

Per Arne Rennestraum, Porsgrunn, Norway

Kyle Clarke, Newport | Daniel Dwan

Frode Knapstad, Bergen, Norway

Sandra Hampson, Norwalk, CT

Rhys Rowlands, Shrewsbury

Terry Speakman - True Blue, Ramsbottom

Wayne Eddie Norris, Gold Coast, Australia

Sean & Jane Riley, Chadderton

Paul Grogan, Middleton | Julie Brannan

Andy Ledward, Ashton Under Lyne

Jamie O'Keeffe, New South Wales

Geoff Wilkinson, Hartlepool

Paul Fiano Fernandez, Helensburgh

Ron Fletcher, Torquay | Matt Cunliffe, Surbiton

Dave Mooney, Manchester

Graham Smith, Nantwich | Ben Cunliffe, Shaw

Mark McCarthy, Donegal | Sem Lima, Norway

Marcin Plucinski, Bamber Bridge

Jason Henshall 'The Snapper'

Dr Anthony Bristow, Macclesfield

Daniel Hammond, Prestatyn

Andy Hill - Blue in Bandit Country, Flixton

David Billings, Ashton-under-Lyne

Steve Rawlings, Eyam | Ziggy Rawlings

Kevin Cummins, London

Arthur Owen, Stockport

Roger Haigh, Southport | Seth Elsworth

Sidney Hague | Danny Killen

Joe Cohen | Neil Fleet, Lancaster

Ramsey Travers, Hyde

John Robertsson, Luxembourg

Jacob Nisnevich, Seattle

Robert Burgess, Aberdeen

Reece Peter Coils, Falkirk

Pete Tierney, Handforth

Steven Wilson, Manchester